The Modern C# Challenge

Become an expert C# programmer by solving interesting
programming problems

Rod Stephens

BIRMINGHAM - MUMBAI

The Modern C# Challenge

Commissioning Editor: Pavan Ramchandani
Acquisition Editor: Sandeep Mishra
Content Development Editor: Akshada Iyer
Technical Editor: Adhithya Haridas
Copy Editor: Safis Editing
Project Coordinator: Prajakta Naik
Proofreader: Safis Editing
Indexer: Aishwarya Gangawane
Graphics: Jisha Chirayil
Production Coordinator: Shraddha Falebhai

First published: October 2018

Production reference: 2021118

Published by Packt Publishing Ltd.
Livery Place
35 Livery Street
Birmingham
B3 2PB, UK.

ISBN 978-1-78953-542-6

www.packt.com

For Amy and Ken

`mapt.io`

Mapt is an online digital library that gives you full access to over 5,000 books and videos, as well as industry leading tools to help you plan your personal development and advance your career. For more information, please visit our website.

Why subscribe?

- Spend less time learning and more time coding with practical eBooks and Videos from over 4,000 industry professionals

- Improve your learning with Skill Plans built especially for you

- Get a free eBook or video every month

- Mapt is fully searchable

- Copy and paste, print, and bookmark content

Packt.com

Did you know that Packt offers eBook versions of every book published, with PDF and ePub files available? You can upgrade to the eBook version at `www.packt.com` and as a print book customer, you are entitled to a discount on the eBook copy. Get in touch with us at `customercare@packtpub.com` for more details.

At `www.packt.com`, you can also read a collection of free technical articles, sign up for a range of free newsletters, and receive exclusive discounts and offers on Packt books and eBooks.

Contributors

About the author

Rod Stephens has been a software developer, consultant, instructor, and author. He has written more than 30 books and 250 magazine articles covering such topics as three-dimensional graphics, algorithms, database design, software engineering, interview puzzles, C#, and Visual Basic.

Rod's popular C# Helper and VB Helper websites receive millions of hits per year and contain thousands of tips, tricks, and example programs for C# and Visual Basic developers. Some of his most recent books include:

- *WPF 3d*: *Three-Dimensional Graphics with WPF and C#*
- *Interview Puzzles Dissected*: *Solving and Understanding Interview Puzzles*
- *Beginning Software Engineering*
- *Essential Algorithms*: *A Practical Approach to Computer Algorithms*

Thanks to Sandeep Mishra, Akshada Iyer, and Adhithya Haridas for helping me put this book together.

About the reviewer

Luis Felipe is a software developer with a degree in software analysis and development, and he is studying for a specialization in software engineering. The main technologies he works with are ASP.NET Core, Angular (2+), SQL Server databases and MongoDB. He has been studying the C# language for almost 10 years and has passed the Microsoft 70-483 certification exam Programming with C#.

He currently works for the public ministry, working with the developing team to build the most important software for the institution of the last years. He also worked as a freelance developer, working on desktop and web applications using C#.

I really must start thanking my mother Luiza, my sister Ingrid and my girlfriend Helora. They were important in helping me to get the reviewing process done, by supporting me. My father, who passed away last year, always motivated me a lot to study and work hard. I thank him a lot. Also, I must thank the publishing team, who helped me a lot in learning the reviewing process to improve the book quality.

Packt is searching for authors like you

If you're interested in becoming an author for Packt, please visit `authors.packtpub.com` and apply today. We have worked with thousands of developers and tech professionals, just like you, to help them share their insight with the global tech community. You can make a general application, apply for a specific hot topic that we are recruiting an author for, or submit your own idea.

Table of Contents

Preface

So you've read an introductory book and perhaps one or two more advanced books. You've worked with C# for a while and now you're ready for something that wasn't written for idiots or dummies. This book may be just the thing!

This book includes 100 problems (with solutions) that you can use to test and hone your C# programming skills. They cover an eclectic assortment of topics, such as mathematical calculations, geometry, dates and times, the filesystem, simulations, and cryptography. These problems won't make you an expert in those fields, but they will give you some experience with a wide variety of useful topics.

As with many skills, the best way to learn programming is to practice. Most programming books cover roughly the same topics, so they don't give you the opportunity to practice skills that fall into the programming nooks and crannies that those books miss. They do a good job of covering basic topics, such as forms, controls, classes, and for loops. More advanced books also cover more specialized topics, such as algorithms (I've written a few algorithms books), databases, web programming, and phone apps. Few books have room for more specialized topics, such as mathematical calculations, simulations, and cryptography. You'll get a brief introduction to those topics here.

In addition to giving you practice with some of programming's less heavily-trodden byways, many of the examples in this book demonstrate important C# programming concepts. They show how to protect your programs from integer and floating point overflow, avoid exhausting stack memory, know when LINQ or PLINQ might hurt performance, handle times in multiple time zones, and use the yield statement.

Two things that this book does *not* cover are console applications and WPF. The example solutions use Windows Forms programs because they are easy to write, and that lets you focus on the concepts behind the user interface instead of spending time fiddling with WPF issues.

Before I get to the problems themselves, the following sections explain some of the details of the book's layout, how to get the most out of the book, and how you can get in touch with the publisher. After you skim that material, find a comfortable chair, possibly in your favorite coffee shop or tea house with a caffeinated beverage and a scone, open your laptop, and get ready to give your brain a workout!

Who this book is for

This book is intended for C# programmers. It does not explain basic C# concepts, so you should have some familiarity with C# programming before you read it. The book does not assume that you are an expert C# developer, however. If you know basic techniques such as creating classes, writing methods, and working with arrays and lists, then you should be able to work through the problems and understand their solutions.

What this book covers

This book includes 100 problems to challenge you and help you develop your C# programming skills. The solutions rely on general programming methods rather than C# language minutiae, so you should have a chance to solve them even if you haven't been programming for decades. They demonstrate useful techniques, not the answers to trivia questions.

Many of the examples also demonstrate important development concepts, such as comparing floating point values, handling integer overflow, avoiding unnecessary recursion, working across time zones, and building simulations. Some examples also show how to use specific advanced C# and .NET Framework tools such as the yield statement, the Transact Parallel Library (TPL), and .NET cryptography classes.

The following paragraphs describe the book's chapters in some detail:

Chapter 1, *Mathematics*, describes problems that ask you to perform mathematical tasks. These include numerical tasks such as calculating statistical functions, factorials, and binomial coefficients. They also include some combinatorial tasks such as finding all of the permutations or combinations from a set of items.

Chapter 2, *Geometry*, presents problems that perform geometric calculations. These ask you to find values such as the roots of equations, the points where lines and circles intersect, and the areas of polygons. Many of these problems ask you to draw shapes such as lines, circles, arrowheads, polygons, and stars.

Chapter 3, *Dates and Times*, includes problems that deal with dates and times. They pay special attention to programs that include multiple time zones or that include times when daylight saving time (or the equivalent in other countries) starts or ends.

Chapter 4, *Randomization*, poses problems that use randomization to produce various kinds of randomized data. For example, they ask you to generate random floating point numbers within a range, pick random items from a list or array, and generate random passwords.

`Chapter 5`, *Strings*, describes problems that manipulate strings. For example, they require you to convert between numbers and roman numerals and between bytes and hexadecimal strings, detect palindromic substrings, validate passwords for correctness, and use the Soundex algorithm to represent word's sound.

`Chapter 6`, *Files and Directories*, covers problems that deal with the filesystem. Its problems ask you to remove blank lines from a file, calculate a directory's total size, detect duplicate files, and generate thumbnails for image files in a directory.

`Chapter 7`, *Advanced C# and .NET Features*, includes problems that deal with more advanced features such as Language Integrated Query (LINQ), Parallel LINQ (PLINQ), Transact Parallel Library (TPL), and the yield statement.

`Chapter 8`, *Simulations*, asks you to write programs that perform simulations. Those range from simple numeric or text-based simulations (such as Dawkins' weasel and finding hailstone sequences), to positional simulations (such as Langton's ant and Life), to simulations that model gravitational force and acceleration.

`Chapter 9`, *Cryptography*, describes cryptographic problems. Some, such as the problems that deal with Caesar and Vigenère ciphers, are interesting mostly for fun and historical perspective. Others, such as those that deal with prime numbers, hashing, and string encryption, demonstrate strong, modern cryptographic methods.

You may not learn something new from *every* problem in the book, but hopefully you'll learn something from many of them.

To get the most out of this book

Programming is best learned by doing rather than by reading, so I strongly encourage you to try to solve a problem before you look at my example solution later in the book. I've tried to include all of the information that you need to solve each problem in its description, so you should be able to take a crack at it before you look at my solution.

Even if you get stuck on a problem, the beginning of the solution's description may help you figure out how to solve it. If you experience an *Ah ha!* moment while you're reading about the solution, stop and give it another try.

Keep in mind that there are always multiple ways to solve any particular problem. Some solutions may be better than others, but most problems can be solved by several different approaches, so don't think your solution is wrong just because it's different from mine. In fact, yours may be better than mine.

The easiest way to read this book is from front to back, tackling each problem in order. The chapters are arranged so the less confusing topics come first. Similarly, the problems within each chapter are arranged with the less demanding first. Some of the material described in one problem's solution may also be used in a later solution, so reading the problems and their solutions in order makes sense.

However, the problems and their example solutions are described separately, so you can jump around if you like. For example, if you are particularly interested in steganography, you can jump straight to Chapter 9, *Cryptography*. The worst that will happen is that an example solution may refer you to an earlier solution for some of its details. You can then go back and read the earlier solution for further details.

Download the example code files

You can download the example code files for this book from your account at www.packt.com. If you purchased this book elsewhere, you can visit www.packt.com/support and register to have the files emailed directly to you.

You can download the code files by following these steps:

1. Log in or register at www.packt.com.
2. Select the **SUPPORT** tab.
3. Click on **Code Downloads & Errata**.
4. Enter the name of the book in the **Search** box and follow the onscreen instructions.

Once the file is downloaded, please make sure that you unzip or extract the folder using the latest version of:

- WinRAR/7-Zip for Windows
- Zipeg/iZip/UnRarX for Mac
- 7-Zip/PeaZip for Linux

The code bundle for the book is also hosted on GitHub at https://github.com/PacktPublishing/The-Modern-CSharp-Challenge. In case there's an update to the code, it will be updated on the existing GitHub repository.

We also have other code bundles from our rich catalog of books and videos available at https://github.com/PacktPublishing/. Check them out!

Download the color images

We also provide a PDF file that has color images of the screenshots/diagrams used in this book. You can download it here: `https://www.packtpub.com/sites/default/files/downloads/9781789535426_ColorImages.pdf`.

Conventions used

There are a number of text conventions used throughout this book.

`CodeInText`: Indicates code words in text, database table names, folder names, filenames, file extensions, pathnames, dummy URLs, user input, and Twitter handles. Here is an example: "Several of the solutions in earlier chapters used the `Random` class to generate random numbers."

A block of code is set as follows:

```
private int FindError(string string1, string string2)
{
    int error = 0;
    for (int i = 0; i < string1.Length; i++)
        error += Math.Abs((int)string1[i] - (int)string2[i]);
    return error;
}
```

When we wish to draw your attention to a particular part of a code block, the relevant lines or items are set in bold:

```
{
    string testSubstring = string1.Substring(startPos, length);
    int testPos = string2.IndexOf(testSubstring);
    if (testPos < 0) break;

    bestLength = length;
    bestSubstring = testSubstring;
}
```

Bold: Indicates a new term, an important word, or words that you see onscreen. For example, words in menus or dialog boxes appear in the text like this. Here is an example: "In the **Add Item** dialog, I selected the MP3 file and clicked **Add**."

Warnings or important notes appear like this.

 Tips and tricks appear like this.

Get in touch

Feedback from our readers is always welcome.

General feedback: If you have questions about any aspect of this book, mention the book title in the subject of your message and email us at customercare@packtpub.com.

Errata: Although we have taken every care to ensure the accuracy of our content, mistakes do happen. If you have found a mistake in this book, we would be grateful if you would report this to us. Please visit www.packt.com/submit-errata, selecting your book, clicking on the Errata Submission Form link, and entering the details.

Piracy: If you come across any illegal copies of our works in any form on the Internet, we would be grateful if you would provide us with the location address or website name. Please contact us at copyright@packt.com with a link to the material.

If you are interested in becoming an author: If there is a topic that you have expertise in and you are interested in either writing or contributing to a book, please visit authors.packtpub.com.

Reviews

Please leave a review. Once you have read and used this book, why not leave a review on the site that you purchased it from? Potential readers can then see and use your unbiased opinion to make purchase decisions, we at Packt can understand what you think about our products, and our authors can see your feedback on their book. Thank you!

For more information about Packt, please visit packt.com.

Mathematics 1

This chapter includes mathematical problems. Some let you calculate useful values such as factorials and statistical functions. Others demonstrate useful programming techniques for managing recursion, value caching, and protecting applications against calculation errors. Finally, some of these problems are just plain fun and interesting.

Problems

Use the following problems to test your mathematical programming prowess. I strongly encourage you to give each problem a try before you turn to the solutions and download the example programs.

1. Statistical functions

Create a `StatisticsExtensions` class that defines extension methods to calculate statistical functions for arrays or lists of numbers. LINQ provides the `Average`, `Max`, and `Min` extension methods to calculate some statistical functions, so you don't need to implement those.

The following list summarizes the statistical functions that you should provide:

- **Truncated mean:** This is the mean (average) after removing an indicated number or percentage of the largest and smallest values. For example, if the values are {1, 1, 3, 5, 7, 7, 9} and you want to remove the two largest and smallest values, the remaining values are {3, 5, 7}.
- **Median:** This is the middlemost value. For example, if the values are {1, 1, 3, 5, 7, 7, 9}, then the median is 5 because half of the values are less than 5 and half are greater. If the set includes an even number of values, the median is the average of the two middlemost values.
- **Mode:** This is the value that occurs most often. In the set {1, 2, 3, 3, 7}, the mode is 3 because it appears twice. If there's a tie, return all of the modes in a list.
- **Sample standard deviation:** This is a measure of how widely spread the values are. The sample standard deviation is defined by the following formula:

$$\sigma = \sqrt{\frac{1}{N-1} \sum_{i=1}^{N} (x_i - \mu)^2}$$

- **Population standard deviation:** This is similar to the sample standard deviation except you divide by N instead of $N - 1$ in the equation.

In the standard deviation equation:

- The lowercase Greek sigma, σ, represents the standard deviation
- N is the number of items in the set
- The uppercase Greek sigma, Σ, means to add up the values to its right (in this case, the sums of the squares of the differences between the x_i values and μ) as i ranges from 1 to N
- The lowercase Greek mu, μ, is the mean (average) of the values

Write a program similar to the one shown in the following screenshot to test your extension methods. This program generates the indicated number of values and displays statistics about them. Each value is the sum of two random values between 1 and 6, so the values give a bell curve. (The shape is more obvious if you generate more than 100 values.):

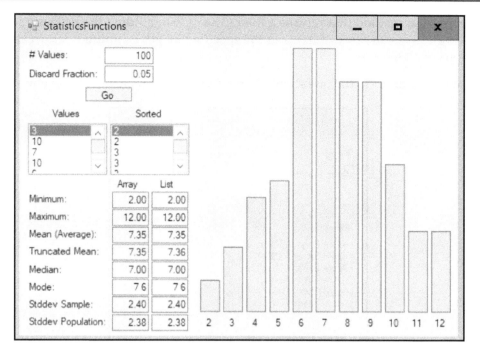

The example solution uses labels to build the histogram, showing the numbers' frequencies.

An extension method can handle both arrays and lists if it takes an
`IEnumerable` as a parameter. You will need to convert the values from an
`IEnumerable` of generic objects into an array of double values for some of
the operations.

2. Permutations

A **permutation** is an ordering of a selection of objects from a set. For example, suppose the
set is {apple, banana, cherry}, then the permutations containing two items are all of the
orderings of two items selected from that set. Those permutations are {apple, banana},
{apple, cherry}, {banana, apple}, {banana, cherry}, {cherry, apple}, and {cherry, banana}.
Notice that {apple, banana} and {banana, apple} contain the same items in different orders.

Write an extension method that returns a `List<List<T>>`, holding the permutations of a specified length from an array of items. If the specified length is omitted, return all permutations of all lengths.

Write a program similar to the one shown in the following screenshot to test your method:

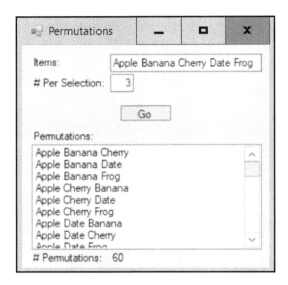

3. Combinations

A **combination** is an unordered selection of objects from a set. For example, if the set is {apple, banana, cherry}, then the combinations containing two items are all of the subsets containing two items in any order. Those combinations are {apple, banana}, {apple, cherry}, and {banana, cherry}. This time, {apple, banana} and {banana, apple} are considered the same, so the combinations only include one of those subsets.

Write an extension method that returns a `List<List<T>>`, holding the combinations of a specified length from an array of items. If the specified length is zero, return all combinations of all lengths.

Write a program similar to the one shown in the following screenshot to test your method:

4. Factorials

The **factorial** of a non-negative integer number, N, is written N! and is given by the equation N! = 1 × 2 × 3 × ... × N. You can also define factorials recursively as N! = N × (N – 1)! By definition, 0! = 1.

Write a program that calculates factorials recursively and non-recursively. Is one version better than the other? What is the limiting factor for calculating factorials?

5. Fibonacci numbers

The following equations define *Fibonacci numbers* recursively:

$$F_0 = 0$$

$$F_1 = 1$$

$$F_N = F_{N-1} + F_{N-2}$$

The last equation applies when N > 1. For example, the first ten Fibonacci numbers are 0, 1, 1, 2, 3, 5, 8, 13, 21, and 34.

Write a program that calculates Fibonacci numbers recursively, non-recursively, and via a cache table holding Fibonacci values.

6. Binomial coefficients

The **binomial coefficient** of N and K gives the number of ways that you can pick N values from a set of K values. The binomial coefficient is usually written as $\binom{N}{K}$ and is pronounced *N choose K*.

For example, suppose you have a set of four values, {A, B, C, D}. The possible ways to select two of those values are {A, B}, {A, C}, {A, D}, {B, C}, {B, D}, and {C, D}. There are six possible ways to select two items from the original set of four items, so $\binom{4}{2}$ =6.

You can use the following formula to calculate binomial coefficients:

$$\binom{N}{K} = \frac{N!}{K!(N-K)!}$$

For the example where we select two items out of four, the formula gives the following:

$$\binom{4}{2} = \frac{4!}{2!(4-2)!} = \frac{24}{2 \times 2} = 6$$

Write a program that calculates binomial coefficients. Test your program by verifying the following values:

$$\binom{4}{2} = 6$$

$$\binom{10}{6} = 210$$

$$\binom{28}{3} = 3,276$$

$$\binom{40}{20} = 137,846,528,820$$

7. Pascal's triangle

Pascal's triangle is a triangle of numbers (you probably guessed that from its name) where each row begins and ends with **1** and every other value is the sum of the two numbers above it. The following diagram shows the first six rows of Pascal's triangle:

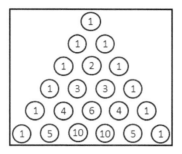

Write a program that displays Pascal's triangle as simple text. For a bigger challenge, display the values graphically centered over each other, as shown in the preceding figure.

The values in Pascal's triangle are binomial coefficients, where the Kth value in row N is $\binom{N}{K}$. Here the rows and entries are numbered starting at zero. For example, the third entry in the fifth row has the value $\binom{4}{2}$=6.

8. Greatest common divisors

The **greatest common divisor** or *GCD* of two integers A and B, which is written GCD(A, B), is the largest integer C that divides both A and B evenly. For example, GCD(84, 36) = 12 because 12 is the largest integer that divides into both 84 and 36 with no remainder.

Write a program that calculates GCDs. Use the program to verify that GCD(10370370276, 82962962964) = 756.

9. Least common multiples

The **least common multiple** or *LCM* of two positive integers A and B, which is written LCM(A, B), is the smallest positive integer that is a multiple of both A and B. For example, LCM(30, 42) is 210 because 210 is the smallest positive integer that is a multiple of 30 (210 = 7 × 30) and 42 (210 = 5 × 42).

Write a program that calculates LCMs. Use the program to verify that LCM(1234567000, 7654321000) = 9,449,772,114,007,000.

10. Sums of multiples

Write a program that calculates the sums of multiples of 3 or 5 between zero and a given maximum value. For example, if the maximum is 30, then the program should calculate 3 + 5 + 6 + 9 + 10 + 12 + 15 + 18 + 20 + 21 + 24 + 25 + 27 + 30 = 225 because those are the multiples of 3 and 5.

11. Primality testing

A **prime number** is an integer greater than 1 that has no factors other than 1 and itself. For example, 17 is prime because the only positive integers that you can multiply to get 17 are 1 and 17. In contrast, 21 is not prime because $3 \times 7 = 21$. Integers greater than 1 that are not prime are called **composite numbers**.

Write a program that determines whether an integer is prime or composite.

12. Prime table

Write a program that builds an array of Booleans that indicates which values up to a specified maximum are prime. For example, if you call the array `Primes`, then `Primes[i]` should be true if `i` is prime. After it builds the table, the program should use it to display the largest prime that it found.

13. Prime factors

A number's **prime factors** are a set of prime numbers that multiply together to give the original number. For example, $60 = 2 \times 2 \times 3 \times 5$. There is only one set of prime numbers that can multiply together to give a particular number, so the prime factorization is unique.

Write a program that prime factors numbers.

14. Unique prime factors

A number's **unique prime factors** are the set of the number's prime factors with duplicates removed. For example, the prime factors of 360 are {2, 2, 2, 3, 3, 5}. Its unique prime factors are {2, 3, 5}.

Write a program that finds a number's unique prime factors.

15. Prime tuples

Mathematicians like playing with prime numbers, so they have come up with several different names for groupings of related primes:

- **Twin primes** are primes {p, p + 2} that differ by two, such as {3, 5}. (Primes that differ by only 1 are not very interesting because 2 and 3 are the only primes that differ by 1.)
- **Cousin primes** are primes {p, p + 4} that differ by 4, such as {3, 7}.
- **Sexy primes** are primes {p, p + 6} that differ by 6, such as {5, 11}. (The name *sexy primes* is a pun because *sex* is Latin for *six*.)

You can also look for different numbers of primes with various spacings. For example, you can look for sexy pairs, sexy triples such as {7, 13, 19}, and so forth.

Write a program that checks numbers up to a maximum value, looking for primes with a given spacing and quantity. For example, the user might set the spacing to six and the number to 3 to look for groups of three primes that are each six apart, such as {5, 11, 17}.

Use your program to see what's special about groups of three or four primes that differ by 6, 12, 18, and other multiples of 3.

16. Proper divisors

A **divisor** of a number N is any number that divides evenly into N. For example, the divisors of 12 are {1, 2, 4, 6, 12}.

The **proper divisors** of a number N are N's divisors, not including N itself. For example, the proper divisors of 12 are {1, 2, 4, 6}.

Write a program that finds a number's proper divisors.

17. Amicable numbers

Two numbers are **amicable numbers** if they are different and the sum of each number's proper divisors equals the other number. For example, the divisors of 220 are {1, 2, 4, 5, 10, 11, 20, 22, 44, 55, 110} and $1 + 2 + 4 + 5 + 10 + 11 + 20 + 22 + 44 + 55 + 110 = 284$. Also, the divisors of 284 are {1, 2, 4, 71, 142} and $1 + 2 + 4 + 71 + 142 = 220$. That means 220 and 284 are amicable numbers.

Write a program that finds amicable numbers between 1 and a specified maximum.

18. Perfect numbers

A **perfect number** equals the sum of its divisors. Basically, a perfect number is amicable with itself. For example, the divisors of 6 are 1, 2, and 3, and $6 = 1 + 2 + 3$.

Write a program that finds perfect numbers between 1 and a specified maximum.

19. Armstrong numbers

A number is an **Armstrong number** if raising its digits to the power of the number of digits and adding the results give the original number. For example, 371 is an Armstrong number because it has three digits and $3^3 + 7^3 + 1^3 = 371$.

Write a program that finds Armstrong numbers between 1 and a specified maximum.

Solutions

The following sections describe solutions to the preceding problems. Remember that there usually isn't a single correct way to solve a particular problem. Also remember that the explanations shown here include only the most interesting and important details needed to solve the problems. Download the example solutions to see additional details and to experiment with the programs at https://github.com/PacktPublishing/The-Modern-CSharp-Challenge/tree/master/Chapter01.

1. Statistical functions

Extension methods must be contained in a `public static` class. This solution uses the following declaration for its `StatisticsExtensions` class:

```
public static class StatisticsExtensions
{
    ...
}
```

Extension methods must also be declared as `public` and `static`. Their first parameter should be marked with the `this` keyword to indicate that the parameter is the object that is being extended.

The following code shows the `TruncatedMean` extension method:

```
// Return the truncated mean of an IEnumerable of numbers.
// Set discardNumber to the number of values to discard at the
// top and bottom. For example, set discardNumber = 5 to
// discard the 5 largest and smallest values.
public static double TruncatedMean<T>(this IEnumerable<T> values,
    int discardNumber)
{
    // Convert the values into an enumerable of doubles.
    IEnumerable<double> doubles =
        values.Select(value => Convert.ToDouble(value));
    double[] doubleArray = doubles.ToArray();

    // Sort the doubles.
    Array.Sort(doubleArray);

    // Find the values that we want to use.
    int minIndex = discardNumber;
    int maxIndex = doubleArray.Length - 1 - discardNumber;

    // Copy the desired items into a new array.
    int numRemaining = maxIndex - minIndex + 1;
    double[] remainingItems = new double[numRemaining];
    Array.Copy(doubleArray, minIndex, remainingItems, 0, numRemaining);

    // Calculate and return the truncated mean.
    return remainingItems.Average();
}
```

This method has a generic type parameter, T, between its name and its parameter list. The first parameter has type IEnumerable<T>, so the method extends that type. Because both arrays and lists implement IEnumerable, this means that the method applies to both arrays and lists.

The method's second parameter indicates the number of largest and smallest items that should be removed for the truncated mean.

Even if the input values are integers, their mean might not be an integer, so the method returns a double.

In order to discard the largest and smallest items, the method must sort the inputs. It cannot do that with objects that have the generic type T, so the code uses a LINQ query to convert the items into a list of double. The method uses the query to make an array of double and sorts it.

If the values are not numeric, this code will throw an exception when it tries to convert the values into doubles.

Next, the code calculates the indices of the first and last items that it should keep when it discards the largest and smallest values. It uses Array.Copy to copy those values into a new array, uses the Average LINQ extension method to calculate the mean of the remaining values, and returns the result.

This extension method takes, as its second parameter, the number of largest and smallest values that it should discard. The following overloaded version of the method takes a discard fraction as a parameter instead:

```
// Return the truncated mean of an IEnumerable of numbers.
// Set discardFraction to the fraction of values to discard at the
// top and bottom. For example, set discardFraction = 0.05 to
// discard the 5% largest and smallest values.
public static double TruncatedMean<T>(this IEnumerable<T> values,
    double discardFraction)
{
    // Calculate the number of items to remove at the top and bottom.
    int discardNumber = (int)(values.Count() * discardFraction);

    // Invoke the previous version of TruncatedMean.
    return TruncatedMean(values, discardNumber);
}
```

This method uses the discard fraction to calculate the number of values that it should discard. It then invokes the previous version of the method.

The following code shows the Median extension method:

```
// Return the median of an IEnumerable of numbers.
public static double Median<T>(this IEnumerable<T> values)
{
    // Convert into an enumerable of doubles.
    IEnumerable<double> doubles =
        values.Select(value => Convert.ToDouble(value));
    double[] doubleArray = doubles.ToArray();

    // Sort the doubles.
    Array.Sort(doubleArray);

    // Calculate and return the median.
    int numValues = doubleArray.Length;
    if (numValues % 2 == 1)
    {
        // There are an odd number of values.
        // Return the middle one.
        return doubleArray[numValues / 2];
    }

    // Return the mean of the two middle values.
    double value1 = doubleArray[numValues / 2 - 1];
    double value2 = doubleArray[numValues / 2];
    return (value1 + value2) / 2.0;
}
```

In order to find the value in the middle of the others, the method must sort the values. To do that, the method converts the values into an array of double and then sorts it, just like the first version of the TruncatedMean method did.

Next, if the resulting array contains an odd number of values, the method calculates the index of the middle value and returns that value.

If the double array contains an even number of values, the method calculates the indices of the two middle values and returns the average of those values.

The following code shows the `Modes` extension method, which finds the values' modes:

```
// Return the mode(s) of an IEnumerable of numbers.
public static List<T> Modes<T>(this IEnumerable<T> values)
{
    // Make a dictionary to hold value counts.
    Dictionary<T, int> counts = new Dictionary<T, int>();

    // Count the values.
    foreach (T value in values)
    {
        if (!counts.ContainsKey(value))
            counts.Add(value, 1);
        else
            counts[value]++;
    }

    // Find the largest count.
    int largestCount = counts.Values.Max();

    // Find the value(s) with that count.
    List<T> modes = new List<T>();
    foreach (KeyValuePair<T, int> pair in counts)
        if (pair.Value == largestCount) modes.Add(pair.Key);
    return modes;
}
```

This method creates a dictionary to hold counts for the values. The dictionary's keys are the original values, and the associated values are the counts.

After it creates the dictionary, the code loops through the values. When it comes to a value that is not already in the dictionary, the code adds it to the dictionary, setting its initial count to 1.

If the dictionary already contains a value, then the code increments its count.

After it has counted all of the values, the code uses the `Max` LINQ extension method to find the largest count.

The code then loops through the key/value pairs in the dictionary. If a pair has a count equal to the largest count, the code adds it to the list of modes.

After it has processed all of the values, the method returns the `modes` list.

This method returns the items in the `values` list that occur the most, even if that value is non-numeric. For example, if the values are names, the method will return the names that occur the most.

The following code shows the final method in the `StatisticsExtensions` class, `StdDev`:

```
// Return the standard deviation of an IEnumerable of numbers.
//
// If the second argument is True, evaluate as a sample.
// If the second argument is False, evaluate as a population.
public static double StdDev<T>(this IEnumerable<T> values,
    bool asSample = false)
{
    // Convert into an enumerable of doubles.
    IEnumerable<double> doubles =
        values.Select(value => Convert.ToDouble(value));

    // Get the number of items and the mean.
    int numValues = doubles.Count();
    double mean = doubles.Average();

    // Get the sum of the squares of the differences between
    // the values and the mean.
    var squaresQuery =
        from double value in doubles
        select (value - mean) * (value - mean);
    double sumOfSquares = squaresQuery.Sum();

    // Return the apppropriate type of standard deviation.
    if (asSample)
        return Math.Sqrt(sumOfSquares / (numValues - 1));
    return Math.Sqrt(sumOfSquares / numValues);
}
```

This method converts the values into a `double` array as usual. It then gets the number of values and their mean.

Next, the code makes a LINQ query that selects the square of the difference between a value in the array and the mean. It then uses the `Sum` method to add all of those differences squared.

Finally, the method divides by the number of values, or one less than the number of values depending on whether it is calculating a sample or population standard deviation.

Now the main program can use extension methods to calculate statistical values. For example, it uses the following code to display the median of the values in the array named `valuesArray`:

```
arrayMedianTextBox.Text = valuesArray.Median().ToString("0.00");
```

The following code shows a useful technique that the program uses to display the mode, which is a list of values:

```
arrayModeTextBox.Text = string.Join(" ",
    valuesArray.Modes().ConvertAll(i => i.ToString()));
```

This statement calls the `Modes` extension method to get the modes. It uses the `ConvertAll` LINQ extension method to convert the list of mode values into a list of strings. It then uses `string.Join` to combine the strings into a single string with the values separated by space characters.

Download the `StatisticalFunctions` example solution to see additional details, such as how the program uses labels to build its histogram.

2. Permutations

This example defines extension methods in the static `ArrangingExtensions` class. The following code shows the main `Permutations` method:

```
// Find permutations containing the desired number of items.
public static List<List<T>> Permutations<T>(this T[] values, int
numPerGroup)
{
    int numValues = values.Count();
    bool[] used = new bool[numValues];
    List<T> currentSolution = new List<T>();
    return FindPermutations(values, numPerGroup, currentSolution,
        used, numValues);
}
```

This method gets the number of values in the array and then creates an array of `bool` with the same size. The program will use that array to keep track of which values are in the solution as the code works on it.

The code then creates a `List<T>` to hold the current solution. It passes the values, the desired number of items in each permutation, the current solution (initially empty), the `used` array (initially all `false`), and the number of values into the following `FindPermutations` helper method:

```
// Find permutations that include the current solution.
private static List<List<T>> FindPermutations<T>(T[] values,
    int numPerGroup, List<T> currentSolution, bool[] used,
    int numValues)
{
    List<List<T>> results = new List<List<T>>();

    // If this solution has the desired length, return it.
    if (currentSolution.Count() == numPerGroup)
    {
        // Make a copy because currentSolution will change over time.
        List<T> copy = new List<T>(currentSolution);
        results.Add(copy);
        return results;
    }

    // Try adding other values to the solution.
    for (int i = 0; i < numValues; i++)
    {
        // See if value[i] is in the solution yet.
        if (!used[i])
        {
            // Try adding this value.
            used[i] = true;
            currentSolution.Add(values[i]);

            // Recursively look for solutions that have values[i]
            // added.
            List<List<T>> newResults =
                FindPermutations(values, numPerGroup, currentSolution,
                    used, numValues);
            results.AddRange(newResults);

            // Remove values[i].
            used[i] = false;
            currentSolution.RemoveAt(currentSolution.Count() - 1);
        }
    }
    return results;
}
```

Before I describe the `FindPermutations` method in detail, it's worth giving you a short overview. The method calls itself recursively to build the permutations. When it is called, the `currentSolution` list holds the beginning of a permutation. The method examines the other items that are not already in the permutation (as determined by their `used` values being `false`) and adds some to the current solution.

Now, on to the method's details. The method begins by checking the number of items in the current solution. If that solution contains the desired number of items, then it is a valid solution so the method returns it.

However, the `currentSolution` list will be changed later as instances of the `FindPermutations` method pass the `currentSolution` variable back and forth. If the method simply returned `currentSolution`, its value would change later and that would destroy the current solution.

In order to preserve the current solution, the method makes a copy of it and returns the copy.

If the current solution isn't long enough, the method loops through all of the items trying to extend the solution. If an item's `used` flag indicates that it is not yet in the solution, the method tries adding it.

The method sets the item's `used` value to `true`, adds it to the current solution, and then recursively calls itself to continue building the solution. Other recursive calls to `FindPermutations` will add more items to the solution until it has the desired length.

After the recursive call returns, the method adds any results returned by that call to the `results` list.

The method then removes the most recently added item from the current solution by setting its `used` value to `false` and removing it from the `currentSolution` list. The method does that so it can consider other items for the next position in the solution.

After it has considered adding all of the items to the solution, the method returns whatever results it has found.

Notice that the method considers all of the items that are not yet part of the solution. For example, suppose the current solution contains three items. The method could place any of the remaining items in the fourth position.

If an item is not used in the fourth position, it might be added later by another recursive call to `FindPermutations`.

In particular, consider the items in positions i and j in the original array of values. The FindPermutations method could add item i and then later add item j, or it could add item j and then later add item i. The values could appear in any positions and in any order. This flexibility of ordering is what makes the result a permutation. You should contrast this with the combinations produced by the next solution.

One special case that is not handled is by the previous Permutations method, that is, when the numPerGroup parameter is omitted. In that case, the Permutations method should return permutations of every possible length. The following overloaded version of the method does just that:

```
// Find permutations containing any number of items.
public static List<List<T>> Permutations<T>(this T[] values)
{
    List<List<T>> results = new List<List<T>>();

    // Get permutations of all lengths.
    for (int i = 1; i <= values.Count(); i++)
        results.AddRange(values.Permutations(i));
    return results;
}
```

This version of the Permutations method loops through all of the possible permutation lengths between 1 and the number of values present. It calls the previous version of the method to find permutations of those lengths, combines the results into a single list, and returns it.

The solution's main program uses the Permutations extension methods to display permutations. The heart of the program is shown in the following code snippet:

```
// Get the inputs.
char[] separators = { ' ' };
string[] values = valuesTextBox.Text.Split(separators,
StringSplitOptions.RemoveEmptyEntries);
int numPerGroup = int.Parse(numPerGroupTextBox.Text);

// Get the permutations.
List<List<string>> permutations;
if (numPerGroup == 0)
    permutations = values.Permutations();
else
    permutations = values.Permutations(numPerGroup);

// Display the results.
foreach (List<string> permutation in permutations)
    resultsListBox.Items.Add(string.Join(" ", permutation.ToArray()));
```

This code gets the values and the number of items that should be in each permutation. Next, the method calls the `Permutations` extension method on the `values` array. It finishes by looping through the permutations, adding each to the result list box. It uses the technique described in the preceding solution to convert the `permutation` list into a string containing values separated by spaces.

Download the `Permutations` example solution to see additional details.

3. Combinations

The `Combinations` method works much like the `Permutations` method did in the preceding section. The main `Combinations` method calls the `FindCombinations` helper method to do most of the work recursively. That method loops through the values, adds them to the growing current solution, and calls itself recursively to build longer combinations.

The following code shows the `Combinations` method:

```
// Find combinations containing the desired number of items.
public static List<List<T>> Combinations<T>(this T[] values,
    int numPerGroup)
{
    int numValues = values.Count();
    bool[] used = new bool[numValues];
    List<T> currentSolution = new List<T>();
    return FindCombinations(values, numPerGroup, currentSolution,
        used, 0, numValues);
}
```

See the description of the `Permutations` method in the preceding section for details about how this method works.

The following code shows the `FindCombinations` method:

```
// Find Combinations that include the current solution.
private static List<List<T>> FindCombinations<T>(T[] values,
    int numPerGroup, List<T> currentSolution, bool[] used,
    int firstIndex, int numValues)
{
    List<List<T>> results = new List<List<T>>();

    // If this solution has the desired length, return it.
    if (currentSolution.Count() == numPerGroup)
    {
```

```
                // Make a copy because currentSolution will change over time.
                List<T> copy = new List<T>(currentSolution);
                results.Add(copy);
                return results;
        }

        // Try adding other values to the solution.
        for (int i = firstIndex; i < numValues; i++)
        {
                // See if value[i] is in the solution yet.
                if (!used[i])
                {
                        // Try adding this value.
                        used[i] = true;
                        currentSolution.Add(values[i]);

                        // Recursively look for solutions that have values[i]
                        // added.
                        List<List<T>> newResults =
                                FindCombinations(values, numPerGroup, currentSolution,
                                        used, i + 1, numValues);
                        results.AddRange(newResults);

                        // Remove values[i].
                        used[i] = false;
                        currentSolution.RemoveAt(currentSolution.Count() - 1);
                }
        }
        return results;
}
```

This method is somewhat similar to the `FindPermutations` method described in the preceding section, with the major exception that it takes a parameter that gives the index of the first item that the method should consider adding to the solution. When the method loops through the values, it only considers the items that have this index or later.

This prevents the method from adding items in orders other than the one in which they appear in the `values` array. For example, suppose i and j are indices of items in the array and that i < j. Then this method would consider adding `values[i]` and then later adding `values[j]`, but it would not consider adding `values[j]` before adding `values[i]` because i < j.

By keeping the values in their sorted order, the method produces combinations rather than permutations.

The following code shows the overloaded version of the `Combinations` method that returns combinations of any length:

```
// Find combinations containing any number of items.
public static List<List<T>> Combinations<T>(this T[] values)
{
    List<List<T>> results = new List<List<T>>();

    // Get combinations of all lengths.
    for (int i = 1; i <= values.Count(); i++)
        results.AddRange(values.Combinations(i));
    return results;
}
```

This method loops through the possible combination sizes, calls the earlier version of the `Combinations` method to get combinations of those lengths, combines them, and returns the result.

The solution's main program is similar to the one for the preceding problem. See the preceding section for more information and download the `Combinations` example solution to see additional details.

4. Factorials

The following code shows a recursive method for calculating factorials:

```
// Calculate the factorial recursively.
private long RecursiveFactorial(long number)
{
    checked
    {
        if (number <= 1) return 1;
        return number * RecursiveFactorial(number - 1);
    }
}
```

This method first checks whether `number` is less than or equal to 1. If `number` ≤ 1, the method returns 1. If `number` is greater than 1, the method calls itself recursively to calculate (`number` – 1)! and then returns `number` times (`number` – 1)!.

The following code shows a non-recursive method for calculating factorials:

```
// Calculate the factorial non-recursively.
private long NonRecursiveFactorial(long number)
{
    checked
    {
        long total = 1;
        for (long i = 2; i <= number; i++) total *= i;
        return total;
    }
}
```

This method initializes the `total` variable to 1. It then enters a loop where it multiples `total` by the values between 2 and `number`. The result is $1 \times 2 \times 3 \times ... \times$ `number`, which is the factorial.

Some recursive programs may have very large depths of recursion where the method calls itself so many times that the stack memory is exhausted and the program crashes. For example, if a program tried to calculate `RecursiveFactorial(1000000)`, the method would call itself 1 million times. That could exhaust the program's stack space and crash the program.

Fortunately (or unfortunately, depending on how you look at it), the factorial function grows extremely quickly, so the number of recursive calls that will work is limited. These methods use 64-bit long integers to perform their calculations, so they can only hold values up to 9,223,372,036,854,775,807. The value 20! is 2,432,902,008,176,640,000 and the value 21! is too big to fit in a 64-bit integer, so the program can only calculate values up to 20! anyway. That means the recursive version can use, at most, 20 levels of recursion, and the program will never exhaust its stack space.

In general, non-recursive versions of methods are often better than recursive versions because they don't make as many demands on stack memory, but in this example the difference doesn't really matter. The limiting factor for this program is the fact that the factorial method grows so quickly that it can exceed the limits of 64-bit integers.

That brings us to the most important lesson in this example. By default, C# does not check integer operations for overflow. If the result of an integer operation is too big to fit inside the appropriate data type, the program normally does not notice. Instead, it continues merrily along using whatever garbage is present in its variables as if nothing was wrong.

You can force C# to check for integer overflow by placing risky statements inside a checked block, as shown in preceding code. If you omit the checked statements, the factorial methods will try to calculate values for numbers greater than 20. For example, they will report that 21! is -4,249,290,049,419,214,848, which is clearly wrong because it's a negative number. If you try to calculate factorials for much larger values such as 10,000 or 1 million, the program will exhaust its stack space.

C# ignores integer overflow for performance reasons, although in my tests, using a checked block only increased runtime by about 10%. The moral of all this is that if a certain calculation may cause an integer overflow, then you should place it inside a checked block.

 A group of checked blocks does not nest across method calls the way try catch blocks do. For example, if a checked block includes a method call and that method might cause an integer overflow, then the method also needs its own checked block because the calling checked block will not protect it.

Download the Factorials example solution to see additional details.

5. Fibonacci numbers

The following code shows a recursive method that calculates Fibonacci numbers:

```
// Calculate the Fibonacci number recursively.
private long RecursiveFibonacci(int number)
{
    checked
    {
        // On 0 or 1, return 0 or 1.
        if (number <= 1) return number;

        // Fibonacci(N) = Fibonacci(N - 1) + Fibonacci(N - 2).
        return
            RecursiveFibonacci(number - 1) +
            RecursiveFibonacci(number - 2);
    }
}
```

This method simply follows the recursive definition of Fibonacci numbers.

Fibonacci numbers grow very quickly (although not as quickly as the factorial function), so the program uses a checked block to protect itself from integer overflow errors.

Unfortunately, this method has a more pressing problem—it recalculates certain values a huge number of times. For example, suppose you want to calculate F_N. To do that, the method calls itself to calculate F_{N-1} and F_{N-2}. Then, to calculate F_{N-1}, the method calls itself to calculate F_{N-2} and F_{N-3}. Here, the method is calculating F_{N-2} twice.

If you follow the recursive calls further, you'll find that the method calls itself to recalculate the same values an enormous number of times. The following diagram shows the calls needed to calculate F5:

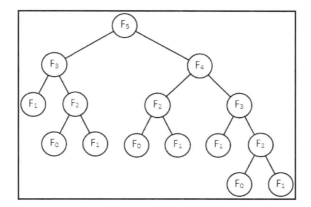

You can see in the preceding diagram that the values F_1 and F_0 are calculated many times. Those values are easy to calculate, but if the tree were bigger, the method would also calculate more complicated values many times. The following table shows the total number of times the method is called while calculating various Fibonacci numbers:

Value	Method Calls
F_5	15
F_{10}	177
F_{15}	1,973
F_{20}	21,891
F_{25}	242,785
F_{30}	2,692,537
F_{35}	29,860,703
F_{40}	331,160,281

You can see from the preceding table that the number of method calls grows very quickly. The method calls itself so many times that it cannot calculate values larger than around F_{45} in a reasonable amount of time.

In cases such as this, you need to remove the need for all of the duplicate calculations. One way to do that is to change the way you think about the recursive definition of Fibonacci numbers. Recall the following definition:

$$F_0 = 0$$

$$F_1 = 1$$

$$F_N = F_{N-1} + F_{N-2} \text{ for } N>1$$

The previous method used a top-down approach, where it started with a large value (say F_{10}) and then recursively called itself to calculate the smaller values needed to build that value (F_9 and F_8).

Alternatively, you can take a bottom-up approach, where you build smaller values and then use them to create larger ones. The following method uses the bottom-up approach:

```
// Calculate the Fibonacci number non-recursively.
private long NonRecursiveFibonacci(int number)
{
    checked
    {
        // On 0 or 1, return 0 or 1.
        if (number <= 1) return number;

        // Start at i = 2.
        long fiboIMinus2 = 0;                      // Fibonacci(0)
        long fiboIMinus1 = 1;                      // Fibonacci(1)
        long fiboI = fiboIMinus1 + fiboIMinus2; // Fibonacci(2)
        for (int i = 2; i < number; i++)
        {
            // Update the values.
            fiboIMinus2 = fiboIMinus1;
            fiboIMinus1 = fiboI;
            fiboI = fiboIMinus1 + fiboIMinus2;
        }
        return fiboI;
    }
}
```

This method uses variables to hold the values F_i, F_{i-1}, and F_{i-2} as it performs its calculations. It enters a loop where it uses F_{i-1} and F_{i-2} to calculate F_i until it has calculated the value it needs.

This version calculates each Fibonacci value once. For example, to calculate F_{40}, it calculates F_0, F_1, and F_2, and so on for a total of 40 calculations instead of the 331 million required by the recursive method.

This non-recursive version is extremely efficient, but it's also rather confusing because it requires you to keep track of which variables hold which values.

A table of values can sometimes make this sort of recursion removal easier to understand. The following method stores values in an array and then fills the array until it has calculated the value that it needs:

```
// Use a table to calculate the Fibonacci number non-recursively.
private long TableFibonacci(int number)
{
    checked
    {
        // Make a table to hold Fibonacci values.
        long[] values = new long[number + 1];

        // Initialize Fibonacci(0) and Fibonacci(1).
        values[0] = 0;
        values[1] = 1;

        // Fill the table.
        for (int i = 2; i <= number; i++)
            values[i] = values[i - 1] + values[i - 2];

        // Return values[number].
        return values[number];
    }
}
```

This version is also fast and effective. Its one drawback is that it recreates the table every time it calculates a Fibonacci value. It might be nice to keep any previously calculated values for later use. The following method uses a cache to hold values in case they are needed later:

```
// Use a cache table to calculate the Fibonacci number non-recursively.
private long[] FibonacciCache = null;
private long CachedFibonacci(int number)
{
    // Initialize the cache if necessary.
```

```
if (FibonacciCache == null)
{
    // Initialize the table to hold all -1 entries.
    // Fibonacci(92) is the largest value that doesn't overflow.
    const int MaxNumber = 92;
    FibonacciCache =
        Enumerable.Repeat(-1L, MaxNumber + 1).ToArray();

    // Initialize Fibonacci(0) and Fibonacci(1).
    FibonacciCache[0] = 0;
    FibonacciCache[1] = 1;
}

// Use the cache to calculate the Fibonacci number.
checked
{
    // We don't have the value. Calculate and save it.
    if (FibonacciCache[number] < 0) FibonacciCache[number] =
        CachedFibonacci(number - 1) +
        CachedFibonacci(number - 2);

    // Return the cached value.
    return FibonacciCache[number];
}
}
```

This code defines the cache array outside the method. When the method starts, it checks the cache to see if it has been initialized. If the cache is `null`, the method creates a new array with each entry set to -1. It then initializes the first two values to $F_0 = 0$ and $F_1 = 1$. (The method gives the array 93 positions with indices 0 through 92 because F_{92} is the largest Fibonacci number that fits in a long integer.)

The method then checks the cache to see if it has already calculated the value that it needs. If the value is not yet in the cache, the method calls itself recursively to store that value in the array. It can then return the desired value.

This method follows the same general approach as the initial recursive approach. The big difference is that it stores any value that it calculates so that it doesn't need to calculate the same values again and again. For example, if you look back at the earlier diagram, you'll see that the tree calculates F_4 twice. The new method would only calculate that value once and save it, so it would chop off the entire F_4 subtree from the calculation. When calculating larger values, the savings are huge.

Even better, after a while the cache table will contain all of the Fibonacci numbers up to F_{92}, so the method will never need to perform new calculations. You could even prefill the table when the program starts so that the method can look up values later.

There's one more point about this example worth mentioning. Fibonacci numbers don't grow as quickly as factorials, but they do grow quickly, so large Fibonacci numbers will overflow 64-bit long integers. For that reason, the methods protect themselves with `checked` blocks.

To summarize, there are several lessons to be learned from this example. First, if a recursive solution works and is easy to understand, then use it. If a recursive approach recalculates the same values many times, try a bottom-up approach. If a bottom-up approach is confusing, consider saving intermediate values in a table. Finally, if you're using a table, ask yourself whether it's worth converting the table into a cache so that you can reuse saved values later.

Download the `FibonacciNumbers` example solution to see additional details.

6. Binomial coefficients

The following method simply uses the formula for calculating the binomial coefficient:

```
// Calculate the binomial coefficient.
private long CalculatedNchooseK(int n, int k)
{
    checked
    {
        return Factorial(n) / Factorial(k) / Factorial(n - k);
    }
}
```

This is quick and easy, but it only works if the factorials are all small enough to be calculated. For example, it is obvious that $\binom{100}{100} = 1$ because there's only one way to pick 100 items out of 100 items, namely picking all of them.

Unfortunately, to use the formula, the method must calculate 100!, and we know from the Solution to Problem 4. *Factorials*, that a program can only calculate factorials up to 20!. Larger values such as 100! cause integer overflow. Even though the final solution may be perfectly reasonable, the formula is impractical if N or K is greater than 20.

The problem statement asked you to verify the following:

$$\binom{28}{3} = 3,276$$

Unfortunately, 28! is too big to fit in a long integer, so this method cannot calculate that value. Fortunately, there's another way to calculate binomial coefficients.

Recall that $\binom{N}{K}$ gives the number of ways that you can pick K items from a set of N items. Now, think about how you might pick K items. The selection could include the first item or not. The total number of ways you could pick K items equals the sum of the numbers of ways the selection could include the first item, plus the number of ways it could not include that item.

Suppose the selection includes the first item. If this is the case, you still need to pick K – 1 items from the remaining N – 1 items to make a full selection. The number of ways to pick K – 1 items from the remaining N – 1 items is the following:

$$\binom{N-1}{K-1}$$

Now, suppose the selection does *not* include the first item. In that case, you still need to pick K items from the remaining N – 1 items to make a full selection. The number of ways to pick K items out of N – 1 items is as follows:

$$\binom{N-1}{K}$$

That means the total number of ways you can pick K items from N items is given by the following formula:

$$\binom{N}{K} = \binom{N-1}{K-1} + \binom{N-1}{K}$$

This formula leads to the following recursive method for calculating binomial coefficients:

```
// Use recursion to find the binomial coefficient.
private long RecursiveNchooseK(int n, int k)
{
    checked
    {
        if (k == 1) return n;
        if (k == n) return 1;
        return
            RecursiveNchooseK(n - 1, k) +
            RecursiveNchooseK(n - 1, k - 1);
    }
}
```

If k is 1, the method returns n because there are n ways to pick 1 value from a set of n values.

Next, if k equals n, the method returns 1 because there is one way to pick n values from a set of n values, namely, pick every item.

If k is neither 1 nor n, the method calls itself recursively to calculate the following:

$$\binom{N-1}{K-1} + \binom{N-1}{K}$$

The method then returns the result.

This method works and does not have a problem with integer overflow, so it can calculate $\binom{28}{3}$. Unfortunately, it has a problem similar to the one encountered by the straightforward method to calculate Fibonacci numbers recursively: it calculates too many intermediate values.

To calculate a value, the method calculates two smaller values. Calculating those values requires the method to calculate two other smaller values, and so forth. If you draw a tree showing the calculations similar to the tree shown earlier for Fibonacci numbers, you get a binary tree with height and business depending on N and K. In the worst case scenario, the tree contains a huge number of nodes, so the calculation takes an extremely long time. The problem statement asked you to calculate $\binom{40}{20}$, and this method is just not up to the challenge.

Solution 5. *Fibonacci Numbers*, described several methods for avoiding this sort of problem with Fibonacci numbers. Unfortunately, a table or cache won't work in this case because the recursive binomial coefficient method calculates a huge number of values but no duplicates.

The other Fibonacci solution takes a bottom-up approach, using smaller values to calculate larger ones. That approach also works here, although it's a bit hard to understand.

To use this approach, consider the original binomial coefficient formula again and rearrange it as follows:

$$\binom{N}{K} = \frac{N!}{K!(N-K)!} = \frac{N(N-1)!}{K(K-1)!((N-1)-(K-1))!} = \frac{N}{K}\binom{N-1}{K-1}$$

This lets you write $\binom{N}{K}$ as the simple fraction N/K times the smaller value $\binom{N-1}{K-1}$. If you repeat this process, you can rewrite the original value as a product of simple fractions:

$$\binom{N}{K} = \frac{N}{K} \times \frac{N-1}{K-1} \times \frac{N-2}{K-2} \times \cdots \times \frac{N-(K-1)}{K-(K-1)}$$

The last term simplifies to $(N - (K - 1)) / 1$, which has the value $N - (K - 1)$.

Now, if you work from right-to-left, you can calculate each value in this sequence in terms of previous values (to the right).

Because each of the intermediate values is also a binomial coefficient, such as $\binom{N-1}{K-1}$, you know that it must be an integer value. (There cannot be 6.3 ways to pick 20 items from a set of 40.) This means that at each stage of calculation, the numbers must cancel out to give an integer result.

All of this gives the following surprisingly simple method for calculating binomial coefficients:

```
// Use canceling to find the binomial coefficient
private long CancelingNchooseK(int n, int k)
{
    checked
    {
        long result = 1;
        for (int i = 1; i <= k; i++)
        {
            result *= n - (k - i);
```

```
            result /= i;
        }
        return result;
    }
}
```

This method is fast, only requiring K steps. The numbers also cancel as the calculation progresses, so there's no integer overflow unless the final result is too big. For example, $\binom{100}{50}$ is just plain huge, no matter how you try to calculate it.

This method can verify the following:

$$\binom{40}{20} = 137,846,528,820$$

You can use the solution to this problem to verify the number of solutions found for Problem 3. *Combinations*. That problem asked you to find combinations of K items picked from a total of N items. This problem asks you to calculate the number of those combinations.

Download the `BinomialCoefficients` example solution to see additional details.

7. Pascal's triangle

The following method generates the indicated number of rows in Pascal's triangle:

```
// Make a Pascal's triangle with the desired number of rows.
private List<List<int>> MakePascalsTriangle(int numRows)
{
    // Make the result list.
    List<List<int>> triangle = new List<List<int>>();

    // Make the first row.
    List<int> prevRow = new List<int>();
    prevRow.Add(1);
    triangle.Add(prevRow);

    // Make the other rows.
    for (int rowNum = 2; rowNum <= numRows; rowNum++)
    {
        // Make the next row.
        List<int> newRow = new List<int>();
        newRow.Add(1);
        for (int colNum = 2; colNum < rowNum; colNum++)
```

```
        {
            newRow.Add(
                prevRow[colNum - 2] +
                prevRow[colNum - 1]);
        }
        newRow.Add(1);

        // Prepare for the next row.
        triangle.Add(newRow);
        prevRow = newRow;
    }
    return triangle;
}
```

This method creates a result list and then adds the top row of the triangle containing the single value 1.

It then enters a loop to calculate each of the remaining rows from the rows above them in the result list.

Alternatively, you could use one of the methods in Solution 6. *Binomial Coefficients*, to calculate each of the triangle's binomial coefficients directly.

The following method converts a triangle's entries from a List<List<int>> into a multiline string:

```
// Convert a Pascal's triangle into a string
private string TriangleToString(List<List<int>> triangle
{
    StringBuilder sb = new StringBuilder();
    foreach (List<int> row in triangle)
    {
        sb.AppendLine(
            string.Join(" ",
                row.ConvertAll(i => i.ToString())));
    }
    return sb.ToString();
}
```

This method creates a StringBuilder and then loops through the triangle's rows. It uses the ConvertAll LINQ extension method to convert the row's values into strings, uses string.Join to concatenate those strings into a single space-delimited string, and adds the row's space-delimited values to the StringBuilder.

After it processes all of the rows, the method returns the text in the StringBuilder.

The following screenshot shows the `PascalsTriangle` example solution, displaying the first 10 rows of Pascal's triangle:

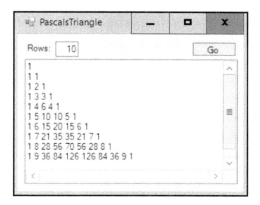

Displaying Pascal's triangle graphically is a bit more challenging. The `PascalsTriangleGraphical` example solution uses the following code to draw Pascal's triangle:

```
// The Pascal's triangle.
private List<List<int>> PascalsTriangle = null;
// Draw the triangle on the PictureBox.
private void DrawTriangle(Graphics gr, int cx)
{
    gr.Clear(Color.White);
    if (PascalsTriangle == null) return;
    gr.TextRenderingHint = TextRenderingHint.AntiAliasGridFit;
    gr.SmoothingMode = SmoothingMode.AntiAlias;

    // The size of an item.
    const int wid = 30;
    const int hgt = 30;
    const int margin = 2;
    // Make a StringFormat to center text.
    using (StringFormat sf = new StringFormat())
    {
        sf.Alignment = StringAlignment.Center;
        sf.LineAlignment = StringAlignment.Center;

        // Make a font to use.
        using (Font font = new Font("Segoe", 9))
        {
            int y = 4;

            // Draw each row.
```

```
int numRows = PascalsTriangle.Count;
for (int rowNum = 1; rowNum <= numRows; rowNum++)
{
    // Start on the left so the row is centered.
    int x = cx - rowNum * wid / 2;

    // Draw the items in this row.
    List<int> row = PascalsTriangle[rowNum - 1];
    for (int colNum = 1; colNum <= rowNum; colNum++)
    {
        Rectangle rect = new Rectangle(
            x + margin, y + margin,
            wid - 2 * margin, hgt - 2 * margin);
        gr.DrawString(row[colNum - 1].ToString(),
            font, Brushes.Blue, rect, sf);
        gr.DrawEllipse(Pens.Black, rect);
        x += wid;
    }
    y += hgt;
}
}
}
```

The `PascalsTriangle` variable holds the solution found by the previous `MakePascalsTriangle` method.

The `DrawTriangle` method first performs some setup chores. It makes a `StringFormat` object that it can use to center text in a rectangle and creates a font. It then initializes the variable `y` to indicate the vertical position of the first row.

The method then loops through the triangle's rows. For each row, the method calculates the row's width, divides that by 2, and subtracts the result from the X coordinate of the center of the `PictureBox`. That gives the X coordinate where the program must start drawing the row in order to center it horizontally.

Next, the code loops through the row to draw its values, updating the variable `x` after each.

To draw a value, the code makes a rectangle at position `(x, y)`, and with the width and height given by the constants `wid` and `hgt`. It offsets the position and dimensions to make a margin between values.

This method draws the value centered inside the rectangle and then uses the same rectangle to draw an ellipse around the value.

The following screenshot shows the `PascalsTriangleGraphical` program in action:

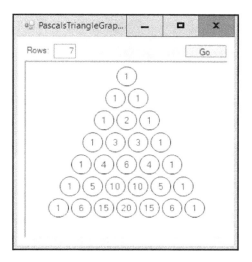

 Note that the program doesn't try to adjust the size of the ellipses depending on the length of the values. For example, the 20th row of the triangle contains the value 92,378, which won't fit in the ellipses drawn by the preceding code. Modifying the program to handle larger values would make an interesting exercise, so I encourage you to give it a try.

Download the `PascalsTriangle` and `PascalsTriangleGraphical` example solutions to see additional details.

8. Greatest common divisors

The most obvious way to calculate GCD(A, B) is to simply try all of the values smaller than A and B and see which ones divide both numbers. That method is straightforward and reasonably fast, although it could take a while if A and B are very large. In particular, using this method to find GCD(10370370276, 82962962964) could take a long time.

A faster alternative would be to factor A and B (I'll talk about factoring later in this chapter) and then determine the factors that they have in common.

An even faster alternative was described by Euclid (pronounced *yoo-klid*) around 300 BC. Because he first described the algorithm, it is called **Euclid's algorithm** or the Euclidean algorithm.

The idea behind the algorithm is that, if A > B and C evenly divides both A and B, then C must also evenly divide A – B. That leads to the following algorithm:

1. Set remainder = A mod B
2. If remainder is 0, then B is the GCD
3. Otherwise set A = B and B = remainder, and then repeat from step 1

For example, the following steps show the calculation for GCD(180, 48):

1. Remainder = 180 % 48 = 36
2. A = 48, B = 36
3. Remainder = 48 % 36 = 12
4. A = 36, B = 12
5. Remainder = 36 % 12 = 0
6. At this point, the remainder is 0, so the GCD is B, which is 12

This calculation found GCD(180, 48) in only six steps.

The following method uses this algorithm to calculate the GCD:

```
// Use Euclid's algorithm to find GCD(a, b).
private long GCD(long a, long b)
{
    a = Math.Abs(a);
    b = Math.Abs(b);

    // Pull out remainders.
    for (;;)
    {
        long remainder = a % b;
        if (remainder == 0) return b;
        a = b;
        b = remainder;
    };
}
```

This code simply takes the absolute values of its inputs a and b, and then follows Euclid's algorithm.

It's interesting to see what happens if a < b when the algorithm starts. I'll let you work through that on your own.

Download the GCD example solution to see additional details.

9. Least common multiples

Once you know how to calculate GCDs, calculating LCMs is easy. To see why, suppose g = GCD(a, b). Then a = g × A and b = g × B for some integers A and B. In that case, LCM(a, b) is given by g × A × B.

You could divide a and b by g to find A and B, but you don't really need to know A and B. Instead, you can simply calculate LCM(a, b) = a × b/g. If you replace a and b in that equation with g × A and g × B, you get (g × A) × (g × B)/g. Canceling and rearranging a bit gives g × A × B, which is LCM(a, b).

That gives us the following simple method for calculating LCMs:

```
// Find LCM(a, b).
private long LCM(long a, long b)
{
    return a * b / GCD(a, b);
}
```

This method has one drawback. In the mathematical expression, the * and / operators have the same precedence, so the program evaluates them in left-to-right order. That means that it first calculates a * b and then divides that result by g. If a * b is too large, it will cause integer overflow. In particular, if you try to use this method to calculate LCM(1234567000, 7654321000), as required by this problem, the result is -8,996,971,959,702,551, which is clearly incorrect.

You can reduce this problem by making two modifications. First, use the checked keyword to ensure that the program looks for overflow. Second, you can rearrange the calculation to keep the intermediate values as small as possible during the calculation.

The following code shows an improved version of this method:

```
// Find LCM(a, b).
private long LCM(long a, long b)
{
    return checked(a / GCD(a, b) * b);
}
```

Now, the method first divides a by GCD(a, b). We know that GCD(a, b) divides evenly into a because it is a divisor of a, so a / GCD(a, b) is an integer. (In fact, that value is the value A that I described earlier.) The method then multiplies that intermediate value by b. The result may still cause overflow if the LCM is too big, but at least the method won't overflow during an intermediate calculation.

This version of the method can verify that LCM(1234567000, 7654321000) = 9,449,772,114,007,000.

There are two lessons here. First, as in earlier problems, use the checked keyword if there is a chance that the program might cause integer overflow. This lets the program detect the problem rather than trying to continue with a nonsensical result.

The second lesson is that you can sometimes rearrange calculations to avoid integer overflow.

Download the LCM example solution to see additional details.

10. Sums of multiples

One obvious approach for finding multiples of three and five is to loop through the numbers between 3 and the maximum value, check each number to see if it is a multiple of 3 or 5, and add the multiples to get a running total. The following method takes this approach into account:

```
private long Method1(long max)
{
    long total = 0;
    checked
    {
        for (long i = 3; i <= max; i++)
            if ((i % 3 == 0) || (i % 5 == 0))
                total += i;
    }
    return total;
}
```

This is straightforward but not very efficient. If the max parameter is large, this method can take a while.

A better approach is to use a variable to keep track of the next multiple of five and then loop through the multiples of 3. If a multiple of 3 is greater than the next multiple of 5, add that multiple to the total and move it to the next multiple of 5. The following method uses this approach:

```
private long Method2(long max)
{
    long total = 0;
    checked
    {
        int next5 = 5;
        for (long i = 3; i <= max; i += 3)
        {
            total += i;
            if (i == next5)
            {
                next5 += 5;
            }
            else if (i > next5)
            {
                total += next5;
                next5 += 5;
            }
        }

        // Check the final few entries.
        for (long i = max; i > max - 3; i--)
        {
            if (i % 3 == 0) break;
            if (i % 5 == 0)
            {
                total += i;
                break;
            }
        }
    }
    return total;
}
```

This method is much faster than the first version for two reasons. First, it only considers values that are multiples of three or five. Second, it uses addition to increase the `i` and `next5` values, so it always knows that those values are multiples of three or five, respectively. That means that it doesn't need to use the relatively slow modulus operator % to see if a value is a multiple.

This method is effective, but it's rather complicated. That means it will be harder to understand, debug, and maintain. You can make a simpler version if you think a bit more about the problem.

You could use two loops—one to add up multiples of three and a second one to add up multiples of 5. If you did that, however, multiples of both 3 and 5 such as 15 and 30 would be counted twice. You could then fix the total by using another loop to subtract those duplicated multiples of 15 so they are counted only once.

One of the lessons from Solution 9. *Least common multiples,* was that the evaluation order can sometimes cause integer overflow and that same lesson applies here. It is possible that adding up the multiples of 3 and then the multiples of 5 could cause an integer overflow. We can avoid that if we subtract the multiples of 15 after adding the multiples of three and before adding the multiples of five, as shown in the following code:

```
private long Method3(long max)
{
    checked
    {
        long total = 0;
        for (long i = 3; i <= max; i += 3) total += i;
        for (long i = 15; i <= max; i += 15) total -= i;
        for (long i = 5; i <= max; i += 5) total += i;
        return total;
    }
}
```

This version is about as fast as the preceding version and won't cause integer overflow unless the final total is too big to fit in a long integer, in which case we're stuck anyway. However, we can do even better!

Once again, we need to think about the problem in a new way. The preceding solution adds up the numbers 3 + 6 + 9 + ... That sum equals 3 times the slightly simpler sum 1 + 2 + 3 + ... You can use the following equation to calculate the simpler sum without adding up the numbers individually:

$$1 + 2 + 3 + \cdots + N = \frac{N(N+1)}{2}$$

Now, you can use that formula to directly calculate the sums of the multiples of 3, 5, and 15 instead of using loops. The following code demonstrates this method:

```
private long Method4(long max)
{
    checked
    {
        long num3s = max / 3;
        long threes = num3s * (num3s + 1) / 2 * 3;
        long num5s = max / 5;
        long fives = num5s * (num5s + 1) / 2 * 5;
        long num15s = max / 15;
        long fifteens = num15s * (num15s + 1) / 2 * 15;
        return threes - fifteens + fives;
    }
}
```

This code first calculates `max / 3` to get the largest multiple of three less than or equal to max. For example, if max is 25, then `max / 3` = 8. (Keep in mind that this is integer division, so the fractional part is discarded.) The code uses the formula to calculate 1 + 2 + ... + 8 and multiplies the result by 3 to get the total 3 + 6 + ... + 24.

The method repeats those steps to calculate the sums of the multiples of 5 and 15 and combines them to get the final result.

This version of the method performs only a few calculations instead of using long loops, so it is *much* faster than any of the previous solutions.

The following screenshot shows the example solution adding multiples between 0 and 100 million:

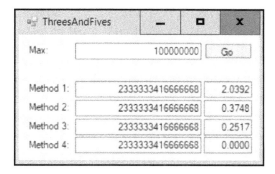

The first solution took around 2 seconds. The second and third approaches took around 0.38 and 0.25 seconds, respectively. Those times are reasonably comparable. The final solution took so little time that it is virtually instantaneous. Unlike the other solutions, the final approach does not depend on the maximum value, so it takes no longer to add up a few values or millions of values.

One lesson to be learned here is that you should (as usual) use the `checked` keyword to look for integer overflow. You should also look at a problem from multiple directions to see if you can restate the problem in a simpler form. In this case, we converted a long, slow loop into a series of faster loops, and then we converted those loops into some simple calculations.

Download the `SumsOfMultiples` example solution to see additional details.

11. Primality testing

One simple way to determine whether a number N is prime is to loop through all of the integers between 2 and N – 1 and use the modulus operator % to see if any of them divide the number evenly. There are a couple of ways that you can improve this approach.

First, note that once you check a potential divisor, you don't need to check any multiples of that divisor. For example, if 2 doesn't divide evenly into N, then 4, 6, 8, and other multiples of 2 also cannot divide evenly into N. To make the basic approach faster, you can test the divisor 2 separately and then make the loop consider only odd numbers.

You can also improve this method by changing the loop's upper limit. The original method considers values between 2 and N – 1, but you can change the upper limit to $\sqrt{N}$. To see why that works, suppose N has a factor A where $A > \sqrt{N}$, so the loop won't find A. In that case, N = A × B for some value, B. If $A > \sqrt{N}$, then B must be less than $\sqrt{N}$, so the loop won't find A, but it will find B.

Making the loop consider only odd numbers and making the loop end at $\sqrt{N}$ gives the following method for determining whether a number is prime:

```
// Return true if the number is prime.
private bool IsPrime(long number)
{
    // Handle 2 separately.
    if (number == 2) return true;
    if (number % 2 == 0) return false;

    // See if the number is divisible by odd values up to Sqrt(number).
```

```
        long sqrt = (long)Math.Sqrt(number);
        for (long i = 3; i <= sqrt; i += 2)
            if (number % i == 0) return false;

        // If we get here, the number is prime.
        return true;
    }
```

Note that this method only uses numbers that are smaller than N, so it cannot cause an integer overflow.

Download the `PrimalityTesting` example solution to see additional details.

12. Prime table

The obvious approach is to loop through all of the values in the array and call the `IsPrime` method, described in the previous solution, to see which values are prime. The following method uses this approach:

```
// Use the IsPrime method to make a table of prime numbers.
private bool[] MakePrimesTable(int max)
{
    // Make the array and mark 2 and odd numbers greater than 1 as
    // prime.
    bool[] isPrime = new bool[max + 1];
    isPrime[2] = true;
    for (int i = 3; i <= max; i += 2) isPrime[i] = IsPrime(i);
    return isPrime;
}
```

This method allocates an array big enough to hold all of the desired values. It then sets `isPrime[2] = true` because 2 is prime. It leaves the other even values alone because they are set to `false` when the array is allocated.

The code then loops through the array's odd numbers and calls the `IsPrime` method, described in the preceding solution, to set each value's array entry. The method finishes by returning the array.

This method is easy to understand, but it's fairly slow. The `IsPrime` method loops over many values, so putting calls to `IsPrime` inside another loop makes the method slow.

While describing the `IsPrime` method in the preceding solution, I mentioned that we could skip multiples of 2 because, if 2 does not divide evenly into a number, then multiples of 2 cannot either.

We can generalize this rule to make building the table of primes faster. After we consider a prime number p, we know that all multiples of p greater than p are non-prime. For example, we know that 2 is prime, so we can conclude that the multiples 2 × 2, 2 × 3, 2 × 4, ... are not prime.

This leads to the *Sieve of Eratosthenes*, named after the Greek mathematician Eratosthenes of Cyrene, who discovered it. The idea is to start with a table that contains an entry for all of the numbers of interest. Initially, we assume that all of the numbers are prime.

Now, you start at entry 2 and cross out the later multiples of 2 to indicate that they are not prime.

You then move from 2 to the next entry that is still marked prime, in this case 3, and you cross out the later multiples of 3.

Again, you move to the next numbers that is still marked as prime. The value 4 was crossed out when we considered multiples of 2. The next prime number is 5, so you cross out later multiples of 5.

You continue these steps, finding the next prime number and crossing out its later multiples, until you have considered all of the values in the table.

The following code implements this method:

```
// Make a sieve of Eratosthenes.
private bool[] MakeSieveOfEratosthenes(int max)
{
    // Make the array and mark 2 and odd numbers greater than 1 as
    // prime.
    bool[] isPrime = new bool[max + 1];
    isPrime[2] = true;
    for (int i = 3; i <= max; i += 2) isPrime[i] = true;

    // Cross out multiples of odd primes.
    for (int i = 3; i <= max; i++)
    {
        // See if i is prime.
        if (isPrime[i])
        {
            // Knock out multiples of i.
            for (int j = i * 2; j <= max; j += i)
                isPrime[j] = false;
        }
    }
    return isPrime;
}
```

When the method allocates the `isPrime` array, its entries are initially `false`. The code marks 2 and the odd numbers as prime, and leaves the remaining even numbers flagged as non-prime.

Next, the code loops through the odd numbers. If a number is marked as prime, the code marks all of its later multiples as non-prime.

This method is much faster than the previous one, which checked each number individually to see if it was prime. The Sieve of Eratosthenes remained state-of-the art for almost 2,000 years until the 18th century when Euler (pronounced *oiler*) discovered a major improvement. Euler noticed that you don't need to cross out all multiples of a prime, p; you only need to cross out multiples p × q where q ≥ p and q is also prime.

For example, when you're crossing out multiples of 7, you cross out 7 × 7, 11 × 7, 13 × 7, 17 × 7, and so forth. You already crossed out multiples of smaller primes when you considered them. For example, you crossed out 5 × 7 when you considered multiples of 5.

Also, you already considered non-prime numbers, q, that are bigger than 7 when you considered the prime factors of those numbers. For example, you crossed out 21 × 7 when you examined multiples of 3.

That's the basic improvement on Eratosthenes' algorithm. When you consider a new prime p, you cross out p times larger values in the table that are still marked as prime.

There's one implementation trick here. When you consider multiples of p, you cannot immediately cross them out because you may need them later. For example, suppose you're considering multiples of 3. You start by crossing out the value 3 × 3 = 9.

The next values of q that you consider are 5 and 7. They're still marked as prime, so you cross out 3 × 5 = 15 and 3 × 7 = 21.

The next value of q that you consider is 9. Unfortunately you just crossed out 9 a little while ago, so it's no longer marked as prime. That means you won't cross out 3 × 9 = 27, and that's a problem because 27 is not prime.

The way Euler handled this was to initially mark multiples of 3 as ready for crossing out, but to leave them in the table until after marking all of the multiples of 3. In this example, the program would mark 9 but not cross it out until after it checked the other multiples including 3 × 9 = 27.

The solution shown here handles this problem in a different way by examining multiples of 3 in decreasing order that lets it consider consider 3 × 9 before it considers 3 × 3.

The following code shows the method that builds Euler's sieve:

```
// Make Euler's sieve.
private bool[] MakeEulersSieve(int max)
{
    // Make the array and mark 2 and odd numbers greater than 1 as
    // prime.
    bool[] isPrime = new bool[max + 1];
    isPrime[2] = true;
    for (int i = 3; i <= max; i += 2) isPrime[i] = true;

    // Cross out multiples of the primes.
    for (int i = 3; i <= max; i += 2)
    {
        // See if i is prime.
        if (isPrime[i])
        {
            // Knock out multiples of p.
            int maxQ = max / i;
            if (maxQ % 2 == 0) maxQ--;      // Make it odd.
            for (int q = maxQ; q >= i; q -= 2)
            {
                // Only use q if it is prime.
                if (isPrime[q]) isPrime[i * q] = false;
            }
        }
    }
    return isPrime;
}
```

This method allocates the `isPrime` array and marks 2 and the odd numbers as prime. It then loops through the odd numbers, looking for those that are still marked as prime.

When it finds a number p that is marked as prime, the code sets the `maxQ` variable to the largest odd number, q, where p × q is within the table. For example, suppose i is 19 and `max` is 1,000. Then the program sets `maxQ` to 51 because 19 × 51 = 969 is the largest odd multiple of 19 that is less than or equal to 1,000.

The program then loops backwards over odd numbers between `maxQ` and i. If one of those numbers is still marked as prime, the program crosses out that value times i.

The following screenshot shows the example program building prime tables program by using the three methods described here. The Sieve of Eratosthenes is much faster than the brute-force approach, but Euler's sieve is even faster:

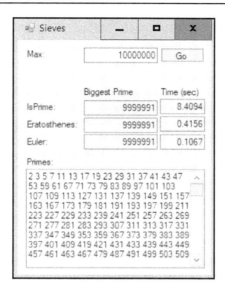

Download the `PrimesTable` example solution to see additional details.

13. Prime factors

The most obvious approach to prime factoring a number is to loop through values less than that number and see if they divide into that number evenly. Each time you find such a factor, you divide it from the number. You continue this process until the modified number equals 1.

The following method uses this approach:

```
// Divide by smaller values up the the square root of the value.
private List<long> Method1(long number)
{
    checked
    {
        List<long> factors = new List<long>();

        // Pull out 2s.
        while (number % 2 == 0)
        {
            factors.Add(2);
            number /= 2;
        }

        // Pull out odd factors.
```

```
long limit = (long)Math.Sqrt(number);
for (long factor = 3; factor <= limit; factor += 2)
{
    while (number % factor == 0)
    {
        factors.Add(factor);
        number /= factor;
        limit = (long)Math.Sqrt(number);
    }
}

// Add the leftover.
if (number != 1) factors.Add(number);
return factors;
}
}
```

The method first uses a loop to pull out factors of 2. As long as the number is divisible by 2, the method adds 2 to the list of factors and divides the number by 2.

Next, the code loops over odd values between 3 and the square root of the number. It doesn't need to consider values greater than the number's square root because, if there is a factor p greater than the square root, then there is another factor, q, less than the square root so that p × q equals the number.

When it finds a factor that divides into the number evenly, the code adds it to the factor list, divides the number by the factor, and then updates the square root for the updated number.

When it finishes examining possible factors, the number is either 1, in which case we have found all of the factors, or it is prime. If the number is prime, the code adds it to the factor list.

This method is reasonably efficient if you only want to factor a single value. If you need to factor a large number of values, however, then you can improve performance by making a pre-calculated table of prime numbers.

The preceding method considers all odd numbers as possible factors, but it really only needs to consider prime numbers as factors. If you build Euler's sieve as was described in the preceding solution, then you can use it to decide which numbers might be factors.

The `PrimeFactors` example solution uses the methods described in the preceding solution to build Euler's sieve. It then uses the following code snippet to convert the sieve into a list containing the prime numbers:

```
// Convert the sieve into a list of primes.
Primes = new List<long>();
Primes.Add(2);
for (int i = 3; i <= max; i += 2)
    if (!isComposite[i]) Primes.Add(i);
```

This code creates a list to hold the prime numbers. It then scans through the sieve stored in the `isComposite` array, adding the primes to the list.

The following method uses the list of prime numbers to factor a value:

```
// Use a pre-made sieve of primes up to MaxNumber.
// Update the limit when we find a prime.
private List<long> Method2(long number)
{
    checked
    {
        List<long> factors = new List<long>();

        // Pull out primes.
        long limit = (long)Math.Sqrt(number);
        foreach (long prime in Primes)
        {
            while (number % prime == 0)
            {
                factors.Add(prime);
                number /= prime;
                limit = (long)Math.Sqrt(number);
            }
            if (prime > limit) break;
        }

        // Add the leftover.
        if (number != 1) factors.Add(number);
        return factors;
    }
}
```

This method is similar to the earlier one, except it only considers prime numbers when looking for factors. It sets `limit` to the square root of the number. It then loops through the precomputed primes list. While a prime evenly divides into the number, the code adds the prime to the factor list, divides the number by the prime, and then updates the limit.

If the prime that the method is considering is greater than the limit, the code breaks out of its loop.

Finally, if the number has not been reduced to 1 by the time the loop ends, the code adds it to the factor list as before.

The following screenshot shows the `PrimeFactors` example solution factoring the number 12,345,678,901,234:

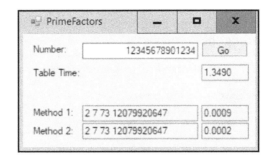

When you enter a value and click **Go**, the program uses the two methods described earlier to factor the number. In the preceding screenshot, you can see that the first method took around 0.0009 seconds and the second method too around 0.0002 seconds when using the second method. The second method is considerably faster, although the absolute times are minuscule, so it would only be worth using the second approach if you needed to factor a *lot* of values. When it started, the program took 1.35 seconds to build a primes list containing numbers up to the square root of 1 × 1015. It can use that list to factor numbers up to 1 × 1015.

Download the `PrimeFactors` example solution to see additional details.

14. Unique prime factors

One obvious way to find a number's unique prime factors is to find all of its prime factors and then remove duplicates. That would be relatively straightforward and fast.

An alternative strategy would be to modify the code that factors numbers so that it only saves one copy of each prime factor. The following method takes this approach:

```
// Find a number's unique prime factors.
private List<long> FindUniquePrimeFactors(long number)
{
    checked
```

```
    {
        List<long> factors = new List<long>();

        // Pull out 2s.
        if (number % 2 == 0)
        {
            factors.Add(2);
            while (number % 2 == 0) number /= 2;
        }

        // Pull out odd factors.
        long limit = (long)Math.Sqrt(number);
        for (long factor = 3; factor <= limit; factor += 2)
        {
            if (number % factor == 0)
            {
                factors.Add(factor);
                while (number % factor == 0)
                {
                    number /= factor;
                    limit = (long)Math.Sqrt(number);
                }
            }
        }

        // Add the leftover.
        if (number != 1) factors.Add(number);
        return factors;
    }
}
```

This method is similar to the one used in the preceding solution, except it only keeps one copy of each prime factor.

Like the preceding solution, you can make this solution faster if you build a prefilled list of prime numbers to use when searching for factors.

The lesson to be learned here is that you can sometimes solve a new problem by reusing an existing solution, but sometimes it's worth modifying the existing solution to make the new approach simpler.

Download the UniquePrimeFactors example solution to see additional details.

15. Prime tuples

This is a relatively straightforward problem. Simply create an Euler's sieve and then search it for primes that have the right spacing and number. The following method takes this approach:

```
// Look for groups of primes.
private List<List<int>> FindPrimeGroups(int max,
    int spacing, int number, bool[] isPrime)
{
    List<List<int>> results = new List<List<int>>();

    // Treat 2 specially.
    List<int> group = GroupAt(2, max, spacing, number, isPrime);
    if (group != null) results.Add(group);

    // Check odd primes to see if a group starts there.
    for (int p = 3; p <= max; p += 2)
    {
        group = GroupAt(p, max, spacing, number, isPrime);
        if (group != null) results.Add(group);
    }

    // Return the groups we found.
    return results;
}
```

This method's final parameter, isPrime, is an Euler's sieve containing primes up to the maximum value, max.

The method calls the GroupAt method, which will be described shortly, to see if there is a group of primes with the desired spacing and number starting with the value 2. Like many programs that deal with primes, this one treats 2 specially because it is the only even prime number, and that lets the code look only at odd values later.

After considering 2, the method loops over odd values up to max and uses the GroupAt method to see if any of them begin the right kind of prime groups.

The following code shows the GroupAt method:

```
// Determine whether the indicated number begins a group.
// Return the group or null if there is no group here.
private List<int> GroupAt(int startIndex, int max,
    int spacing, int number, bool[] isPrime)
{
    // See if there is room for a group.
```

```
    if (startIndex + (number - 1) * spacing > max)
        return null;

    // If there is no group here, return null.
    for (int i = 0; i < number; i++)
        if (!isPrime[startIndex + i * spacing])
            return null;

    // We found a group. Return it.
    List<int> result = new List<int>();
    for (int i = 0; i < number; i++)
        result.Add(startIndex + i * spacing);
    return result;
}
```

This method first checks to see if there is room before the `max` value for the desired primes. For example, if `max` is 100 and we're looking for a group of two primes spaced four apart, then there's no need to check for a group starting at position 97 because 97 + 4 = 101 is greater than `max`. (This check is important because it prevents the program from trying to access `isPrime[101]`, which would cause an `IndexOutOfRangeException`.)

The method then loops through the desired number of values with the indicated spacing. For example, if `spacing` is 6, `number` is 3, and `startIndex` is 17, then the program would examine the values 17, 23, and 29.

If the `isPrime` array shows that any of the values are not prime, the method returns `null`.

If all of the examined values are prime, the method returns them in a list.

If you experiment with the program for a while, you'll notice something interesting about the values. If you look for *two* primes with any even spacing (as in {p, p + 2}, {p, p + 4}, {p, p + 6}, and so on), you'll find lots of results. However, if you look for three or four primes (as in {p, p + 2, p + 4} or {p, p + 6, p + 12}), you'll only get interesting results if the spacing is a multiple of three.

To see why, suppose we're looking for three primes and the spacing is 2, so we're looking for a set {p, p + 2, p + 4}. In that case, one of those three values must be a multiple of three, so that value cannot be prime. (Unless the first value *is* 3, as in {3, 5, 7} or {3, 7, 11}.) This means that you won't find groups of three or more with a spacing of 2.

The same argument works if the spacing is some other value that is not a multiple of three.

In contrast, if the spacing *is* a multiple of three, then either all of the values are multiples of three, or none of them are. If none of them are multiples of three, then they *might all* be prime.

Download the `PrimeTuples` example solution to see additional details.

16. Proper divisors

An obvious method for finding the proper divisors of the number N is to consider all of the values between 1 and N/2 and see which ones divide into N evenly. The following method takes this approach:

```
// Examine values between 1 and number / 2.
private List<long> Method1(long number)
{
    checked
    {
        List<long> divisors = new List<long>();
        long limit = number / 2;
        for (long factor = 1; factor <= limit; factor++)
        {
            if (number % factor == 0)
                divisors.Add(factor);
        }
        return divisors;
    }
}
```

This method is straightforward, but it can be slow if the number is large. For example, if the number is 10 billion, then the method must examine 5 billion values.

In contrast, the prime factoring algorithms described earlier in this chapter only needed to examine values up to the square root of the number. For example, if the number is 10 billion, then its square root is 100,000, which is 50,000 times smaller than the 5 billion numbers examined by the preceding code.

The reason why prime factoring code only needs to examine values up to the square root of the number is that each larger factor would be paired with a smaller factor. If the number N = p × q and p > $\sqrt{N}$, then q < $\sqrt{N}$. If we only examine values up to $\sqrt{N}$, we won't find p, but we will find q.

We can use similar logic when we look for divisors. Continuing from the previous example, if we only examine values up to $\sqrt{N}$, we still won't find p. However, when we find q, we can use it to calculate p because N = p × q. That gives us the following method for finding divisors:

```
// Examine values between 2 and Sqrt(number).
private List<long> GetProperDivisors(long number)
{
    checked
    {
        List<long> divisors = new List<long>();
        divisors.Add(1);
        long limit = (long)Math.Sqrt(number);
        for (long divisor = 2; divisor <= limit; divisor++)
        {
            if (number % divisor == 0)
            {
                divisors.Add(divisor);
                long divisor2 = number / divisor;
                if (divisor != divisor2) divisors.Add(divisor2);
            }
        }
        divisors.Sort();
        return divisors;
    }
}
```

This method creates the `divisors` list and adds 1 to it. It then loops over values between 2 and the square root of the number.

If a value divides evenly into the number, then it is a divisor, so the method adds it to the `divisors` list.

The number divided by the divisor is also a divisor, so the method also adds it to the list. The only trick here is that the two divisors might be the same if the number is a perfect square. For example, if the number is 49, then the method will find the two divisors 7 and 49/7 = 7. The method checks that the second divisor is different from the first before adding it to the list.

Because the method adds small and large divisors in pairs, the final list is not sorted, so the method sorts the list before returning it.

The following screenshot shows the `ProperDivisors` example solution finding the 71 proper divisors of the number 123,456,780. You can see that the second method is much faster than the first:

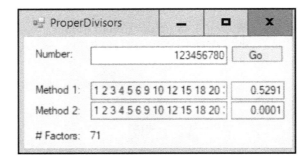

The trick to this solution was to think about the earlier technique used by the factoring algorithms and then find a way to apply a similar technique to this problem. Examining values only up to the square root of the number saved a huge amount of time.

Download the `ProperDivisors` example solution to see additional details.

17. Amicable numbers

The obvious approach to this problem is to examine each pair of values between 1 and the maximum and see if the sums of their proper divisors equal each other. There are two problems with this method.

First, there are a *lot* of pairs of values. If the maximum number is 100,000, then there are 100,000 numbers that can be paired with 99,999 other numbers, making a total of 100,000 × 99,999 = 9,999,900,000, or almost 10 billion pairs to consider.

The second problem is that this technique would recalculate the sum of each value's divisors every time it considered that value. For 100,000 numbers, that means finding and adding divisors almost 20 billion times, once for both values in every pair.

To solve the first problem, you can change the question slightly. Instead of asking whether a pair is amicable, you could ask, for a given value, what other value would be its pair if it has one. For example, when you consider the value 123, you would add its divisors {1, 3, 41} to get 1 + 3 + 41 = 45. You would then examine the value 45 and add *that* number's divisors {1, 3, 5, 9, 15} to get 1 + 3 + 5 + 9 + 15 = 33. This result, 33, is not the original value, 123, so the two numbers 123 and 45 are not amicable.

This greatly reduces the number of calculations we need to make. Instead of examining almost 10 billion pairs, we only examine 100,000 values and their potential pairs, making this around 200,000 calculations instead of 20 billion.

We can even reduce the second problem somewhat by pre-calculating each number's sum of divisors. We know that we will need to calculate every value's sum at least once, so we won't be performing any extra calculations by pre-calculating those values. That will also allow us to avoid calculating the sum for the second value in each potential pair, so we save roughly half of those calculations.

These two enhancements give us the following method for finding amicable pairs:

```
// Find amicable numbers <= max.
private List<List<long>> FindAmicablePairs(long max)
{
    // Get the array of sums.
    long[] sums = GetSumsOfDivisors(max);

    // Look for pairs.
    List<List<long>> pairs = new List<List<long>>();
    for (int value = 1; value <= max; value++)
    {
        long sum = sums[value];
        if ((sum > value) && (sum <= max) && (sums[sum] == value))
        {
            List<long> pair = new List<long>();
            pair.Add(value);
            pair.Add(sums[value]);
            pairs.Add(pair);
        }
    }
    return pairs;
}
```

The method first calls the GetSumsOfDivisors method, which is described shortly, to build an array of every value's sum of divisors. It then loops through the values between 1 and the maximum number. For each value, the code looks up the value's sum of divisors to find its potential pair. It then compares the pair's sum with the current value. If the two match, then this is an amicable pair.

The code performs two other tests before it accepts the pair. First, it checks that the second value is greater than the original value. This prevents the code from deciding that a number is its own pair. (The definition of amicable numbers says that they are two different numbers.)

This test also ensures that we find each pair only once. For example, the program won't find the pair {220, 284} and then later find {284, 220}.

The second test also ensures that the second number in the potential pair is no greater than the maximum value. This guarantees that it is small enough to lie within the sums array, so we can look at its sum without causing an IndexOutOfRange exception.

The following code shows the GetSumsOfDivisors method:

```
// Calculate the sums of the divisors of numbers between 1 and max.
private long[] GetSumsOfDivisors(long max)
{
    // Make room for the sums.
    long[] sums = new long[max + 1];

    // Fill in the sums.
    for (long i = 1; i <= max; i++)
        sums[i] = GetProperDivisors(i).Sum();

    // Return the result.
    return sums;
}
```

This method creates an array to hold the sums and then loops through the values. It calls the GetProperDivisors method (which was used in the previous solution) for each value, adds the divisors, and saves the result in the sums array.

This technique is fast enough that the program can examine the first one million numbers for amicable pairs in just a few seconds. The two tricks here are to invert the problem so that we only need to examine the numbers once instead of looking at all of the pairs of numbers, and storing pre-calculated values so that we don't need to calculate them multiple times.

Download the AmicableNumbers example solution to see additional details.

18. Perfect numbers

You can modify the preceding solution to find perfect numbers. Because you only need to calculate the sum of each value's divisors once, there's no need to pre-calculate those values and store them in an array. That wouldn't cost you much time, but it would use up a bunch of unnecessary memory.

The following code shows a method that finds perfect numbers:

```
// Find perfect numbers <= max.
private List<long> FindPerfectNumbers(long max)
{
    // Look for perfect numbers.
    List<long> values = new List<long>();
    for (int value = 1; value <= max; value++)
    {
        long sum = GetProperDivisors(value).Sum();
        if (value == sum) values.Add(value);
    }
    return values;
}
```

This method loops through the values that are less than the maximum. For each value, it calls the `GetProperDivisors` method, which is used in the previous solution, and calls `Sum` to add the divisors. If the sum equals the original number, the code adds the number to its list of perfect numbers.

Download the `PerfectNumbers` example solution to see additional details.

19. Armstrong numbers

The obvious approach to this problem is to loop through the candidate numbers, convert each into a string, pull apart its digits, raise the digits to the correct power, and see if they add up to the original number.

The following method loops through values up to the desired maximum to build a list of Armstrong numbers:

```
// Look for Armstrong numbers <= max.
private List<long> FindArmstrongNumbers(long max)
{
    List<long> values = new List<long>();
    for (long i = 1; i <= max; i++)
        if (IsArmstrong(i)) values.Add(i);
    return values;
}
```

This method calls the following `IsArmstrong` method to see if a value is an Armstrong number:

```
// Return true if this is an Armstrong number.
private bool IsArmstrong(long number)
{
    // Get the number's digits.
    long copy = number;
    List<long> digits = new List<long>();
    while (copy > 0L)
    {
        digits.Add(copy % 10L);
        copy = copy / 10L;
    }

    // Add the digits' powers.
    long total = 0;
    long numDigits = digits.Count;
    foreach (long digit in digits)
        total += (long)Math.Pow(digit, numDigits);
    return (total == number);
}
```

The only non-obvious pieces in this method are the two statements that calculate the digit and update the copy of the number. The calculation `copy % 10L` returns the number's least significant digit. For example, 417 % 10L returns 7.

The calculation `copy / 10L` returns the number with its least significant digit removed. For example, 417 % 10L returns 41.

Download the `ArmstrongNumbers` example solution to see additional details.

2
Geometry

This chapter includes geometric problems. Some ask you to calculate values such as π or the area below a curve. Others demonstrate useful techniques such as Monte Carlo algorithms. Finally, some are directly useful if you need to perform geometric operations such as drawing arrowheads or finding intersections between line segments.

Many of these problems have intuitive graphical purposes. In those cases, the solutions may include graphical components that draw the problem and its solution. The graphics code usually isn't necessary to solve the problems, however; it just makes visualizing the solution easier, so I won't describe that code in detail. Download the solutions to see all of the details.

Problems

Use the following problems to test your geometric programming skills. Give each problem a try before you turn to the solutions and download the example programs. If you have trouble with the graphical part, try to implement the non-graphical pieces. Then, you can download the example solutions and replace the key parts of the program with your code.

20. Monte Carlo π

A Monte Carlo algorithm uses randomness to approximate the solution to a problem. Often, using more random samples gives you a more accurate approximated solution or gives a greater probability that the solution is correct.

For this problem, use a Monte Carlo algorithm to approximate π. To do that, generate random points in the square (0 ≤ X, Y ≤ 1) and then see how many fall within a circle centered in that square.

21. Newton's π

Various mathematicians have developed many different ways to approximate π over the years. Sir Isaac Newton devised the following formula to calculate π:

$$\pi = 6 \sum_{n=0}^{\infty} \frac{(2n)!}{2^{4n+1}(n!)^2(2n+1)}$$

Use Newton's method to approximate π. Let the user enter the number of terms to calculate. Display the approximation and its error.

How does this value compare to the fraction 355/113? Do you need to use `checked` blocks to protect the code?

22. Bisection root-finding

Root-finding algorithms find values (*y*) for which an equation *y* = *F(x)* equals zero. For example, the equation $y = x^2 - 4$ has roots at *x* = 2 and *x* = -2 because at those values *y* = 0.

To find roots using binary subdivision, the program starts with an interval, $x_0 \leq x \leq x_1$, which we suspect contains a root. For the method to work, $F(x_0)$ and $F(x_1)$ must have different signs. In other words, one must be greater than zero and one must be less than zero.

To look for the root, the method picks the middle X value, $x_{new} = (x_0 + x_1) / 2$, and then calculates $F(x_{new})$. If the result is greater than zero, then you know that the root lies between x_{new} and whichever of x_0 and x_1 gives a value less than zero.

Similarly, if the result is less than zero, you know that the root lies between x_{new} and whichever of x0 and x1, whichever gives a value greater than zero.

Now, you update x_0 and x_1 to bound the new interval. You then repeat the process until $F(x_0)$ and $F(x_1)$ are within some maximum allowed error value.

Write a program that uses binary subdivision to find roots for equations. Make the equation a delegate parameter to the main method so you can easily pass the method different equations. Use the program to find the roots for the following equations:

$$y = x^2 - 4$$

$$y = x^3 - x^2 + 3$$

$$y = \frac{(x^4 + 2x^3 - 12x^2 - 2x + 6)}{10}$$

For extra credit, make the program draw the equations and their roots.

23. Newton's method

Binary subdivision uses intervals to quickly converge on an equation's root. Newton's method, which is also called the **Newton-Raphson method**, uses a different technique to converge even more quickly.

The method starts with a value (x). As long as *F(x)* is not close enough to zero, the method uses the derivative of the function to find the slope *F'(x)*. It then follows the tangent line at that point to the new point *x'* where the line intersects the X axis. The value *x'* becomes the method's next guess for the root. The program continues calculating new values until *F(x)* is close enough to 0.

Finding the point of intersection between the tangent line and the X axis is easier than you might think. If you start with the value x_i, you simply use the following equation to find the next value, x_{i+1}:

$$x_{i+1} = x_i - \frac{F(x_i)}{F'(x_i)}$$

Here, *F* is the function and *F'* is its derivative.

Write a program that uses Newton's method to find roots for equations. Make the equation and its derivative delegate parameters to the main method so you can easily pass different equations to the method. Use the program to find the roots for the following equations:

$$y = x^2 - 4$$

$$y = x^3 - x^2 + 3$$

$$y = \frac{(x^4 + 2x^3 - 12x^2 - 2x + 6)}{10}$$

In case you don't remember your calculus, the derivatives of those functions are the following:

$$y' = 2x$$

$$y' = 3x^2 - 2x$$

$$y = \frac{(4x^3 + 6x^2 - 24x - 2)}{10}$$

For extra credit, make the program draw the equations and their roots.

24. Gaussian elimination

Bisection and Newton's method let you find solutions to an equation of the form $F(x) = 0$. **Gaussian elimination** lets you find the solution to a system of linear equations of the following form:

$$A_1 \cdot x_1 + B_1 \cdot x_2 + \cdots + N_1 \cdot x_n = C_1$$
$$A_2 \cdot x_1 + B_2 \cdot x_2 + \cdots + N_2 \cdot x_n = C_2$$
$$\vdots$$
$$A_n \cdot x_1 + B_n \cdot x_2 + \cdots + N_n \cdot x_n = C_n$$

For example, consider the following equations where n is 2:

$$9 \cdot x_1 + 4 \cdot x_2 = 7$$
$$4 \cdot x_1 + 3 \cdot x_2 = 8$$

The solution to these equations includes the values for x_1 and x_2 that make both of the equations true. In this example, you can plug in the values $x_1 = -1$ and $x_2 = 4$ to verify that those values form a solution.

This problem asks you to use Gaussian elimination to solve systems of equations. Unfortunately, you need to know a fair amount of background to use Gaussian elimination.

To perform Gaussian elimination, you first represent the equations as a matrix multiplied by a vector of variables $x_1, x_2, \dots , x_n$ giving a vector of constants $C_1, C_2, \dots , C_n$, as shown in the following matrix equation:

$$
\begin{vmatrix}
A_1 & B_1 & \cdots & N_1 \\
A_2 & B_2 & \cdots & N_2 \\
 & & \ddots & \\
A_n & B_n & \cdots & N_n
\end{vmatrix}
\times
\begin{vmatrix}
x_1 \\
x_2 \\
\vdots \\
x_n
\end{vmatrix}
=
\begin{vmatrix}
C_1 \\
C_2 \\
\vdots \\
C_n
\end{vmatrix}
$$

Next, you convert this into an **augmented matrix** that holds the original coefficients plus two extra columns, one to hold the C values and one to hold the final solution. Initially, that final column should be initialized to all zeros, as shown in the following matrix:

$$
\begin{vmatrix}
A_1 & B_1 & \cdots & N_1 & C_1 & 0 \\
A_2 & B_2 & \cdots & N_2 & C_2 & 0 \\
 & & \ddots & & & \\
A_n & B_n & \cdots & N_n & C_n & 0
\end{vmatrix}
$$

Now you perform row operations to reduce this augmented matrix into an upper triangular form.

In a **row operation**, you can add multiples of one row to another row. For example, if you add $-A_2/A_1$ times the first row to the second row, then the new second row has a 0 in its first position. That row's other positions will depend on the other values in the two rows. For example, the entry in its second column will be $B_2 - A_2/A_1 \times B_1$.

The important thing about row operations is that they do not change the truth of the system of equations. If a set of values $(x_1, x_2, ..., x_n)$ solves the original equations, then those values also solve the equations after you perform row operations.

Start by using row operations on the first row to zero out the first entries in all rows after row zero. Next, use row operations with the second row to zero out the entries in the second column below that row. Continue using the kth row to zero out the entries in column k in the rows that follow until the augmented matrix has an upper triangular form, like the following:

$$\begin{vmatrix} A_1' & B_1' & \cdots & N_1' & C_1' & 0 \\ 0 & B_2' & \cdots & N_2' & C_2' & 0 \\ & & \ddots & & & \\ 0 & 0 & \cdots & N_n' & C_n' & 0 \end{vmatrix}$$

You may run into a problem when you try to put the augmented matrix into upper triangular form. When you're considering row k, you may find that it has a 0 in column k. In that case, you cannot use that row to zero out column k in the following rows because that would require you to divide by zero.

In that case, simply swap row k with a later row that does not have a 0 in column k. Then you can continue converting the matrix into upper triangular form. If you ever find that all of the remaining rows have 0 in column k, then there is no unique solution to the system of equations.

After the augmented matrix is in upper triangular form, you are ready to pull out the solution. At this point, the augmented array represents the following system equations:

$$A_1' \cdot x_1 + B_1' \cdot x_2 + \cdots + N_1' \cdot x_n = C_1'$$
$$0 \cdot x_1 + B_2' \cdot x_2 + \cdots + N_2' \cdot x_n = C_2'$$
$$\vdots$$
$$0 \cdot x_1 + 0 \cdot x_2 + \cdots + N_n' \cdot x_n = C_n'$$

Now, you can easily solve the last equation and get $x_n = C'_n / N'_n$. You can save that value in the final column of the augmented matrix's last row. Then, you can plug the value for x_n into the second-to-last equation to find x_{n-1} and save the result in the second-to-last row's final column.

Next, you plug x_n and x_{n-1} into the third-to-last equation to find x_{n-2}.

You continue using the values that you have found so far to find new values farther up in the augmented matrix until you have found all of the values and saved them in the matrix's final column. This process is called **backsolving**.

Now that you understand how Gaussian elimination works, here's your problem. Write a program similar to the one shown in the following screenshot that allows the user to enter the coefficients for a set of linear equations and then solves them:

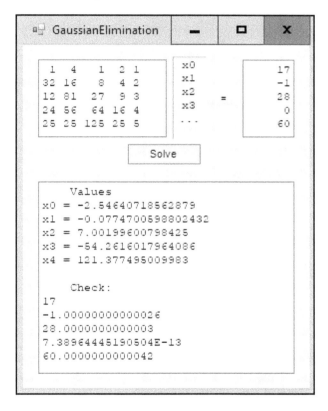

Use the program to solve the following systems of equations:

$$\begin{vmatrix} 1 & -3 & 1 \\ 2 & -8 & 8 \\ -6 & 3 & -15 \end{vmatrix} \times \begin{vmatrix} x_1 \\ x_2 \\ x_3 \end{vmatrix} = \begin{vmatrix} 4 \\ -2 \\ 9 \end{vmatrix}$$

$$\begin{vmatrix} 9 & 3 & 4 \\ 4 & 3 & 4 \\ 1 & 1 & 1 \end{vmatrix} \times \begin{vmatrix} x_1 \\ x_2 \\ x_3 \end{vmatrix} = \begin{vmatrix} 7 \\ 8 \\ 3 \end{vmatrix}$$

$$\begin{vmatrix} 1 & 1 & 1 & 1 & 1 \\ 32 & 16 & 8 & 4 & 2 \\ 243 & 81 & 27 & 9 & 3 \\ 1024 & 256 & 64 & 16 & 4 \\ 3125 & 625 & 125 & 25 & 5 \end{vmatrix} \times \begin{vmatrix} x_1 \\ x_2 \\ x_3 \\ x_4 \\ x_5 \end{vmatrix} = \begin{vmatrix} 1 \\ -1 \\ 8 \\ -56 \\ 569 \end{vmatrix}$$

$$\begin{vmatrix} 2 & -1 & 1 \\ 3 & 2 & -4 \\ -6 & 3 & -3 \end{vmatrix} \times \begin{vmatrix} x_1 \\ x_2 \\ x_3 \end{vmatrix} = \begin{vmatrix} 1 \\ 4 \\ 2 \end{vmatrix}$$

$$\begin{vmatrix} 1 & -1 & 2 \\ 4 & 4 & -2 \\ -2 & 2 & -4 \end{vmatrix} \times \begin{vmatrix} x_1 \\ x_2 \\ x_3 \end{vmatrix} = \begin{vmatrix} -3 \\ 1 \\ 6 \end{vmatrix}$$

25. Monte Carlo integration

Integration is the process of calculating the area inside a region. Typically, this is the area under a curve defined by some function $y = F(x)$. For example, in the following diagram, the goal is to calculate the shaded area under the curve in the domain -2 ≤ x ≤ 1.5:

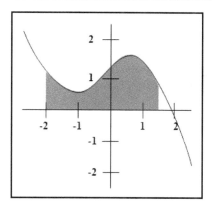

You can use calculus to integrate the area under a curve, at least if you remember your calculus and the function is reasonably well-behaved. If you cannot apply calculus, then you can use **Monte Carlo integration**.

From the name and your experience with Monte Carlo approximation for π, you may be able to guess how this works. Pick a rectangle that includes the area of interest. Then, randomly generate points within the rectangle and see how many lie within the range and between the curve and the X axis. Finally, use the fraction of points in that area to estimate the area beneath the curve.

Write a program that performs Monte Carlo integration. As in the previous examples, pass the function into the method as a parameter so you can easily change it. Use your program to estimate the areas below the following functions within the indicated domains:

Function	Domain
$y = x^2 + 1$	$-1.5 \le x \le 1.5$
$y = x^3 - 2x^2 + 2$	$-1 \le x \le 2$
$y = \sin(x) + \cos(2x) + 2.5$	$-4 \le x \le 3$

If you remember your calculus, make the program calculate the areas exactly and compare the calculated result and the result approximated by Monte Carlo integration.

26. Rectangle rule integration

Monte Carlo integration is relatively simple, but it's also not repeatable. If you perform the same test multiple times with a different selection of random points, you'll get slightly different results.

Another method for estimating an area is to use a **Riemann sum**. (The method is named after the 19th century German mathematician Bernhard Riemann who made great contributions to integral geometry and other fields.) To calculate a Riemann sum, also known as applying the **rectangle rule**, you divide the area into thin slices and add up the areas of the slices. The following diagram shows an area being approximated by a Riemann sum:

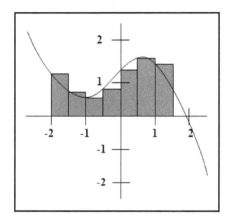

In this example, the height of each rectangle is given by the function's value at the rectangle's left edge, so this is sometimes called the **left Riemann sum**. Other variations use the function's value at the rectangle's right edge (the **right Riemann sum**) or in the rectangle's middle (the **midpoint rule**).

The widths of the rectangles depend on the number of rectangles. Using more, thinner rectangles gives a closer approximation to the actual area.

Write a program that uses the left Riemann sum to approximate the area under a function. Use your program to estimate the areas for the curves described in the preceding problem.

If you remember your calculus, make the program calculate the areas exactly and compare the calculated and estimated results.

27. Trapezoid rule integration

In addition to the left, right, and middle Riemann sum variations, a fourth variation divides an area into trapezoids instead of rectangles, as shown in the following diagram:

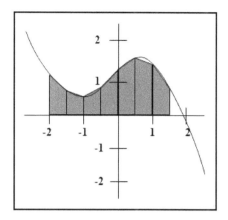

Write a program that uses the trapezoid rule to approximate the area under a curve. Use your program to estimate the areas for the curves described in Problem 25. *Monte Carlo integration.*

28. Arrowheads

Write a program that lets the user click and drag to define a line segment. Add a tail to the segment's starting point and an arrowhead to its ending point, as shown in the following screenshot:

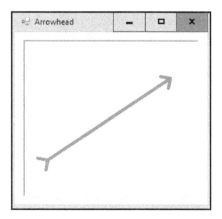

Hint: If $<vx, vy>$ is a vector, then $<vy, -vx>$ and $<-vy, vx>$ are two vectors perpendicular to the original vector.

29. Line-line intersection

Write a program that determines where two lines intersect. Let the user left-click twice to define one line and right-click twice to define another. Be sure that the program can handle horizontal and vertical lines, and the case when the lines are parallel.

Hint: Use a parametric definition for the lines as in $p = p_0 + t \times v$ where p_0 is a point on the line, v is a vector pointing in the direction of the line, and t is a real number parameter. If that doesn't make sense to you, then read the solution. You may want to stop after the explanation and try to implement the code yourself before you read the entire solution.

30. Point-line distance

Write a program that determines the closest point and shortest distance between a point and a line. Let the user left-click twice to define the line and right-click once to define the point. Draw the line and point, and a dashed line showing the shortest distance, as shown in the following screenshot:

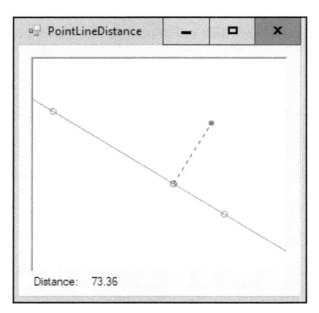

31. Point-segment distance

Write a program that determines the closest point and shortest distance between a point and a line segment. Let the user left-click twice to define the segment and right-click once to define the point. Draw the segment and point, and a dashed line showing the shortest distance, as shown in the following screenshot:

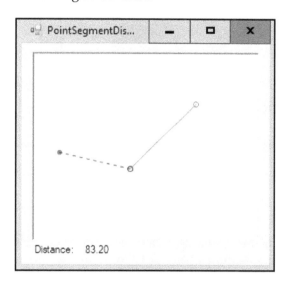

32. Segment-segment distance

Write a program that finds the shortest distance between the two line segments defined by the user. Let the user left- and right-click twice to define the two segments.

33. Circle selection

Write a program that lets the user define a circle by clicking three points.

Hint: The key to solving this problem is to find a circle that passes through the users' three points. There are several approaches that you can take, but the one I use is to note that the perpendicular bisectors of a chord of a circle always pass through the circle's center.

The following diagram shows three points on a circle **A**, **B**, and **C**. The dashed lines show perpendicular bisectors for the segments **AB** and **BC**. The point where the bisectors intersect is the circle's center:

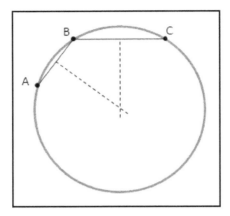

34. Line-circle intersection

Write a program that finds the intersection between a line and a circle. Let the user left-click three times to define the circle and right-click twice to define the line.

35. Circle-circle intersection

Write a program that finds the points where two circles intersect. Let the user left- and right-click three times to define the two circles.

36. Circle-line tangents

Write a program that lets the user click to define a point and a circle. It should then find tangent lines between the two.

(Hint: Look at Solution 35. *Circle-circle intersection*)

37. Polygon area

Write a program that lets the user left-click to add points to a polygon. When the user right-clicks, close the polygon and calculate its area.

 Hint: Consider the trapezoids defined by the polygon's edges, the X axis, and sides dropped vertically from the polygon's vertices to the X axis.

38. Point in a polygon

Write a program that lets the user right-click to add points to a polygon. When the user right-clicks, finalize the polygon and determine whether the clicked point lies inside the polygon. If the user right-clicks again, determine whether the new point lies within the existing polygon. If the user left-clicks after the polygon has been finalized, start a new polygon.

39. Convexity testing

Write a program that lets the user left-click to add points to a polygon. When the user right-clicks, finalize the polygon and determine whether the polygon is convex.

40. Stars

Write a program that lets the user enter a number of sides and a skip number. It should then draw a regular polygon with the indicated number of sides. It should also draw a star by connecting each of the polygon's vertices to the vertex that is the skip number of steps away around the perimeter of the polygon.

For example, the following screenshot shows the Stars example solution drawing a pentagon and a five-pointed star. The skip number is two, so the program draws the star by connecting each vertex with the point that is two positions away from it around the edge of the polygon:

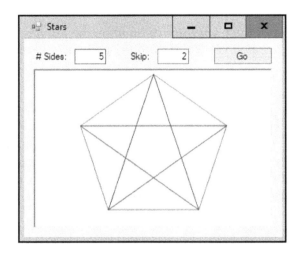

If you experiment with the program, you'll find that some skip numbers produce disconnected stars. In other words, the points on the star are not all joined by a continuous sequence of connected line segments. For example, try a 12-sided polygon with the skip number 8. What is the relationship between the skip number and the number of polygon sides for these disconnected stars?

Solutions

The following sections describe solutions to the preceding problems. You can download the example solutions to see additional details and to experiment with the programs at
`https://github.com/PacktPublishing/The-Modern-CSharp-Challenge/tree/master/`
`Chapter02.`

20. Monte Carlo π

The following code uses a Monte Carlo algorithm to estimate π:

```
// Use Monte Carlo simulation to estimate pi.
private double MonteCarloPi(long numPoints)
{
    Random rand = new Random();

    // Make a bitmap to show points.
    int wid = pointsPictureBox.ClientSize.Width;
    int hgt = pointsPictureBox.ClientSize.Height;
    Bitmap bm = new Bitmap(wid, hgt);
    using (Graphics gr = Graphics.FromImage(bm))
    {
        gr.Clear(Color.White);
        gr.DrawEllipse(Pens.Black, 0, 0, wid - 1, hgt - 1);
    }

    // Make the random points.
    int numHits = 0;
    for (int i = 0; i < numPoints; i++)
    {
        // Make a random point 0 <= x < 1.
        double x = rand.NextDouble();
        double y = rand.NextDouble();

        // See how far the point is from (0.5, 0.5).
        double dx = x - 0.5;
        double dy = y - 0.5;
        if (dx * dx + dy * dy < 0.25) numHits++;

        // Plots up to 10,000 points.
        if (i < 10000)
        {
            int ix = (int)(wid * x);
            int iy = (int)(hgt * y);
            if (dx * dx + dy * dy < 0.25)
                bm.SetPixel(ix, iy, Color.Gray);
            else
                bm.SetPixel(ix, iy, Color.Black);
        }
    }

    // Display the plotted points.
    pointsPictureBox.Image = bm;
```

```
        // Get the hit fraction.
        double fraction = numHits / (double)numPoints;

        // Estimate pi.
        return 4.0 * fraction;
    }
```

The method starts by creating a `Random` object that it can use to generate random numbers. It then creates a bitmap to fit the program's `PictureBox`, associates a `Graphics` object with it, clears the bitmap, and draws a circle centered in the bitmap.

Next, the code uses a loop to generate the desired number of random points within the square *0 ≤ X, Y ≤ 1*. The `NextDouble` method of the `Random` class returns a value between 0 and 1, so generating the point's *X* and *Y* coordinates is relatively easy.

The code then determines whether the point lies within the circle that fills the square *0 ≤ X, Y ≤ 1*. To do that, the method calculates the distance from the random point to the center of the circle (*0.5, 0.5*). It then determines whether that distance is less than the circle's radius.

Actually, the code doesn't really find the distance between the point and (*0.5, 0.5*). To do that, it would use the distance formula to find the distance and then use the following equation to determine whether the result is less than the circle's radius 0.5:

$$\sqrt{dx^2 + dy^2} \leq 0.5$$

Calculating square roots is relatively slow, however, so the program squares both sides of the equation and uses the following equation instead:

$$dx^2 + dy^2 \leq 0.5^2$$

The value 0.5 squared is 0.25, so the program actually tests whether:

$$dx^2 + dy^2 \leq 0.25$$

The program then plots the point on the bitmap in either gray or black, depending on whether the point lies within the circle. The code also uses the `numHits` variable to keep track of the number of points that lie within the circle.

After it finishes generating points, the code makes its approximation for π. The square $0 \leq X, Y \leq 1$ has an area of 1.0 and the circle should have the area $\pi \times R^2$ where R is the circle's radius. In this example, R is 0.5, so the fraction of points that fall inside the circle should be the following:

$$fraction = \frac{\pi \times 0.5^2}{1.0} = 0.25\pi$$

If you solve this equation for π, you get the following:

$$\pi = \frac{fraction}{0.25} = 4 \times fraction$$

The code gets the fraction of the points that fell within the circle, multiples that by 4.0, and returns the result as its estimate for π.

The following screenshot shows the `MonteCarloPi` example solution approximating π. After generating 10,000 random points, its approximation for π is off by around 1%. Using more points produces better approximations for π. The result with million points is correct within about 0.1–0.2%, and the result with 100 million points is correct to within around 0.01%:

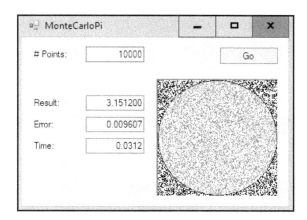

Download the `MonteCarloPi` example solution to see additional details.

21. Newton's π

The following code implements Newton's method for calculating π:

```
// Use Newton's formula to calculate pi.
private double NewtonPi(int numTerms)
{
    double total = 0;
    for (int i = 0; i < numTerms; i++)
    {
        total +=
            Factorial(2 * i) /
            Math.Pow(2, 4 * i + 1) /
            (Factorial(i) * Factorial(i)) /
            (2 * i + 1);
    }

    double result = 6 * total;
    Debug.Assert(!double.IsInfinity(result));
    return result;
}
```

This method simply loops over the desired number of terms, calculates the appropriate term values, and adds them to the result.

To allow the program to work with larger values, it uses the following `Factorial` method:

```
// Return number!
private double Factorial(int number)
{
    double total = 1;
    for (int i = 2; i <= number; i++) total *= i;
    return total;
}
```

This is a normal factorial, except it stores its total in a `double` variable, which can hold larger values than a `long` variable can.

The value *355/113* is approximately 3.1415929, which is remarkably close to π. Newton's method converges very quickly on values close to π, only needing nine terms before it is more accurate than *355/113*.

This method runs into problems when `numTerms` is greater than 86. In that case, the value `Factorial(2 * i)` is too big to fit in a `double` variable. Because the problem occurs in a `double` variable instead of an integer, a `checked` block won't detect the problem.

As is the case with integers, C# doesn't notify you if the value doesn't fit in a `double` variable. Instead, it sets the variable equal to one of the special value, values `double.Infinity` or `double.NegativeInfinity`. The `NewtonPi` method uses a `Debug.Assert` statement to see if this happened.

> The `Debug` class is defined in the `System.Diagnostics` namespace, so the program includes the directive `using System.Diagnostics` to make using that class easier.

The lesson to be learned here is that you should use the `double.IsInfinity` method to check `double` variables for overflow to infinity or negative infinity if that might be an issue.

Some double calculations, such as `total = Math.Sqrt(-1)`, may result in the special value `double.NaN`, which stands for **Not a Number**. You can use the `double.IsNaN` method to check for that situation.

Download the `NewtonPi` example solution to see additional details.

22. Bisection root-finding

Finding roots by using bisection is relatively straightforward, although there are a couple of tricky details. One of the most important is realizing that it's not always obvious what interval to use when looking for a root.

For example, if the function's value at the interval's endpoints, x_0 and x_1, are both positive or both negative, then the interval may contain no roots, one root, or several roots. The following diagram shows three functions. All three start and end with function values greater than zero. The curve on the left has no roots because it does not cross the X axis, the middle curve has a single root where it touches the X axis, and the curve on the right has four roots because it crosses the X axis four times:

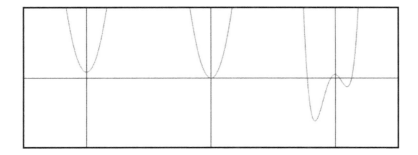

One way to find roots is to manually pick the intervals that the algorithm should examine. That works, but it requires you to know something about the general shape of the function and the locations of its roots.

The approach I took was to allow you to specify a series of intervals. The program then considers each interval, looking for roots.

The following FindRoots method starts the process:

```
// Find roots for the equation within the range xmin <= x <= xmax.
private List<double> FindRoots(Func<double, double> F,
    double xmin, double xmax, int numTests,
    double maxError, out List<double> xmins)
{
    xmins = new List<double>();
    List<double> roots = new List<double>();
    double dx = (xmax - xmin) / numTests;
    for (int i = 0; i < numTests; i++)
    {
        double x = xmin + dx * i;
        xmins.Add(x);
        double root = BinarySubdivision(F, x, x + dx, maxError);
        if (!double.IsNaN(root) &&
            !roots.Contains(root, maxError)) roots.Add(root);
    }
    return roots;
}
```

This method's xmin and xmax parameters define a large range xmin $\leq x \leq$ xmax that should contain all of the roots. The numTests parameter indicates the number of intervals into which the program should divide this larger domain to find the roots. The code calculates the size of the intervals and then loops through them, calling the BinarySubdivision method described shortly to look for a root in each interval.

If the BinarySubdivision method returns a number, the FindRoots method calls the Contains extension method to determine whether the root is already in the roots list. The following code shows the Contains method:

```
public static bool Contains(this List<double> values,
    double target, double maxDiff)
{
    foreach (double value in values)
        if (Math.Abs(value - target) <= maxDiff)
            return true;
    return false;
}
```

The problem here is that a list of `double` values might contain two values that should be the same but that are slightly different due to rounding errors. The `Contains` extension method extends `List<double>` objects to determine whether the list contains two values that are very close to each other.

The method simply loops through the list, examining items. It subtracts each item from the target value, takes the absolute value, and determines whether the difference is smaller than the maximum allowed difference. The method returns `true` if the list contains the item and `false` otherwise.

The following code shows the `BinarySubdivision` method, which uses binary subdivision to search an interval for a root:

```
// Search this interval for a root.
private double BinarySubdivision(Func<double, double> F,
    double xmin, double xmax, double maxError)
{
    // Make sure that F(xmin) and F(xmax) have different signs.
    if (Math.Sign(F(xmin)) == Math.Sign(F(xmax)))
        return double.NaN;

    for (;;)
    {
        double x = (xmin + xmax) / 2.0;
        double y = F(x);
        double error = Math.Abs(y);
        if (error < maxError) return x;

        if (Math.Sign(y) == Math.Sign(F(xmin)))
            xmin = x;
        else
            xmax = x;
    }
}
```

This method verifies that the function has values on opposite sides of the X axis at the two endpoints `xmin` and `xmax`. If the function's values at both points are either above or below the X axis, the method returns `double.NaN` to indicate that it did not find a root.

If the function crosses the X axis, the method enters a loop. Each time it goes through the loop, the program calculates the function's `y` value at the interval's midpoint `x`. If `y` is within `maxError` of zero, the code returns `x` as the function's root.

If y is not close enough to zero, the method compares the sign of the function at this point and at xmin. If the two signs are the same, the method moves xmin to the new position x. If the signs of y and F(xmin) are different, then the method updates xmax to the position x.

Eventually, the interval shrinks until y is close enough to zero and the method returns it.

The following screenshot shows the BisectionSubdivisionRoots example solution:

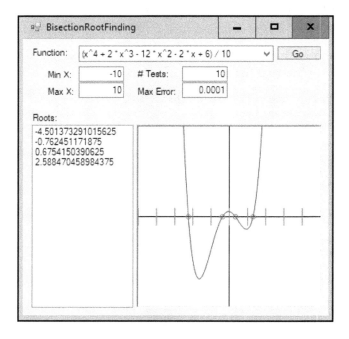

Here the program found the roots for the following equation:

$$F(x) = \frac{x^4 + 2x^3 - 12x^2 - 2x + 6}{10}$$

The short vertical lines crossing the X axis in the screenshot show the intervals that the program used to find the roots. In this example, the program used 10 intervals to find the roots.

Download the BisectionRootFinding example solution to see additional details, such as how the program lets you select a function and how it draws the graph of that function.

23. Newton's method

This program's `FindRoots` method is almost the same as the version used by the preceding solution. The only difference is that the new version calls the following method instead of the `BinarySubdivision` method:

```
// Search this interval for a root.
private double NewtonsMethod(
    Func<double, double> F, Func<double, double> FPrime,
    double x, double maxError, double maxTrials)
{
    for (int trial = 0; trial < maxTrials; trial++)
    {
        x = x - F(x) / FPrime(x);
        double y = F(x);
        double error = Math.Abs(y);
        if (error < maxError) return x;
    }
    return double.NaN;
}
```

Because this method uses a single variable, x, to keep track of its current estimate for the root, it does not need to check that an interval's endpoints lie on opposite sides of the X axis the way the `BinarySubdivision` method does. Instead, it simply enters a loop where it uses the equation in the problem statement to update x. When `F(x)` is close enough to zero, the method returns x.

One place where this method differs from the `BinarySubdivision` method is that it only performs its loop at most `maxTrials` times. Under certain conditions that depend on the function being studied, Newton's method may produce a sequence of repeating or diverging values that don't converge to a root. Limiting the loop prevents the program from being stuck in an infinite loop.

Newton's method converges very quickly, so the example solution sets `maxTrials` to only 1,000. After 1,000 trials, the method has either already found a root or it is probably not converging.

The `NewtonsMethod` example solution looks the same as the `BinarySubdivisionRoots` program shown in the earlier screenshot, so I won't show it here. Download the example to see additional details.

24. Gaussian elimination

The GaussianElimination example solution is fairly complicated, partly because Gaussian elimination is complicated, but also because it must convert user-entered text into an augmented matrix.

The program uses the following code to build the augmented matrix from the user's text. It gets the equations' coefficients from the coefficientsTextBox control. It gets the equations' results (the Cs on the right in the problem description) from the valuesTextBox control:

```
// Load the augmented array.
// Column numCols holds the result values.
// Column numCols + 1 will hold the final values after
// backsolving.
private double[,] LoadArray(out int numRows, out int numCols)
{
    // Build the augmented matrix.
    string[] valueRows = valuesTextBox.Text.Split(
        new string[] { "\r\n" },
        StringSplitOptions.RemoveEmptyEntries);
    string[] coefRows = coefficientsTextBox.Text.Split(
        new string[] { "\r\n" },
        StringSplitOptions.RemoveEmptyEntries);
    string[] oneRow = coefRows[0].Split(
        new string[] { " " }, StringSplitOptions.RemoveEmptyEntries);
    numRows = coefRows.GetUpperBound(0) + 1;
    numCols = oneRow.GetUpperBound(0) + 1;
    double[,] arr = new double[numRows, numCols + 2];
    for (int r = 0; r < numRows; r++)
    {
        oneRow = coefRows[r].Split(
            new char[] { ' ' }, StringSplitOptions.RemoveEmptyEntries);
        for (int c = 0; c < numCols; c++)
        {
            arr[r, c] = double.Parse(oneRow[c]);
        }
        arr[r, numCols] = double.Parse(valueRows[r]);
    }

    return arr;
}
```

This method gets the multiline string of values in `valuesTextBox`, splits the entries delimited by the carriage return/line feed combination, removes any empty entries, and saves the values in the `valueRows` array. It then uses a similar technique to load the rows of coefficients into the `coefRows` array. The method then splits the first row of coefficients delimited by spaces to save that row's coefficients in the `oneRow` array.

The code uses the length of the `coefRows` array to get the number of rows. It uses the length of the `oneRow` array to get the number of columns. Note that the number of columns includes only the equations' coefficients; it does not include the value column or the final result column in the augmented array.

After it knows the numbers of rows and columns, the code creates the `arr` array to hold the augmented matrix. It loops through the values to fill in the array and returns it.

The following `GaussianEliminate` method solves an augmented matrix:

```
// Perform Gaussian elimination.
// Note that arr should be the augmented array.
// Initially the second-to-last column should hold the result values.
// In the end, the final column will hold the final values after
   backsolving.
private void GaussianEliminate(double[,] arr)
{
    const double tiny = 0.00001;

    // Get the number of rows and columns.
    int numRows = arr.GetUpperBound(0) + 1;
    int numCols = arr.GetUpperBound(1) - 1;

    // Start solving.
    for (int r = 0; r < numRows - 1; r++)
    {
        // Zero out all entries in column r after this row.
        // See if this row has a non-zero entry in column r.
        if (Math.Abs(arr[r, r]) < tiny)
        {
            // Too close to zero. Try to swap with a later row.
            for (int r2 = r + 1; r2 < numRows; r2++)
            {
                if (Math.Abs(arr[r2, r]) > tiny)
                {
                    // This row will work. Swap them.
                    for (int c = 0; c <= numCols; c++)
                    {
                        double tmp = arr[r, c];
                        arr[r, c] = arr[r2, c];
```

```
                    arr[r2, c] = tmp;
                }
                break;
            }
        }
    }

    // If this row has a non-zero entry in column r, use it.
    if (Math.Abs(arr[r, r]) > tiny)
    {
        // Zero out this column in later rows.
        for (int r2 = r + 1; r2 < numRows; r2++)
        {
            double factor = -arr[r2, r] / arr[r, r];
            for (int c = r; c <= numCols; c++)
            {
                arr[r2, c] = arr[r2, c] + factor * arr[r, c];
            }
        }
    }
}

// Display the upper-triangular array. (For debugging.)
PrintArray(arr);

// See if we have a solution.
if (arr[numRows - 1, numCols - 1] == 0)
{
    // We have no solution.
    // If all entries in this row are 0, then there is no solution.
    // Otherwise the solution is not unique.
    for (int c = 0; c <= numCols + 1; c++)
        if (arr[numRows - 1, c] != 0)
            throw new Exception("There is no solution");
    throw new Exception("The solution is not unique");
}

// We have a solution. Backsolve.
for (int r = numRows - 1; r >= 0; r--)
{
    double tmp = arr[r, numCols];
    for (int r2 = r + 1; r2 < numRows; r2++)
    {
        tmp -= arr[r, r2] * arr[r2, numCols + 1];
    }
    arr[r, numCols + 1] = tmp / arr[r, r];
}
}
```

This method first gets the number of rows and columns. Note that the numColumns value does not include the augmented matrix's last two columns, which hold the equations' values and the final results.

The method then loops through the rows, using the r row to zero out the r column values in the following rows. Before it uses the r row, the program verifies that it has a non-zero entry in the column r. If the row has a zero in that position, the code swaps it with a later row that has a non-zero entry in that column.

Notice *has a zero in that position* really means *has a small value that could cause overflow when used as a denominator*. It is important to check that floating point numbers are not too small before you divide by them.

After it has finished converting the matrix into upper-triangular form, the code calls the PrintArray method to display the array's values in the Console window. That method is straightforward, so I won't include it here. Download the example solution to see the details.

Next, the code checks the final row to see if it has a non-zero entry in its final coefficient column. If that entry is zero, then there is no solution for the original set of equations and the method throws an exception.

If the final row has a non-zero entry for its final coefficient, the method backsolves to find the final solution.

The result is passed back to the calling code through the modified array.

The following code shows how the program uses the GaussianEliminate method when you click the program's **Solve** button:

```
// Solve the system of equations.
private void solveButton_Click(object sender, EventArgs e)
{
    // Build the augmented matrix.
    // The values numRows and numCols are the number of rows
    // and columns in the matrix, not the augmented matrix.
    int numRows, numCols;
    double[,] arr = LoadArray(out numRows, out numCols);
    double[,] origArr = LoadArray(out numRows, out numCols);

    // Display the initial arrays.
    PrintArray(arr);
    PrintArray(origArr);
```

```
// Perform Gaussian elimination.
try
{
    GaussianEliminate(arr);
}
catch (Exception ex)
{
    MessageBox.Show(ex.Message);
}

// Display the modified array in the Console window.
PrintArray(arr);

// Display the results on the form.
StringBuilder sb = new StringBuilder();
sb.AppendLine("    Values");
for (int r = 0; r < numRows; r++)
{
    sb.AppendLine("x" + r.ToString() + " = " +
        arr[r, numCols + 1].ToString());
}

// Verify.
sb.AppendLine();
sb.AppendLine("    Check:");
for (int r = 0; r < numRows; r++)
{
    double tmp = 0;
    for (int c = 0; c < numCols; c++)
        tmp += origArr[r, c] * arr[c, numCols + 1];
    sb.AppendLine(tmp.ToString());
}
resultsTextBox.Text = sb.ToString();
}
```

The code first calls the LoadArray method to load the values entered by the user. It calls the method twice to make two copies of the array. It will use one for Gaussian elimination and it will save the other so it can later check the results to verify that the solution works.

The code calls the PrintArray method to display the initial augmented matrix and then calls GaussianEliminate to solve the system of equations.

After the `GaussianEliminate` method returns, the code calls `PrintArray` again to display the finished augmented matrix. It then uses `StringBuilder` to make a string showing the solution.

The method then multiples the original matrix's entries by the solution values to verify that the solution is correct. It adds the results to `StringBuilder` and finally displays the result.

The following table shows the solutions to the systems of equations mentioned in the problem description:

System of Equations	Solution
$\begin{vmatrix} 1 & -3 & 1 \\ 2 & -8 & 8 \\ -6 & 3 & -15 \end{vmatrix} \times \begin{vmatrix} x_1 \\ x_2 \\ x_3 \end{vmatrix} = \begin{vmatrix} 4 \\ -2 \\ 9 \end{vmatrix}$	{3, -1, -2}
$\begin{vmatrix} 9 & 3 & 4 \\ 4 & 3 & 4 \\ 1 & 1 & 1 \end{vmatrix} \times \begin{vmatrix} x_1 \\ x_2 \\ x_3 \end{vmatrix} = \begin{vmatrix} 7 \\ 8 \\ 3 \end{vmatrix}$	{-0.2, 4, -0.8}
$\begin{vmatrix} 1 & 1 & 1 & 1 & 1 \\ 32 & 16 & 8 & 4 & 2 \\ 243 & 81 & 27 & 9 & 3 \\ 1024 & 256 & 64 & 16 & 4 \\ 3125 & 625 & 125 & 25 & 5 \end{vmatrix} \times \begin{vmatrix} x_1 \\ x_2 \\ x_3 \\ x_4 \\ x_5 \end{vmatrix} = \begin{vmatrix} 1 \\ -1 \\ 8 \\ -56 \\ 569 \end{vmatrix}$	{7.87, -82.75, 302.17, -446.75, 220.47}
$\begin{vmatrix} 2 & -1 & 1 \\ 3 & 2 & -4 \\ -6 & 3 & -3 \end{vmatrix} \times \begin{vmatrix} x_1 \\ x_2 \\ x_3 \end{vmatrix} = \begin{vmatrix} 1 \\ 4 \\ 2 \end{vmatrix}$	Has no solution
$\begin{vmatrix} 1 & -1 & 2 \\ 4 & 4 & -2 \\ -2 & 2 & -4 \end{vmatrix} \times \begin{vmatrix} x_1 \\ x_2 \\ x_3 \end{vmatrix} = \begin{vmatrix} -3 \\ 1 \\ 6 \end{vmatrix}$	Has no unique solution

Download the `GaussianElimination` example solution to see additional details.

25. Monte Carlo integration

Monte Carlo integration is actually fairly easy. Most of the example solution's code draws the curve and sample points, lets the user select functions, determines the rectangle where integration should occur, and performs other user interface tasks.

The example solution uses the following method to perform the Monte Carlo integration. The code used by the example solution is heavily interspersed with graphics code, which I have omitted here to save space and to make the integration code easier to understand:

```
// Use Monte Carlo integration to find the area under the curve.
private double MonteCarloIntegrate(Func<double, double> F,
    double xmin, double xmax, double ymin, double ymax, int numPoints)
{
    Random rand = new Random();
    int numHits = 0;

    // Make the random points.
    for (int i = 0; i < numPoints; i++)
    {
        // Make a random point xmin <= x <= xmax, ymin <= y <= ymax.
        double x = rand.NextDouble(xmin, xmax);
        double y = rand.NextDouble(ymin, ymax);

        // See if the point is below the function.
        if ((y >= 0) && (y <= F(x))) numHits++;
    }

    // Get the hit fraction.
    double fraction = numHits / (double)numPoints;

    // Estimate the area.
    return fraction * (xmax - xmin) * (ymax - ymin);
}
```

This code enters a loop to generate the required number of random points within the sample rectangle $xmin \leq x \leq xmax$, $ymin \leq y \leq ymax$. If the point (x, y) lies below the point on the function $(x, F(x))$ and above the X axis, the code increments its hit count.

After it finishes generating the points, the method calculates the fraction of the points that were hits. It then multiplies that fraction by the area of the sample rectangle to estimate the area under the curve.

The following screenshot shows the example solution in action:

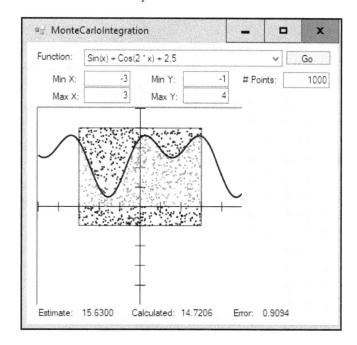

Download the MonteCarloIntegration example solution to see additional details, such as how the program lets the user select the function, how the program draws the curve and sample points, and how the code uses calculus to make a calculated value for comparison with the estimated value.

26. Rectangle rule integration

The following equation shows the total area of the rectangles used to approximate the function's area:

$$area = \sum_{i=0}^{N-1} F(x_i)(x_{i+1} - x_i)$$

Here the sum is over N slices. The value $F(x_i)$ gives the length of the i-th rectangle's left side. The value $(x_{i+1} - x_i)$ is the width of that rectangle.

If all of the rectangles have the same width, dx, then you can factor out that value from each term in the sum to give the following slightly simpler equation:

$$area = dx \sum_{i=0}^{N-1} F(x_i)$$

The following code calculates this sum:

```
// Use the rectangle rule to find the area under the curve.
private double RectangleRuleIntegrate(Func<double, double> F,
    double xmin, double xmax, double ymin, double ymax, int numSlices)
{
    double total = 0;
    double dx = (xmax - xmin) / numSlices;
    double x = xmin;
    for (int i = 0; i < numSlices; i++)
    {
        // Add the height at x.
        total += F(x);
        x += dx;
    }
    return total * dx;
}
```

The code sets dx to the width of the rectangles. It then loops through the rectangles, adding the height of the function at each rectangle's left edge and incrementing the x value by dx to move to the next slice.

After it adds up all of the rectangles' heights, the method multiplies the total by dx and returns the result.

The following screenshot shows the `RectangleRuleIntegration` example solution estimating the area under the same curve shown in the preceding screenshot:

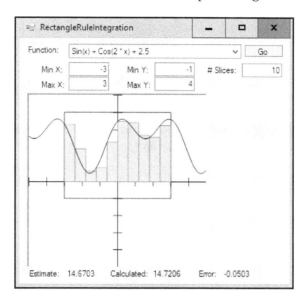

If you look closely at the earlier screenshot, you'll see that Monte Carlo integration used 1,000 random points to estimate the area with an error of roughly 0.9. The new program uses only 10 rectangles to estimate the area with an error of only -0.05.

Download the `RectangleRuleIntegration` example solution to see additional details.

27. Trapezoid rule integration

A **trapezoid** is a quadrilateral (four-sided polygon) that has two parallel sides. The parallel sides are called its **bases** and the other two sides are called its **legs**. The trapezoid's height is the distance between the two bases.

If a trapezoid has a height of *h* and base lengths *b1* and *b2*, then its area is *h × (b1 + b2) / 2*. The following equation gives the sums of the areas used to approximate the area under a function:

$$area = \sum_{i=0}^{N-1} (x_{i+1} - x_i) \frac{F(x_i) + F(x_{i+1})}{2}$$

If we assume that all of the trapezoids have the same height, $dx = (x_{i+1} - x_i)$, then we can factor out the dx and the factor of ½ to get the following:

$$area = \frac{dx}{2} \sum_{i=0}^{N-1} F(x_i) + F(x_{i+1})$$

This is simple, but we can make it even simpler if we notice that most of the x values appear twice in the sum, once as an x_i term and once as an x_{i+1} term. The exceptions are the first (leftmost) and last (rightmost) values, x_0 and x_N, which each appear only once. Using that observation, we can rewrite the equation to get the following version:

$$area = \frac{dx}{2} \left(F(x_0) + F(x_N) + 2 \times \sum_{i=1}^{N-1} F(x_i) \right)$$

Finally, we can rearrange this slightly to get the following:

$$area = dx \left(\frac{F(x_0) + F(x_N)}{2} + \sum_{i=1}^{N-1} F(x_i) \right)$$

The following code calculates this value:

```
// Use the rectangle rule to find the area under the curve.
private double TrapezoidRuleIntegrate(Func<double, double> F,
    double xmin, double xmax, double ymin, double ymax, int numSlices)
{
    double total = 0;
    double dx = (xmax - xmin) / numSlices;
    double x = xmin + dx;
    for (int i = 1; i < numSlices; i++)
    {
        // Add the height at x.
        total += F(x);
        x += dx;
    }
    total = total + (F(xmax) + F(xmin)) / 2;
    return total * dx;
}
```

This code calculates dx and then uses a loop to add up the x values, except for the first and last values. After the loop, it adds the first and last values divided by two. Finally, it multiples that sum by dx and returns the result.

28. Arrowheads

This problem is relatively straightforward, but I'm going to describe the solution in some detail because it demonstrates some techniques that will be useful for later problems. This problem has two parts: allowing the user to draw a segment and drawing the segment as an arrow.

The first problem is relatively simple, at least as long as you've seen this sort of thing before. The `Arrowhead` example solution uses the following code to let the user select the segment:

```
// The segment's endpoint. If they are the same, there's no segment.
private Point StartPoint, EndPoint;

// True while dragging.
private bool Drawing = false;

// Start drawing.
private void arrowPictureBox_MouseDown(object sender, MouseEventArgs e)
{
    Drawing = true;
    StartPoint = e.Location;
    EndPoint = e.Location;
    arrowPictureBox.Refresh();
}

// Continue drawing.
private void arrowPictureBox_MouseMove(object sender, MouseEventArgs e)
{
    if (!Drawing) return;

    EndPoint = e.Location;
    arrowPictureBox.Refresh();
}

// Stop drawing.
private void arrowPictureBox_MouseUp(object sender, MouseEventArgs e)
{
```

```
        if (!Drawing) return;
        Drawing = false;

        EndPoint = e.Location;
        arrowPictureBox.Refresh();
    }
```

The `StartPoint` and `EndPoint` fields hold the segment's endpoints. The program needs some way to tell whether the user has made a selection. This program does that by checking whether the two endpoints are the same.

The `Drawing` field is `true` while the user is in the process of drawing a segment. When the user presses the mouse button down to start drawing a segment, the `MouseDown` event handler executes. It sets `Drawing` to `true` so the program knows that a draw is in progress. It sets `StartPoint` and `EndPoint` to the mouse's current location and refreshes the program's `PictureBox` control. You'll see shortly how that makes the program draw the arrow.

When the user moves the mouse over the program's `PictureBox`, the `MouseMove` event handler executes. If `Drawing` is `false`, then the user is moving the mouse with the mouse button up, so no draw is in progress. In that case, the event handler simply exits. However, if `Drawing` is `true`, the code updates `EndPoint` to hold the mouse's new location and refreshes the `PictureBox`.

When the user releases the mouse button, the `MouseUp` event handler executes. The program again checks `Drawing` to see whether a draw is in progress and exits if it is not. It then sets `Drawing` to `false` to indicate that the current draw is over. It updates `EndPoint` and refreshes the program's `PictureBox`.

When the `PictureBox` needs to redraw itself, for example when it is refreshed, the following `Paint` event handler executes:

```
// Draw the arrow.
private void arrowPictureBox_Paint(object sender, PaintEventArgs e)
{
    if (StartPoint == EndPoint) return;

    e.Graphics.Clear(Color.White);
    e.Graphics.SmoothingMode = SmoothingMode.AntiAlias;

    // Make a thick pen.
    using (Pen pen = new Pen(Color.Red, 5))
    {
        pen.LineJoin = LineJoin.Round;
        pen.EndCap = LineCap.Round;
```

```
pen.StartCap = LineCap.Round;

// Draw the segment.
e.Graphics.DrawLine(pen, StartPoint, EndPoint);

// Draw the arrowhead and tail.
DrawArrowPart(e.Graphics, pen, StartPoint, EndPoint, 15,
    false);
DrawArrowPart(e.Graphics, pen, EndPoint, StartPoint, 15, true);
    }
}
```

If `StartPoint` and `EndPoint` are the same, then no segment has been defined, so the method simply returns. Otherwise, if a segment has been defined, the code clears the drawing area and sets the `Graphics` object's `SmoothingMode` property to produce smooth lines.

Next, the code creates a thick red pen, setting its properties so line joins and end caps are rounded.

The program then draws a line segment connecting `StartPoint` and `EndPoint`. It finishes by calling the `DrawArrowPart` method described shortly to draw the arrow's head and tail. Before I describe that method, however, I'll explain how it works.

A vector, *<vx, vy>*, represents a direction. For example, the vector *<1, 2>* means you should move one unit to the right in the *X* direction and two units up in the *Y* direction—sort of north-northeast.

As I mentioned in the hint, if *<vx, vy>* is a vector, then *<vy, -vx>* and *<-vy, vx>* are two vectors perpendicular to the original vector. The following diagram shows a vector in bold and its two perpendicular vectors created by this method:

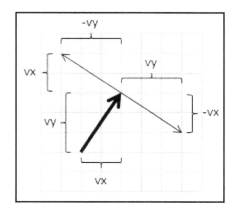

This is all a bit upside down if you remember that Y coordinates increase downward in C#. For now, think of using a normal mathematical coordinate system where Y increases upward. If you add two vectors, the result is a third vector. The result is the same as if you had followed one vector and then the other.

For this problem, you can make an arrowhead or tail by adding a vector parallel to the arrow segment plus a vector perpendicular to it. For example, to create the right side of the arrowhead, you find the right-pointing perpendicular vector shown in the preceding diagram. You add that vector to a vector pointing in the direction opposite that of the line segment to get the dashed vector shown in the following diagram:

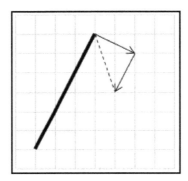

You then add the dashed vector's components to the endpoint of the line segment to get the point at the tip of that side of the arrowhead.

To get the left side of the arrowhead, you repeat the same operations but using the other perpendicular vector on the left side of the original segment.

To create an arrow's tail, you perform similar operations except you reverse the parallel vector's direction.

The final technique that you need to use to make nice arrowheads and tails is scaling a vector. If you multiply a vector's x and y components by a number, you scale its length by that amount. In particular, if you want a vector to have a specific length, L, you can divide it by its current length and then multiply it by L. The result is a vector pointing in the same direction as the original one but with the desired length.

The following code shows how the `Arrowhead` example solution uses these techniques to add an arrowhead or tail to a line segment:

```
// Draw an arrowhead wedge at point p1.
// If reversed is true, make an arrow tail.
private void DrawArrowPart(Graphics gr, Pen pen, Point p0, Point p1,
```

```
        float sideLength, bool reversed)
{
    // Get a vector along the arrow's length.
    float vx = p1.X - p0.X;
    float vy = p1.Y - p0.Y;

    // If this should be a tail, reverse the vectors.
    if (reversed)
    {
        vx = -vx;
        vy = -vy;
    }

    // Get perpendicular vectors.
    float p0x = vy;
    float p0y = -vx;
    float p1x = -vy;
    float p1y = vx;

    // Get arrowhead/tail vectors.
    float headX0 = p0x - vx;
    float headY0 = p0y - vy;
    float headX1 = p1x - vx;
    float headY1 = p1y - vy;

    // Set the vectors' lengths.
    float length0 = (float)Math.Sqrt(headX0 * headX0 + headY0 *
        headY0);
    headX0 *= sideLength / length0;
    headY0 *= sideLength / length0;
    float length1 = (float)Math.Sqrt(headX1 * headX1 + headY1 *
        headY1);
    headX1 *= sideLength / length1;
    headY1 *= sideLength / length1;

    // Draw it.
    PointF[] points =
    {
        new PointF(p1.X + headX0, p1.Y + headY0),
        p1,
        new PointF(p1.X + headX1, p1.Y + headY1),
    };
    gr.DrawLines(pen, points);
}
```

The method starts by finding a vector <vx, vy> that points along the user's line segment from point p0 to point p1. If the method should draw a tail instead of an arrowhead, the code reverses that vector.

Next, the code finds perpendicular vectors <p0x, p0y> and <p1x, p1y>. (Here, the **p** stands for **perpendicular**.)

The method then adds the parallel and perpendicular vectors as described earlier to make the vectors that give the sides of the arrowhead or tail. It calculates the lengths of those vectors, divides them by their lengths, and multiplies them by the method's sideLength parameter to give them the desired final lengths.

Next, the method adds the vectors to the segment's endpoint to find the locations of the arrowhead/tail's points. It saves the points in an array and uses the array to draw the arrowhead/tail.

These are the main pieces of the program. Download the Arrowhead example solution to see additional details.

The following list shows the key techniques that you should take from this example:

- You can use the MouseDown, MouseMove, and MouseUp event handlers to let the user draw. (You should also consider MouseClick if you only need to let the user select points instead of drawing.)
- If you subtract the components of point *p0* from point *p1*, you get the components for a vector pointing from *p0* to *p1*.
- If *<vx, vy>* is a vector, then *<vy, -vx>* and *<-vy, vx>* are perpendicular to it.
- You can scale a vector by multiplying its components by a number. In particular, you can divide the vector by its length to get a vector of length one. Then, you can multiply it by a desired length if you like.
- If you add a point's coordinates to a vector's components, you get a new point as if you had started at the original point and then moved in the direction and distance given by the vector.

You may find these techniques handy for solving later problems and when facing everyday programming challenges.

29. Line-line intersection

There are several ways you can approach this problem. One approach that doesn't work well is to use slope-intercept equations of the form $y = m \times x + b$ for the lines. The problem with that approach is that it doesn't work for vertical lines. If a line is vertical, then the equation's slope, *m*, is effectively infinite.

The approach that I use defines a line by giving a point *p0* on the line and a vector *v* that points in the direction of the line. Then the following equation defines the points on the line:

$$point = p0 + t \times v$$

Here, *t* is any real number. For example, if *t* = 0, then the point is *p0*.

 This is a **parametric equation**. In a parametric equation, a parameter generates a set of points. In this example, the parameter *t* generates the points on a line.

If *v* is the vector between two points, *p0* and *p1*, then you can use this equation to generate the points along the line segment between those points by setting *t* to values between 0 and 1.

Note that the preceding vector equation really represents two equations involving X and Y coordinates. If *v* = <*vx, vy*>, then the vector equation really represents the following two equations:

$$pointx = p0x + t \times vx$$

$$pointy = p0y + t \times vy$$

Now, assume you have two line segments, one defined by points *p00* and *p01* and the other defined by points *p10* and *p11*, so their parametric equations are the following:

$$point = p00 + t0 \times v0$$

$$point = p10 + t1 \times v1$$

When the two lines intersect, their parametric equations give the same point. Setting the two equations equal to each other and considering the equations' *x* and *y* components gives us the following two equations with two unknowns *t0* and *t1*:

$$p00x + t0 \times v0x = p10x + t1 \times v1x$$

$$p00y + t0 \times v0y = p10y + t1 \times v1y$$

You can rearrange these to get the following:

$$p00x + t0 \times v0x - p10x = t1 \times v1x$$

$$p00y + t0 \times v0y - p10y = t1 \times v1y$$

Now, multiply the first equation by *v1y* and the second equation by *–v1x* to get the following:

$$(p00x + t0 \times v0x - p10x)v1y = (t1 \times v1x)v1y$$

$$(p00y + t0 \times v0y - p10y)(-v1x) = (t1 \times v1y)(-v1x)$$

If you add these two equations, the *t1* terms cancel leaving the following:

$$(p00x + t0 \times v0x - p10x)v1y + (p00y + t0 \times v0y - p10y)(-v1x) = 0$$

Grouping the *t0* terms gives the following equation:

$$t0(v0x \times v1y - v0y \times v1x) + v1y(p00x - p10x) - v1x(p00y - p10y) = 0$$

Now, you can solve for *t0*:

$$t0 = \frac{v1y(p00x - p10x) - v1x(p00y - p10y)}{v0y \times v1x - v0x \times v1y}$$

You can solve for *t1* similarly:

$$t1 = \frac{v0y(p10x - p00x) - v0x(p10y - p00y)}{-(v0y \times v1x - v0x \times v1y)}$$

If the denominator is zero, then you cannot calculate *t1* and *t2* because you would need to divide by zero. In that case, the two lines are parallel so they never intersect.

In practice, you don't need to specifically check to see if the denominator is zero. Instead, you can calculate *t0* and use `float.IsInfinity` to see if the result is undefined.

The `LineLineIntesection` example solution uses the following method to determine where two lines intersect:

```
// Find the point of intersection between lines p00-p01 and p10-p11.
private PointF IntersectLines(PointF p00, PointF p01, PointF p10,
    PointF p11)
{
    // Get the segments' parameters.
    float v0x = p01.X - p00.X;
    float v0y = p01.Y - p00.Y;
    float v1x = p11.X - p10.X;
    float v1y = p11.Y - p10.Y;

    // Solve for t0 and t1.
    float denominator = v0y * v1x - v0x * v1y;

    float t0 = (v1y * (p00.X - p10.X) - v1x * (p00.Y - p10.Y))
        / denominator;
    if (float.IsInfinity(t0))
        throw new Exception("The lines are parallel");

    PointF p0 = new PointF(
        p00.X + t0 * v0x,
        p00.Y + t0 * v0y);

    // Check.
    float t1 = (v0y * (p10.X - p00.X) - v0x * (p10.Y - p00.Y))
        / -denominator;
    PointF p1 = new PointF(
        p10.X + t1 * v1x,
        p10.Y + t1 * v1y);
    Debug.Assert(Math.Abs(p0.X - p1.X) < 0.0001);
    Debug.Assert(Math.Abs(p0.Y - p1.Y) < 0.0001);

    return p0;
}
```

This method fist calculates the *X* and *Y* components of the lines' direction vectors *v0* and *v1*. It then solves for *t0*. Notice the check that uses the `float.IsInfinity` method to see if the denominator is zero.

The code then uses *t0* to find the point of intersection. The method doesn't really need to calculate *t1*, but it does so anyway. It uses *t1* to calculate the point of intersection again and verifies that the two calculations give the same point.

The method finishes by returning the point it calculated.

Download the `LineLineIntersection` example solution to see additional details.

30. Point-line distance

There are several ways that you can attack this problem. I'm going to use a parameterized approach similar to the one used for Problem 29. *Line-line intersection.*

Suppose the point is (px, py) and the line is given by $p0 + t \times v$. Then the distance between the point and a point on the line is given by the following:

$$distance = \sqrt{(p_x - (p_{0x} + t \times v_x))^2 + (p_y - (p_{0y} + t \times v_y))^2}$$

We need to find the value of t that minimizes this equation. You can do that with one trick and a little calculus.

The trick is to note that the minimum of this equation has the same X coordinate that minimizes the equation squared. The following shows the squared equation:

$$distance^2 = (p_x - (p_{0x} + t \times v_x))^2 + (p_y - (p_{0y} + t \times v_y))^2$$

Here comes the calculus. To minimize this equation, we take the derivative of the equation with respect to it, set it equal to zero, and solve for t. The following code shows the new equation:

$$2(p_x - p_{0x} - t \times v_x)v_x + 2(p_y - p_{0y} - t \times v_y)v_y = 0$$

We can divide both sides by 2 and rearrange a bit to get the following:

$$-t(v_x^2 + v_y^2) + v_x(p_x - p_{0x}) + v_y(p_y - p_{0y}) = 0$$

Now we can solve for t:

$$t = \frac{v_x(p_x - p_{0x}) + v_y(p_y - p_{0y})}{v_x^2 + v_y^2}$$

The denominator is zero (and hence the fraction cannot be calculated) only if the vector v has zero length. In that case, the line isn't really a line, so the calculation doesn't make sense.

After you use this equation to solve for t, you can use it to find the point on the line that is closest to the target point p.

Download the `PointLineDistance` example solution to see additional details.

31. Point-segment distance

There are two cases to consider when solving this problem. First, the point on the segment that is closest to the target point might lie on the line segment. In that case, Solution 30 solves this problem.

The second case occurs if the point found by Solution 30 does not lie on the segment but only lies on the line that contains the segment. In that case, the point on the segment that is closest to the point is one of the segment's endpoints.

The following `PointSegmentClosestPoint` method finds the point on a segment that is closest to the target point. It also returns a Boolean through the `isOnSegment` output parameter, indicating whether that point lies on the segment:

```
// Find the point on the line p0-p1 that is closest to point p.
private PointF PointSegmentClosestPoint(PointF p, PointF p0, PointF p1,
    out bool isOnSegment)
{
    float vx = p1.X - p0.X;
    float vy = p1.Y - p0.Y;
    float numerator = vx * (p.X - p0.X) + vy * (p.Y - p0.Y);
    float denominator = vx * vx + vy * vy;
    float t = numerator / denominator;

    // See if the point is on the segment.
    isOnSegment = ((t >= 0) && (t <= 1));
    if (isOnSegment) return new PointF(p0.X + t * vx, p0.Y + t * vy);

    // The point we found is not on the segment.
    // See which end point is closer.
    float dx0 = p.X - p0.X;
    float dy0 = p.Y - p0.Y;
    float dist0squared = dx0 * dx0 + dy0 * dy0;
```

```
float dx1 = p.X - p1.X;
float dy1 = p.Y - p1.Y;
float dist1squared = dx1 * dx1 + dy1 * dy1;

if (dist0squared <= dist1squared) return p0;
return p1;
}
```

This method uses the technique used by Solution 30 to find the point on the segment's line that is closest to the target point. If the parameter *t* lies between 0 and 1, then this point also lies on the segment so the method returns it.

If *t* does not lie between 0 and 1, the method calculates the distances squared between the segment's endpoints and the target point. It then returns whichever endpoint is closer to the target point.

Download the `PointSegmentDistance` example solution to see additional details.

32. Segment-segment distance

If you think about how two segments can be arranged, you'll realize that there are a lot of special cases. The segments could intersect or they could be parallel. If the segments don't intersect and are not parallel, then the closest points could be on the segments' endpoints, in the segments' interiors, or a combination of the two.

Although the problem seems complicated, there are really only two cases that you need to worry about: when the segments intersect and when they don't.

If the segments intersect, then you can use the techniques used by Solution 29, *Line-line intersection*, to find the point of intersection.

If the segments don't intersect, then at least one of the segments' endpoints is the point closest to the other segment. In that case, you can use the method described for the preceding solution, *Point-segment distance*, to find the closest points. Any of the four segment endpoints could be one of the closest points, but you can simply try them all and see which produces the best result.

The last thing you might consider is the special case where the segments are parallel. In that case, multiple endpoints might give the same shortest distance. There may also be pairs of points that give the same shortest distance even though neither of them is an endpoint.

All of these cases give the same shortest distance, however, so it doesn't really matter which one you pick. Unless you have special needs, such as a requirement to find *all* pairs of points that give the shortest distance, then you may as well use the closest points that you find by using the *Point-segment distance* techniques.

The following code shows the SegmentSegmentClosestPoints method, which forms the heart of the example solution:

```
// Find the points where the segments p00-p01 and p10-p11 are closest.
private void SegmentSegmentClosestPoints(
    PointF p00, PointF p01, PointF p10, PointF p11,
    out PointF closestPoint0, out PointF closestPoint1,
    out bool isOnSegment0, out bool isOnSegment1)
{
    closestPoint0 = new PointF(-1, -1);
    closestPoint1 = new PointF(-1, -1);
    isOnSegment0 = false;
    isOnSegment1 = false;

    // Look for an intersection.
    PointF intersection = IntersectLines(p00, p01, p10, p11,
        out isOnSegment0, out isOnSegment1);
    if (isOnSegment0 && isOnSegment1)
    {
        closestPoint0 = intersection;
        closestPoint1 = intersection;
        return;
    }

    // See which segment end points are closest to the other segment.
    float testDist, bestDist = float.MaxValue;
    PointF testPoint;
    bool testIsOnSegment;

    // Check p00.
    testPoint = PointSegmentClosestPoint(p00,
        p10, p11, out testIsOnSegment);
    testDist = DistanceSquared(p00, testPoint);
    if (testDist < bestDist)
    {
        closestPoint0 = p00;
        closestPoint1 = testPoint;
        isOnSegment0 = true;
        isOnSegment1 = testIsOnSegment;
        bestDist = testDist;
    }
```

```
        // Check p01.
        testPoint = PointSegmentClosestPoint(p01,
            p10, p11, out testIsOnSegment);
        testDist = DistanceSquared(p01, testPoint);
        if (testDist < bestDist)
        {
            closestPoint0 = p01;
            closestPoint1 = testPoint;
            isOnSegment0 = true;
            isOnSegment1 = testIsOnSegment;
            bestDist = testDist;
        }

        // Check p10.
        testPoint = PointSegmentClosestPoint(p10,
            p00, p01, out testIsOnSegment);
        testDist = DistanceSquared(p10, testPoint);
        if (testDist < bestDist)
        {
            closestPoint0 = testPoint;
            closestPoint1 = p10;
            isOnSegment0 = testIsOnSegment;
            isOnSegment1 = true;
            bestDist = testDist;
        }

        // Check p11.
        testPoint = PointSegmentClosestPoint(p11,
            p00, p01, out testIsOnSegment);
        testDist = DistanceSquared(p11, testPoint);
        if (testDist < bestDist)
        {
            closestPoint0 = testPoint;
            closestPoint1 = p11;
            isOnSegment0 = testIsOnSegment;
            isOnSegment1 = true;
            bestDist = testDist;
        }
    }
```

This method uses the IntersectLines method to see whether the segments intersect. That method is similar to the one used in Solution 29. *Line-line intersection,* modified to not throw an exception if the lines are parallel. See that solution for more information about the method.

Next, the `SegmentSegmentClosestPoints` method uses the `PointSegmentClosestPoint` method to see which of the segments' endpoints is closest to the other segment. That method is similar to the one used in Solution *31. Point-segment distance*, so you can read more about it there.

That's all there is to this solution. It simply combines methods used by previous solutions to find the closest points. Download the `SegmentSegmentDistance` example solution and look at the previous solutions to see additional details.

33. Circle selection

The hint said that the perpendicular bisectors of a chord of a circle pass through the circle's center. To apply that hint to this problem, find a perpendicular bisector for the segment connecting two of the points selected by the user. That bisector passes through the circle's center.

The following `FindBisector` helper method finds a perpendicular bisector for a segment:

```
// Find a bisector for the segment connecting the two points.
private void FindBisector(PointF p0, PointF p1,
    out PointF b0, out PointF b1)
{
    // Find the midpoint.
    b0 = new PointF(
        (p0.X + p1.X) / 2,
        (p0.Y + p1.Y) / 2);

    // Find the p0-p1 direction vector.
    float dx = p1.X - p0.X;
    float dy = p1.Y - p0.Y;

    // Add <dy, -dx> to b0 to get b1.
    b1 = new PointF(
        b0.X + dy,
        b0.Y - dx);
}
```

The method first averages the two points, `p0` and `p1`, to find the point at the center of the segment. The bisector must pass through that point.

Next, the code finds the <dx, dy> direction vector that points in the direction of the original segment. The two vectors <dy, -dx> and <-dy, dx> are perpendicular to <dx, dy>, one pointing to the left and the other to the right. The code adds <dy, -dx> to the segment's center point to get a new point that lies along the perpendicular bisector.

The following FindCircle method uses the FindBisector helper method to find the circle that passes through three points:

```
// Return a RectangleF that defines a circle
// passing through the three points.
private RectangleF FindCircle(PointF p0, PointF p1, PointF p2)
{
    // Find a bisector for p0-p1.
    PointF b00, b01;
    FindBisector(p0, p1, out b00, out b01);

    // Find a bisector for p1-p2.
    PointF b10, b11;
    FindBisector(p1, p2, out b10, out b11);

    // Find the bisectors' point of intersection.
    bool linesAreParallel;
    PointF center = IntersectLines(b00, b01, b10, b11,
        out linesAreParallel);
    if (linesAreParallel)
    {
        MessageBox.Show("The circle's points are colinear");
        return new RectangleF(-1, -1, -1, -1);
    }

    // Return the circle.
    float radius = Distance(center, p0);
    return new RectangleF(
        center.X - radius, center.Y - radius,
        2 * radius, 2 * radius);
}
```

This method calls the FindBisector helper method to find the chord bisectors. It then calls IntersectLines to see where the bisectors intersect.

The two bisectors will be parallel if the user's three points are co-linear. In that case, there is no circle that includes all three points.

Next, the method uses the `Distance` helper method to find the distance between the center point and one of the user's points. (The `Distance` method simply calculates the distance between two points. It's straightforward so I won't show it here.) That distance gives the radius of the circle.

The method finishes by a `RectangleF` that defines the circle. (You could store the circle's center point and radius instead, but the program's `Paint` event handler uses a `RectangleF` to draw the circle, so it's convenient to represent the circle as `RectangleF`.)

The rest of the program is reasonably straightforward if you use the tools provided by the previous solutions. Download the `CircleSelection` example program to see additional details.

34. Line-circle intersection

Suppose the line is defined by the following parametric equations:

$$x(t) = p_0 x + t \times vx$$

$$y(t) = p_0 y + t \times vy$$

Here, $p_0 = (p_0x, p_0y)$ is a point on the line and $<vx, vy>$ is a vector pointing in the line's direction. If the second point on the line is $p_1 = (p_1x, p_1y)$, then you can use $<p_1x - p_0x, p_1y - p_0x>$ as the vector.

If the circle is centered at point (cx, cy) and has the radius r, then the following equation defines the circle:

$$(x - cx)^2 + (y - cy)^2 = r^2$$

If we plug the line's parametric equations into the circle's equation, we get the following equation:

$$(p_0 x + t \times vx - cx)^2 + (p_0 y + t \times vy - cy)^2 = r^2$$

If you multiply this out and group the terms containing t, you get the following rather untidy result:

$$t^2 (vx^2 + vy^2) + 2t(vx(p_0 x - cx) + vy(p_0 y - cy)) + (p_0 x - cx)^2 + (p_0 y - cy)^2 = r^2$$

This may look messy, but remember that all of the values vx, vy, $p0$, cx, cy, and r are part of the problem statement so we know their values. That means this equation simplifies to the following quadratic:

$$At^2 + Bt + C = 0$$

Here the following is true:

$$A = vx^2 + vy^2$$

$$B = 2(vx(p_0 x - cx) + vy(p_0 y - cy))$$

$$C = (p_0 x - cx)^2 + (p_0 y - cy)^2 - r^2$$

Now we can use the quadratic formula to solve for t:

$$t = \frac{-B \pm \sqrt{B^2 - 4AC}}{2A}$$

The value inside the square root is called the equation's **discriminant** because it discriminates among different possible solutions. If the discriminant has a positive, zero, or negative value, the equation has two, one, or zero real solutions respectively. Those correspond to the line cutting through the circle, touching the circle tangentially, or missing the circle entirely.

The following code shows the `FindLineCircleIntersections` method, which finds the points of intersection between a line and a circle:

```
// Find the point of intersection between a circle defined by
// points p0, p1, p2 and the line define by points 10, 11.
private List<PointF> FindLineCircleIntersections(
    PointF c0, PointF c1, PointF c2,
    PointF p0, PointF p1)
{
    // Make a list to hold the points of intersection.
    List<PointF> results = new List<PointF>();
```

```
// Find the circle.
RectangleF circleRect = FindCircle(c0, c1, c2);

// If the points don't define a circle, return the empty results
// list.
if (circleRect.Width < 0) return results;

// Get the circle's center and radius.
float radius = circleRect.Width / 2;
PointF c = new PointF(
    circleRect.X + radius,
    circleRect.Y + radius);

// Find the intersection.
float vx = p1.X - p0.X;
float vy = p1.Y - p0.Y;
float A = vx * vx + vy * vy;
float B = 2 * (vx * (p0.X - c.X) + vy * (p0.Y - c.Y));
float C =
    (p0.X - c.X) * (p0.X - c.X) +
    (p0.Y - c.Y) * (p0.Y - c.Y) -
    radius * radius;

float discriminant = B * B - 4 * A * C;
if (discriminant < 0)
{
    Console.WriteLine("No real solutions");
    return results;
}

if (Math.Abs(discriminant) < 0.0001)
{
    Console.WriteLine("One solution");
    float t = -B / (2 * A);
    results.Add(new PointF(
        p0.X + t * vx,
        p0.Y + t * vy));
}
else
{
    Console.WriteLine("Two solutions");
    float root = (float)Math.Sqrt(discriminant);

    float t0 = (-B + root) / (2 * A);
    results.Add(new PointF(
        p0.X + t0 * vx,
        p0.Y + t0 * vy));
```

```
        float t1 = (-B - root) / (2 * A);
        results.Add(new PointF(
            p0.X + t1 * vx,
            p0.Y + t1 * vy));
    }

    return results;
}
```

The method starts by creating a `results` list to hold any intersections that it finds. It then calls the `FindCircle` method used by the preceding solution to find the circle that the user selected. If the user's points don't define a circle because they are colinear, the method returns the empty results list.

If the `FindCircle` method did find a circle, the code uses its results to find the circle's radius and center.

Next, the method finds the `<vx, vy>` vector pointing from the line's first point to its second. The method uses the values that it has to calculate *A*, *B*, and *C* for use in the quadratic formula.

The code then calculates and checks the quadratic formula's discriminant to see whether we have zero, one, or two solutions. The code calculates the appropriate number of solutions and adds them to the `results` list. The method finishes by returning that list.

The rest of the example solution uses methods defined by previous solutions to perform other tasks, such as finding the circle that the user selected. Download the `LineCircleIntersection` example solution to see additional details.

35. Circle-circle intersection

As is usually the case, you can take several approaches to solving this problem. For example, you could write the equation for one of the circles, solve for *x* and *y*, and plug those values into the equation for the second circle. Then, you would solve the new equation for *x* and *y*.

Unfortunately, as you saw in the preceding solution, the equation for a circle centered at the point *(cx, cy)* is fairly complicated, so solving that equation for *x* and *y* isn't trivial. When you plug those values into the equation for the other circle, things really get complicated.

Instead of using that method, I'm going to use a geometric approach. Take a look at the circles shown in the following diagram. Our goal is to find the points of intersection between the two circles with the centers *C0* and *C1* and radii *R0* and *R1*:

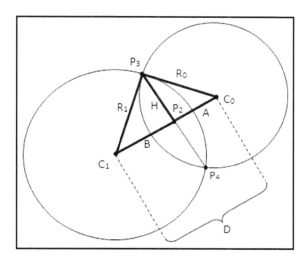

Let D be the distance between the circles' centers. There are several possible scenarios:

- If $D > R_0 + R_1$, then the circles are so far apart that they do not intersect
- If $D < |\ R_0 - R_1|$, then one circle lies inside the other so, again, the circles do not intersect
- If $D = 0$ *and* $R_0 = R_1$, then the circles are the same
- If $D = R_0 + R_1$, then the circles touch at a single point
- Otherwise, the circles intersect at two points

If you look at the triangle $\Delta C_0 P_2 P_3$, the Pythagorean theorem gives us the equation $H^2 = R_0^2 - A^2$. Similarly, if you look at the triangle $\Delta C_1 P_2 P_3$, the Pythagorean theorem gives us $H^2 = R_1^2 - B^2$. Setting these equations as equal gives the following:

$$R_0^2 - A^2 = R_1^2 - B^2$$

We know that $D = A + B$. If we solve for A, that gives us $A = D - B$. If we substitute this value into the preceding equation, we get the following:

$$R_0^2 - (D - B)^2 = R_1^2 - B^2$$

Multiplying this out gives the following:

$$R_0^2 - D^2 + 2BD - B^2 = R_1^2 - B^2$$

If you cancel the $-B^2$ terms on both sides and solve for B, you get the following:

$$B = \frac{R_1^2 - R_0^2 + D^2}{2D}$$

Now, if you go back to the equations given by the Pythagorean theorem and solve for A instead of B, you get the following:

$$A = \frac{R_0^2 - R_1^2 + D^2}{2D}$$

The only difference between these two equations is that the roles of R_0 and R_1 are switched.

We know all of these values, so we can use these equations to find A and B. All that remains is to use those values to find the points of intersection P_3 and P_4.

Let the vector *<vx, vy>* be the vector between the two circles' centers. Then, the vectors *<vy, -vx>* and *<-vy, vx>* are perpendicular to that vector. We can add multiples of those perpendicular vectors to the point P_2 to find the points P_3 and P_4.

To reach the points P_3 and P_4, we need the perpendicular vectors to have the lengths H. We can achieve that by dividing the vectors by their current lengths and then multiplying them by H. We add those vectors to P_2 and we have the points of intersection.

`FindCircleCircleIntersections` uses this method to find the points where two circles intersect:

```
// Find the points of intersection between the circles defined
// by points p00, p01, p02 and p10, p11, p12.
private List<PointF> FindCircleCircleIntersections(
    Point p00, Point p01, Point p02,
    Point p10, Point p11, Point p12)
{
    const float tiny = 0.0001f;

    List<PointF> results = new List<PointF>();

    // Find the two circles, their centers, and their radii.
    Circle0 = FindCircle(p00, p01, p02);
    float R0 = Circle0.Width / 2;
```

```
PointF C0 = new PointF(
    Circle0.X + R0,
    Circle0.Y + R0);

Circle1 = FindCircle(p10, p11, p12);
float R1 = Circle1.Width / 2;
PointF C1 = new PointF(
    Circle1.X + R1,
    Circle1.Y + R1);

// Find the distance between the centers.
double D = Distance(C0, C1);

// See how many solutions there are.
if (D > R0 + R1)
{
    Console.WriteLine(
        "No intersections, the circles are too far apart");
}
else if (D < Math.Abs(R0 - R1))
{
    Console.WriteLine(
        "No intersections, one circle contains the other");
}
else if ((Math.Abs(D) < tiny) && (Math.Abs(R0 - R1) < tiny))
{
    Console.WriteLine(
        "No intersections, the circles are the same");
}
else
{
    // Find A and H.
    double A = (R0 * R0 - R1 * R1 + D * D) / (2 * D);
    double H = Math.Sqrt(R0 * R0 - A * A);

    // Find P2.
    double P2x = C0.X + A * (C1.X - C0.X) / D;
    double P2y = C0.Y + A * (C1.Y - C0.Y) / D;

    // Get the point P3.
    results.Add(new PointF(
        (float)(P2x + H * (C1.Y - C0.Y) / D),
        (float)(P2y - H * (C1.X - C0.X) / D)));

    // See if we a second solution.
    if (Math.Abs(D - (R0 + R1)) >= tiny)
    {
        // Add the second solution with the +/- signs switched.
```

```
                    results.Add(new PointF(
                        (float)(P2x - H * (C1.Y - C0.Y) / D),
                        (float)(P2y + H * (C1.X - C0.X) / D)));
                }

                Console.WriteLine(results.Count.ToString() + " intersections");
            }

            // Return whatever results we found.
            return results;
        }
```

The method starts by using the points that define the circles to find their centers and radii. It then uses the Distance helper method to find the distance between the two centers.

The code then uses a sequence of if statements to determine the correct number of intersections. If there are any intersections, the code calculates A and H, as described earlier and uses them to find the point P_2.

Next, the code uses P_2 to find the first point of intersection, P_3, and adds it to the results list.

The method then checks whether D equals $R_0 + R_1$. If the two values are equal, then P_3 is the only point of intersection. If D does not equal $R_0 + R_1$, then the code finds the other point of intersection, P_4 and adds it to the results list.

The method finishes by returning any points of intersection that it found.

Download the CircleCircleintersection example solution to see additional details.

36. Circle-line tangents

The following diagram shows a circle and point P with their two tangent lines:

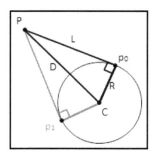

You can calculate the distance between the point P and the circle's center C by using the distance formula. If the point P is at (Px, Py) and the circle's center C is at (Cx, Cy), then the following formula gives the distance between the two points:

$$D = \sqrt{(Cx - Px)^2 + (Cy - Py)^2}$$

A tangent line meets the circle's radius at a 90°. We know D and R, so we can use the Pythagorean theorem to find L:

$$L = \sqrt{D^2 - R^2}$$

At this point, you're basically done. The points p_0 and p_1 are the distance L away from the point P, so they lie on a circle of radius L centered at point P. They also lie on the original circle. Now, you can use the techniques described in Solution 35. *Circle-circle intersection*, to find the points where those two circles intersect, and that gives you the points p_0 and p_1.

The following `FindTangentPoints` method finds the tangent points between a point and a circle:

```
// Find the tangent points for this circle and external point.
private List<PointF> FindLineCircleTangents(PointF center,
    float radius, PointF point)
{
    // Find the distance between center and point.
    float D = Distance(center, point);
    if (D <= radius) return new List<PointF>();

    // Find the distance from point to the tangent points.
    float L = (float)Math.Sqrt(D * D - radius * radius);

    // Find the points of intersection between the original circle
    // and the circle with center point and radius L.
    return FindCircleCircleIntersections(center, radius, point, L);
}
```

This method calculates the distances D and L shown in the preceding diagram. It then calls the `FindCircleCircleIntersections` method to find the intersections of the two circles described earlier.

Note that this version of `FindCircleCircleIntersections` has been modified to take the circles' centers and radii as parameters. Download the `CircleLineTangents` example solution to see the new version of the method and other details.

37. Polygon area

The hint said to consider the trapezoids defined by the polygon's edges, the X axis, and sides dropped vertically from the polygon's vertices to the X axis. The following diagram shows a polygon with one of those trapezoids shaded:

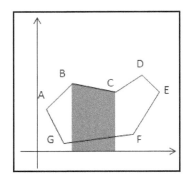

Recall that a trapezoid's bases are its parallel sides. Also recall that a trapezoid with height *h* and base lengths *b1* and *b2* has an area of *h × (b1 + b2) / 2*. To calculate a polygon's area, you can simply add the areas of its trapezoids.

You need to understand two non-obvious facts to make this work. First, notice that the shaded trapezoid in the preceding diagram includes an area between the polygon and the X axis that obviously should not be included in the polygon's area. To see why this isn't a problem, note that the X coordinate of point F is greater than the X coordinate of point G, so when you subtract *Gx − Fx*, you get a negative number. That means the trapezoid that uses the F-G segment as its top subtracts some of the area that lies below the polygon.

The trapezoids that use the polygon's top edges add the extra space below the polygon, but then the trapezoids that use the polygon's bottom edges subtract that space out again leaving only the polygon's area.

The second non-obvious fact is that the sum of the trapezoids' areas may be negative depending on the polygon's orientation. In the preceding diagram, the polygon is oriented clockwise so, for example, the X coordinate of point C is greater than the X coordinate of point B. That means the top trapezoids such as the shaded one have positive areas.

If the polygon's points were oriented counter-clockwise, then those trapezoids would have negative areas. When you add all of the areas, the final result will be negative. If the result is negative, simply take its absolute value and you'll have the polygon's correct area.

This effect is reversed in C# because *Y* coordinates increase from the top down instead of from the bottom up.

The following `PolygonArea` method uses this technique to calculate a polygon's area:

```
// Calculate the polygon's area.
private float PolygonArea(List<Point> points)
{
    int numPoints = points.Count;
    if (numPoints < 3)
        throw new Exception(
            "The polygon must have at least three vertices");

    // Repeat the first point at the end for convenience.
    points.Add(points[0]);

    // Loop over the polygon's segments.
    float area = 0;
    for (int i = 0; i < numPoints; i++)
    {
        float width = points[i + 1].X - points[i].X;
        area += width * (points[i + 1].Y + points[i].Y) / 2f;
    }

    // Remove the repeated first point.
    points.RemoveAt(numPoints);

    return Math.Abs(area);
}
```

This method first verifies that the polygon has at least three points and throws an exception if it does not.

It then copies the polygon's first point to the end of the polygon's point list to make it easier to loop over the polygon's edges.

Next, the method loops over the polygon's edges and adds the areas of their trapezoids to a total. After it finishes, the method removes the copy of the first point that it added to the point list and returns the total area.

Download the `PolygonArea` example solution to see additional details.

38. Point in a polygon

One way to determine whether a point lies inside a polygon is to add up the angles that it makes with the polygon's vertices. If the test point is *P* and *A* and *B* are two adjacent polygon points, then you look at the angle ∠*APB*.

If you add up all of the angles between the test point and each of the polygon's edges, the result will be either 0, 2π, or –2π. If the total is 2π or –2π, then the point is inside the polygon. If the total is 0, then the point lies outside of the polygon. You can probably convince yourself that this works if you draw a few examples. For example, try placing points inside and outside of a square, draw the angles, and estimate their values.

The idea is straightforward. The hard part is calculating the angles. One way to do that is to use dot products and cross products.

The **dot product** of two vectors, *v0* and *v1*, which is written *v0* • *v1*, equals |*v0*| × |*v1*| *cos(θ)*, where |*v0*| and |*v1*| mean the lengths of the vectors *v0* and *v1*, and θ is the angle between the two vectors.

One nice thing about dot products is that they are easy to calculate. If the vectors have the components *v0* = <*v0x, v0y*> and *v1* = <*v1x, v1y*>, then their dot product is simply *v0x* * *v1x* + *v0y* * *v1y*. If you calculate a dot product and then divide by the lengths of the two vectors, then the result is the cosine of the angle between the vectors.

Unfortunately, the cosine isn't quite enough to determine the angle because *cos(θ) = cos(-θ)*. Even after you find the cosine, you still don't know which angle to use.

That's where the cross product comes in. The **cross product** of two vectors, *v0* and *v1*, which is written *v0* × *v1*, gives you a new vector that is perpendicular to both *v0* and *v1*. For example, if *v0* and *v1* lie in the plane of your table, then *v0* × *v1* pokes straight up out of (or down into) the table. The length of the new vector is |*v0*| × |*v1*| *sin(θ)*.

If you write the vectors in three dimensions as <*v0x, v0y, v0z*> and <*v1x, v1y, v1z*>, then the cross product of the vectors is <*rx, ry, rz*>, where:

$$rx = v0y \times v1z - v0z \times v1y$$

$$ry = v0z \times v1x - v0x \times v1z$$

$$rz = v0x \times v1y - v0y \times v1x$$

If you assume that the vectors v0 and v1 lie in the *X-Y* plane, then their *Z* coordinates are zero, so the *rx* and *ry* values are also zero. That makes sense because the result of the cross product is a vector that is perpendicular to the plane containing v0 and v1, so it's X and Y components should be zero. Because this vector has only one non-zero component, *rz*, its length is simply *rz = v0x * v1y − v0y * v1x*.

After you calculate the cross product, you simply divide by the lengths of the two original vectors and you know sin(θ).

Finally, after you know cos(θ) and sin(θ), you can use the `arctangent` function to find θ.

Now that you know how to find the angle θ, it's time to look at some code. The following methods calculate the dot and cross products:

```
// Return the cross product AB x BC.
// Note that |AB x BC| = |AB| * |BC| * Sin(theta).
public static float CrossProductLength(Point A, Point B, Point C)
{
    // Get the vectors' components.
    float ABx = A.X - B.X;
    float ABy = A.Y - B.Y;
    float BCx = C.X - B.X;
    float BCy = C.Y - B.Y;

    // Calculate the Z coordinate of the cross product.
    return (ABx * BCy - ABy * BCx);
}

// Return the dot product AB · BC.
// Note that AB · BC = |AB| * |BC| * Cos(theta).
private static float DotProduct(Point A, Point B, Point C)
{
    // Get the vectors' components.
    float ABx = A.X - B.X;
    float ABy = A.Y - B.Y;
    float BCx = C.X - B.X;
    float BCy = C.Y - B.Y;

    // Calculate the dot product.
    return (ABx * BCx + ABy * BCy);
}
```

These methods take as parameters three points *A*, *B*, and *C*, and calculate *AB · BC* and *AB ×
BC*, respectively.

The following `GetAngle` method uses the `DotProduct` and `CrossProduct` methods to find the angle ∠*ABC:*

```
// Return angle ABC between PI and -PI.
// Note that the value is the opposite of what you might
// expect because Y coordinates increase downward.
public static float GetAngle(Point A, Point B, Point C)
{
    // Get the dot product.
    float dotProduct = DotProduct(A, B, C);

    // Get the cross product.
    float crossProduct = CrossProductLength(A, B, C);

    // Calculate the angle.
    return (float)Math.Atan2(crossProduct, dotProduct);
}
```

The method calls the `DotProduct` and `CrossProduct` methods to get the dot and cross products. It then uses the `Math.Atan2` method to find the corresponding angle.

Finally, the following code shows the `PointIsInPolygon` method:

```
// Return true if testPoint lies inside the polygon.
private bool PointIsInPolygon(List<Point> points, Point testPoint)
{
    int numPoints = points.Count;
    if (numPoints < 3)
        throw new Exception(
            "The polygon must have at least three vertices");

    // Repeat the first point at the end for convenience.
    points.Add(points[0]);

    // Loop over the polygon's segments.
    float total = 0;
    for (int i = 0; i < numPoints; i++)
        total += GetAngle(points[i], testPoint, points[i + 1]);

    // Remove the repeated first point.
    points.RemoveAt(numPoints);

    // See if total is +/-2*pi.
    const float tiny = 0.0001f;
    return (Math.Abs(total) > tiny);
}
```

This method first verifies that the polygon contains at least three points and throws an exception if it doesn't. It then adds a copy of the first point to the end of the polygon's point list to make looping through the polygon's edges easier.

Next, the code loops through the polygon's edges. For each edge, it calls the `GetAngle` method to get the corresponding angle and adds it to the total.

After it has processed all of the edges, the method removes the copy of the first point from the end of the point list. It finishes by returning `true` if the total angle is not close to 0, which means it is either 2π, or -2π.

Download the `PointInPolygon` example solution to see additional details.

39. Convexity testing

A **convex polygon** is one where each of its internal angles is less than 180°. Another way to think of it is that you can pass a line through any two adjacent polygon vertices and the line will not cut into the polygon's body.

The `GetAngle` method described in the preceding solution calculates an angle. Unfortunately, it doesn't return angles greater than 180°. Instead, if an angle is greater than 180°, the method returns 360 minus the angle so the result is always between –180° and 180°.

The method has one other issue that complicates the situation: the sign of the angles depends on the orientation of the points. If *A*, *B*, and *C* are points, then `GetAngle(A, B, C) = -GetAngle(C, B, A)`.

The solution to these problems is to look at the signs of the angles. The `GetAngle` method returns positive or negative values depending on whether an angle bends to the left or right. If `GetAngle` returns all positive or all negative values for a polygon's angles, then the polygon is convex. If `GetAngle` returns some positive values and some negative values, then the polygon is not convex.

The following `PolygonIsConvex` method returns `true` if a polygon is convex:

```
// Return true if the polygon is convex.
private bool PolygonIsConvex(List<Point> points)
{
    int numPoints = points.Count;
    if (numPoints < 3)
        throw new Exception(
            "The polygon must have at least three vertices");
```

```
    // Duplicate the first two points.
    points.Add(points[0]);
    points.Add(points[1]);

    // Get the sign of the first angle.
    int sign = Math.Sign(GetAngle(points[0], points[1], points[2]));

    // Loop through the angles.
    bool isConvex = true;
    for (int i = 1; i < numPoints; i++)
    {
        if (Math.Sign(GetAngle(points[i], points[i + 1], points[i +
          2]))
            != sign)
        {
            isConvex = false;
            break;
        }
    }

    // Remove the duplicates that we added.
    points.RemoveAt(numPoints);
    points.RemoveAt(numPoints);

    return isConvex;
}
```

The method first verifies that the polygon contains at least three points. It then adds copies of the first two points to the end of the point list to make it easier to loop through the polygon's angles.

The code then gets the sign of the first angle and saves it in the sign variable. Next, the code sets the isConvex variable to true and loops through the polygon's remaining angles. If any angle's sign doesn't agree with the value stored in the sign variable, the method sets isConvex to false and breaks out of the loop.

After it finishes the loop, the method removes the duplicate points that it added to the point list and returns the value stored in isConvex.

Download the IsConvex example solution to see additional details.

40. Stars

This is a relatively simple exercise in keeping track of points. To find the polygon's vertices, you can make a `theta` variable loop over angles using sines and cosines to find the vertices.

Because of the way C# calculates angles, and because of the fact that Y coordinates increase downward, `theta` should initially have the value $-\pi/2$ if you want the peak of an odd-sided polygon to be on the top.

When you enter the number of sides and the skip number and click **Go**, the example solution executes the following code:

```
// Get the parameter to draw a new start and refresh.
private void PrepareStar()
{
    NumSides = int.Parse(numSidesTextBox.Text);
    Skip = int.Parse(skipTextBox.Text);
    starPictureBox.Refresh();
}
```

This event handler simply parses the values that you entered and then refreshes the program's `PictureBox` to make it draw using the new parameters. The following code shows how the program draws its polygon and star:

```
// Draw the star.
private void starPictureBox_Paint(object sender, PaintEventArgs e)
{
    e.Graphics.Clear(Color.White);
    e.Graphics.SmoothingMode = SmoothingMode.AntiAlias;

    // Get positioning values.
    PointF center = new PointF(
        starPictureBox.ClientSize.Width / 2f,
        starPictureBox.ClientSize.Height / 2f);
    const float margin = 5;
    float radius = Math.Min(
        starPictureBox.ClientSize.Width / 2f,
        starPictureBox.ClientSize.Height / 2f) - margin;

    // Draw the poylgon.
    double theta = -Math.PI / 2.0;
    double dtheta = 2 * Math.PI / NumSides;
    PointF[] points = new PointF[NumSides];
    for (int i = 0; i < NumSides; i++)
    {
        points[i] = new PointF(
```

```
                (float)(center.X + radius * Math.Cos(theta)),
                (float)(center.Y + radius * Math.Sin(theta)));
            theta += dtheta;
        }
        e.Graphics.DrawPolygon(Pens.Red, points);

        // Draw the star.
        for (int i = 0; i < NumSides; i++)
            e.Graphics.DrawLine(Pens.Blue,
                points[i], points[(i + Skip) % NumSides]);
    }
```

This code finds the center of the program's `PictureBox`. It then calculates a radius for the polygon. It sets the radius, which is the distance between the polygon's center and its vertices, to be half of the smaller of the `PictureBox` control's width and height, minus a margin.

Next, the code initializes the `theta` variable to –π/2. It sets `dtheta` to 2π divided by the polygon's number of sides. The loop can use that value to make `theta` cover 2π values as the program draws the polygon.

The code then loops over the polygon's sides. It uses `theta` to find the next vertex and then increases `theta` by `dtheta`.

After it generates the polygon's vertices, the program simply draws them to display the polygon.

To draw the star, the program loops through the polygon's points, and draws a line between each point and the one that comes `Skip` positions later. The code uses the modulus operator `%` to ensure that the points' indices remain within the `points` array.

Download the `Stars` example solution to see additional details. If you experiment with the program, you'll find that it produces a disconnected star if the greatest common divisor of the number of polygon sides and the skip number lies between those values. In other words, if the polygon has P sides and the skip number is S, then the star is disconnected if $1 < GCD(P, S) < P$.

3
Dates and Times

Usually, dates and times aren't too hard to use, but they get tricky when you need to work with different locales or multiple time zones. This chapter describes problems with regard to working with dates and times. They will show you how to work with days of the week, time zones, Daylight Saving Time (or Summer Time), and localized dates and times.

Problems

Use the following problems to test your skills at working with dates, times, time zones, and date and time localization. Give each problem a try before you turn to the solutions and download the example programs.

41. Days of the week

Write a program that lets the user pick a birthdate from a `MonthCalendar` control. When the user clicks a button, display the days of the week for the next 10 birthdays after today's date.

42. Date and time picker

Normally, the `DateTimePicker` control lets the user display a date or a time, but not both. If you want to let the user select both a date and time in a single control, you need to set its `Format` and `CustomFormat` properties.

Write a program that lets the user select a date and time from a `DateTimePicker` control with a long date format and a short time format. These formats differ depending on the computer's locale. On my system, localized for the United States, the result would have the format `Wednesday, April 1, 2020 4:13 PM`.

When the user changes the selection, use a label to display the selected date and time, both in long formats. On my system, the result looks like `Wednesday, April 1, 2020 4:13:24 PM`. Make sure that all of the values are entered and displayed correctly for the computer's locale.

43. Time zone chart

Write a program that lets the user select a date and two time zones. When the user changes the selections, use a `ListView` control to show how the hours on the date in the first time zone match up with those in the second, as shown in the following screenshot. When the program builds its chart, initially select the row that corresponds to the user's current local time:

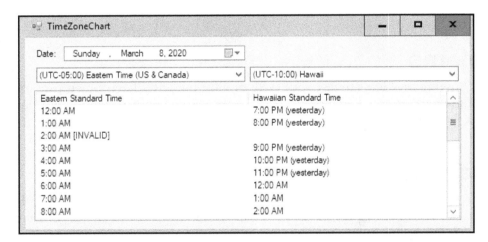

44. Scheduling meetings

Modify the program that you wrote for Problem *43. Time zone chart,* so that it uses a different background color to highlight the hours that lie between 9:00 AM and 5:00 PM in both of the selected time zones. In other words, highlight times when you could schedule a meeting with people in both time zones during their respective work days.

Note that the program will not use the highlighted color if there are no hours between 9:00 AM and 5:00 PM in both time zones.

45. Time zone clocks

Write a program that displays the current time every second in New York, Paris, London, Tokyo, and Sydney, as shown in the following screenshot:

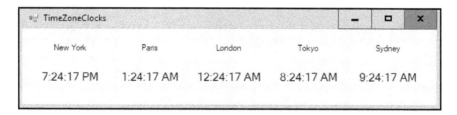

Hint: Use the `TimeZoneInfo` class's `FindSystemTimeZoneById` method to find the necessary `TimeZoneInfo` objects.

46. Local time zone clocks

If you look at the preceding screenshot, you'll notice that all of the times are displayed in the same format. My computer is localized for the United States, so the times use the United States time format.

Modify the program you wrote for problem *45. Time zone clocks*, so that it displays each city's time in its local format, as shown in the following screenshot:

47. Calculating duration

Write a program that lets the user select two dates and times. When the user presses a button, the program should calculate the time between the selected times in hours. It should then convert the times into UTC times and repeat the calculation.

Test the program by verifying that the time between 1:00 PM March 7, 2020 and 1:00 PM March 8, 2020 is 23 hours because Daylight Saving Time starts at 2:00 AM on March 8, 2020.

 If your computer isn't localized to use Daylight Saving Time, use times that span the beginning of Summer Time or whatever other time change your locale observes. If your locale doesn't change the clocks, consider yourself lucky and try converting the local times to Easter Standard Time for testing.

48. Calculating age

Write a program that lets the user pick a birthdate and then displays the person's age in years, months, and days.

Solutions

The following sections describe solutions to the preceding problems. You can download the example solutions to see additional details and to experiment with the programs at `https:/` `/github.com/PacktPublishing/The-Modern-CSharp-Challenge/tree/master/Chapter03`.

41. Days of the week

This is a relatively straightforward exercise in manipulating dates and times, but it also requires some knowledge about the `MonthCalendar` control. By default, this control lets the user select a range of up to seven dates. To make the user select a single date, set the control's `MaxSelectionCount` property to 1, either at design time or at runtime.

When you select a birthdate and click **Go**, the example solution uses the following code to build its list of birthdays:

```
// Show the next 10 birthdays.
private void goButton_Click(object sender, EventArgs e)
{
    datesListBox.Items.Clear();
```

```
    // Get the birthdate.
    DateTime birthdate = birthdateMonthCalendar.SelectionStart;

    // Get the first birthdate that is today or later.
    DateTime startdate = new DateTime(
        DateTime.Now.Year,
        birthdate.Month,
        birthdate.Day);
    if (startdate < DateTime.Now)
        startdate = startdate.AddYears(1);

    // Display the next 10 birthdays.
    for (int i = 0; i < 10; i++)
    {
        datesListBox.Items.Add(
            startdate.AddYears(i).ToLongDateString());
    }
}
```

This code clears the program's list box. It then gets the selected birthdate from its
MonthCalendar control.

If you have not used the MonthCalendar control before, it's worth
spending a few minutes experimenting with it. Using this control prevents
the user from entering invalid dates in a text box such as April 31,
2020 or February 29, 2023.

You can click the left and right arrow buttons on the top of the control to
move to the previous or next month. If you click on the control's top
center, you can zoom in and out of various timescales relatively quickly.
For example, if you click the month, the control zooms out to show the
months of the year. If you click on the year, it zooms out to show the years
in a decade. If you click on the decade, the control shows a list of decades.
From that extremely zoomed-out state, you can select any date with just a
few clicks.

After the program gets the selected date, it creates a new DateTime variable that is
initialized with the birthdate's month and day, but the current date's year. If the current
date is after that date, the code adds one year to that date to get the next birthdate.

The code then loops from 0 to 10, adding that number of years to the starting birthdate and
displaying the result in the computer's long date format.

The `DateTime`, `ToShortDateString`, `ToLongDateString`, `ToShortTimeString`, and `ToLongTimeString` methods are locale-aware, so they display dates and times in a format that is appropriate for the computer's locale. For that reason, it is better to use them rather than hardcoding in date and time formats as in `date.ToString("mm/dd/yyyy")`.

Download the `DaysOfTheWeek` example program to see additional details.

42. Date and time picker

When the example solution starts, it uses the following code to prepare the `DateTimePicker` control to allow the user to select both a date and time:

```
using System.Globalization;
using System.Threading;
...
// Make the DateTimePicker use a custom format
// that includes both date and time in localized long formats.
private void Form1_Load(object sender, EventArgs e)
{
    // Uncomment to test in German.
    //Thread.CurrentThread.CurrentCulture = new CultureInfo("de-DE");

    // Get the computer's culture info.
    CultureInfo info = Thread.CurrentThread.CurrentCulture;

    // Set the format to use long date and short time.
    dateAndTimePicker.Format = DateTimePickerFormat.Custom;
    dateAndTimePicker.CustomFormat =
        info.DateTimeFormat.LongDatePattern + "     " +
        info.DateTimeFormat.ShortTimePattern;

    // Display the initial date and time.
    dateAndTimeLabel.Text = dateAndTimePicker.Value.ToString("F");
}
```

The code begins with `using` directives for the `System.Globalization` and `System.Threading` namespaces because it needs those namespaces to work with localization information.

The form's `Load` event handler begins with a commented statement that sets the thread's culture to German. Uncomment that code to see how the program would behave if it were set up to use the German locale.

Note that this only changes the way the code displays the selected date and time. It does not make the `DateTimePicker` use the German names for months and days of the week because the control has already been created before this code executes.

Next, the code gets the thread's `CultureInfo` object. That object holds localization information, including such things as the formats that the locale uses for dates, times, numbers, and currency.

The code sets the `DateTimePicker` control's `Format` property to `Custom`. It then sets the control's `CustomFormat` property to the locale's long date pattern, followed by some spaces and the locale's short time pattern. Because it takes the date and time patterns from the `CultureInfo` object, the `DateTimePicker` displays the date and time appropriately for the current locale.

The event handler finishes by displaying the initial date and time in a label control. The `"F"` format flag indicates that `ToString` should use the full format with long date and time values. Standard format specifiers such as this one are locale-aware, so the result is displayed appropriately for the computer's locale. (In contrast, custom specifiers such as `"mm/dd/yyyy"` are not locale-aware, so they may be confusing to users in some locales.)

When the user changes the value selected in the `DateTimePicker` control, the following event handler updates the label to show the new selection:

```
// Display the selected date and time in long formats.
private void dateAndTimePicker_ValueChanged(object sender, EventArgs e)
{
    dateAndTimeLabel.Text = dateAndTimePicker.Value.ToString("F");
}
```

This code simply displays the selected time in the form's label control.

The following screenshot shows the example program in action:

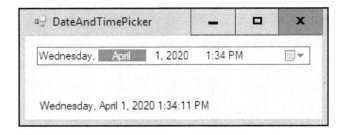

Notice that the `DateTimePicker` control allows the user to select the date, hours, and minutes, but not seconds. However, the label displays `11` seconds after the minute. If you don't let the user set all of the control's value fields, be aware that some of them, such as the seconds in this example, may not be zero.

If you click on the drop-down icon on the `DateTimePicker` control's right, a `MonthCalendar` control appears. If you don't want the user to see that drop-down, set the `DateTimePicker` control's `ShowUpDown` property to `true` to make the control replace the drop-down icon with tiny up and down buttons.

Download the `DateAndTimePicker` example solution to see additional details.

43. Time zone chart

This problem highlights several techniques and difficulties that arise when dealing with multiple time zones. When the example solution starts, it uses the following code to prepare the program for use:

```
// Display the time zones.
private void Form1_Load(object sender, EventArgs e)
{
    // Don't hide the selection when the ListView doesn't have focus.
    timesListView.HideSelection = false;
    timesListView.FullRowSelect = true;

    // List the time zones.
    foreach (TimeZoneInfo info in TimeZoneInfo.GetSystemTimeZones())
    {
        timeZone0ComboBox.Items.Add(info);
        timeZone1ComboBox.Items.Add(info);
    }
```

```
// In the first ComboBox, select the computer's time zone.
timeZone0ComboBox.SelectedItem = TimeZoneInfo.Local;

// In the second ComboBox, select the first time zone.
timeZone1ComboBox.SelectedIndex = 0;

// Display the first time chart.
MakeTimeChart();
}
```

The form displays its time zone chart in a `ListView` control. This code first sets that control's `HideSelection` property to `false` so the control keeps its selected row highlighted, even when the control loses the focus. The code also sets the control's `FullRowSelect` property to `true`, so clicking on any part of one of the control's rows selects the entire row.

Next, the code loops through the system's time zone information and adds the information to the form's two `ComboBox` controls.

 Sometimes, you can simply assign a `ComboBox` or `ListView` control's `DataSource` property to a collection holding the choices that you want to display. If you do that, however, any controls that use the collection are bound to it. In this example, that would mean that if you selected an entry in one `ComboBox`, then the other `ComboBox` would select the same entry. That won't work if you want to let the user select two different time zones.

The code then selects the computer's current time zone in the first `ComboBox` and the first time zone choice in the second.

The code finishes by calling the following `MakeTimeChart` method to display the time zone table:

```
// Make the time chart.
private void MakeTimeChart()
{
    timesListView.Items.Clear();

    // Make sure we have the values we need.
    if (timeZone0ComboBox.SelectedIndex == -1) return;
    if (timeZone1ComboBox.SelectedIndex == -1) return;

    // Get the selected time zones.
    TimeZoneInfo timeZone0 =
        timeZone0ComboBox.SelectedItem as TimeZoneInfo;
    TimeZoneInfo timeZone1 =
        timeZone1ComboBox.SelectedItem as TimeZoneInfo;
```

```
// Get midnight in the time zones.
DateTime time0 = new DateTime(
    dateTimePicker1.Value.Year,
    dateTimePicker1.Value.Month,
    dateTimePicker1.Value.Day,
    0, 0, 0, DateTimeKind.Unspecified);
DateTime time1 = TimeZoneInfo.ConvertTime(time0, timeZone0,
 timeZone1);

// Display the time zone names in the ListView column headers.
if (timeZone0.IsDaylightSavingTime(time0))
    timesListView.Columns[0].Text = timeZone0.DaylightName;
else
    timesListView.Columns[0].Text = timeZone0.StandardName;
if (timeZone1.IsDaylightSavingTime(time1))
    timesListView.Columns[1].Text = timeZone1.DaylightName;
else
    timesListView.Columns[1].Text = timeZone1.StandardName;

// Process 24 hours.
for (int hour = 1; hour <= 24; hour++)
{
    // Display the time in the first time zone.
    string text0 = time0.ToShortTimeString();
    if (timeZone0.IsAmbiguousTime(time0)) text0 += " [AMBIGUOUS]";
    if (timeZone0.IsInvalidTime(time0)) text0 += " [INVALID]";
    ListViewItem item = timesListView.Items.Add(text0);

    // Display the time in the second time zone.
    if (!timeZone0.IsInvalidTime(time0))
    {
        time1 = TimeZoneInfo.ConvertTime(time0, timeZone0,
         timeZone1);
        string text1 = time1.ToShortTimeString();
        if (timeZone1.IsAmbiguousTime(time1)) text1 += "
         [AMBIGUOUS]";
        if (timeZone1.IsInvalidTime(time1)) text1 += " [INVALID]";
        if (time0.Date < time1.Date) text1 += " (tomorrow)";
        else if (time0.Date > time1.Date) text1 += " (yesterday)";
        item.SubItems.Add(text1);
    }

    // Move to the next hour.
    time0 = time0.AddHours(1);
}

// Select the current hour.
DateTime localTime = new DateTime(
```

```
            dateTimePicker1.Value.Year,
            dateTimePicker1.Value.Month,
            dateTimePicker1.Value.Day,
            DateTime.Now.Hour,
            0, 0, DateTimeKind.Unspecified);
        localTime = TimeZoneInfo.ConvertTime(localTime,
            TimeZoneInfo.Local, timeZone0);
        timesListView.Items[localTime.Hour].Selected = true;
        timesListView.EnsureVisible(localTime.Hour);
    }
```

This method first clears the `ListView` control. It then verifies that both time zone choices have been made. (When the program is first loading, this method may be called before both `ComboBox` controls have been initialized. If that happens, the method simply returns.)

Next, the code gets the two selected time zones. Because the program added `TimeZoneInfo` objects to the `ComboBox` controls, the code can convert the selected items back into `TimeZoneInfo` objects.

The method then gets the date selected by the program's `DateTimePicker` control. The `DateTime` structure has a `Kind` field that indicates the type of time value. That property can be `Local` (to the computer), `Utc` (Coordinated Universal Time), or `Unspecified`. This program starts with times in the time zone selected in the first `ComboBox`. Because that is not necessarily the computer's local time zone, we need to work with an `Unspecified` time. Unfortunately, the `DateTimePicker` control assumes that it is working with local times, so its `Value` property gives a `Local` time.

To fix that, the code sets `time0` to a new `DateTime`, initialized with the same year, month, and day selected by the user. It sets the hours, minutes, and seconds to zero, so the time represents midnight on the morning of the selected date.

Now that is has an `Unspecified` time, the code uses the `TimeZoneInfo.ConvertTime` method to convert the time from the first time zone to the second.

The time zone values displayed in the `ComboBox` controls are somewhat unwieldy, so the code displays the time zone names in the `ListView` control's columns. Notice how the code displays different names depending on whether the selected time is observing Daylight Saving Time.

Next, the method loops over 24 hours to create its table. First, it formats `time0` as a short time string. It then checks whether that time is *ambiguous* or *invalid*. This is one of the trickiest issues when working with time.

In the United States, if Daylight Saving Time starts on the selected date, then the clocks skip forward an hour at 2:00 AM on that date so the times between 1:59 AM and 3:00 AM do not exist in that time zone. If you look closely at the screenshot in the problem statement, you'll see that 2:00 AM in the first time zone is marked as invalid.

Conversely, if Daylight Saving Time ends on the selected date, then the clocks skip backward an hour at 2:00 AM so that times between 1:00 AM and 1:59 AM occur twice on that day. That makes those hours ambiguous. (If you schedule an appointment for 1:00 AM, do you mean the first one or the second one?)

In the European Union, Summer Time begins and ends at 1:00 UTC. In much of Africa and Asia, and parts of South America, countries do not change their clocks seasonally. Fortunately, you don't need to know all of the rules for every country. You can simply create the appropriate `DateTime` structure and then use the `TimeZoneInfo` object's `IsAmbiguousTime` and `IsInvalidTime` methods to determine whether a time is ambiguous or invalid.

After it composes a reasonable string for the first time zone, the method adds it to the `ListView` control.

Next, if the time is valid in the first time zone, the code uses the `TimeZoneInfo.ConvertTime` method to convert it to the second time zone. (The `ConvertTime` method throws an exception if the time is invalid.) The code then performs similar steps to build a string for the second time zone. If the new time is during the previous or following day in the second time zone, the code also adds an indication to the new string. After it composes the string for the second time zone, the method displays it as a `ListView` sub-item.

The code then adds one hour to `time0` and repeats the loop until it has displayed the full 24 hours.

The method finishes by selecting the current hour on the selected date. To do that, it creates a new `DateTime` variable named `localTime` that represents the selected date's year, month, and day, plus the current hour. It then uses `TimeZoneInfo.ConvertTime` to convert that time into the first time zone. The method selects the `ListView` item that corresponds to that hour and ensures that the item is visible.

Download the `TimeZoneChart` example solution to see additional details.

44. Scheduling meetings

This is a relatively simple modification to the preceding solution. The new solution adds the following code to its loop, right after the code that displays the time in the second time zone:

```
// Highlight the row if both hours are valid, unambiguous,
// and between 9 AM and 4 PM.
if ((time0.Hour >= 9) && (time0.Hour <= 16) &&
    (time1.Hour >= 9) && (time1.Hour <= 16) &&
    !timeZone0.IsAmbiguousTime(time0) &&
    !timeZone1.IsAmbiguousTime(time1) &&
    !timeZone1.IsInvalidTime(time1))
    item.BackColor = Color.LightBlue;
else
    item.BackColor = Color.Pink;
```

This code checks the two times to see if they lie between 9:00 AM and 4:00 PM. (The hour that starts at 5:00 PM lies outside the range of 9 AM to 5 PM. You could have a meeting then, but it would need to end immediately.) It also checks whether the first time is ambiguous and whether the second time is ambiguous or invalid. If the time passes all of those tests, the code gives the `ListView` item a light blue background. If the time fails any of those tests, the code gives the item a pink background.

Note that the code does not check whether the first time is valid. This code is inside an `if` block that only executes if that time is valid, so the program already knows that the first time is valid.

See the preceding solution and download the `ScheduleMeetings` example solution to see additional details.

45. Time zone clocks

When the example solution starts, it uses the following code to get the `TimeZoneInfo` objects that it will use later:

```
// Arrays holding the clock labels and their TimeZoneInfo objects.
private Label[] ClockLabels;
private TimeZoneInfo[] TimeZoneInfos;

// Initialize the clock labels and time zone IDs.
private void Form1_Load(object sender, EventArgs e)
{
    // Save references to the clock labels.
```

```
ClockLabels = new Label[]
{
    newYorkLabel,
    parisLabel,
    londonLabel,
    tokyoLabel,
    sydneyLabel,
};

// Get the corresponding TimeZoneInfo objects.
string[] ids =
{
    "Eastern Standard Time",
    "Romance Standard Time",
    "GMT Standard Time",
    "Tokyo Standard Time",
    "AUS Eastern Standard Time",
};
TimeZoneInfos = new TimeZoneInfo[ids.Length];
for (int i = 0; i < ids.Length; i++)
    TimeZoneInfos[i] = TimeZoneInfo.FindSystemTimeZoneById(ids[i]);

// Start the timer.
clockTimer.Enabled = true;
}
```

The code first declares an array of `Label` controls and an array of `TimeZoneInfo` objects. The form's `Load` event handler fills the `ClockLabels` array with the `Label` controls that will display the times.

The code then builds an array holding the IDs of the time zones corresponding to the cities. It loops through the IDs and uses the `TimeZoneInfo` class's `FindSystemTimeZoneById` method to get the corresponding `TimeZoneInfo` objects and saves them in the `TimeZoneInfos` array.

You can use example Solution 43. *Time zone chart*, to help find time zone IDs. Set a breakpoint inside the `ComboBox` controls' `SelectedIndexChanged` event handler. When you select a time zone, look at the selected object's `Id` property.

The event handler finishes by enabling the form's `Timer`. When the `Timer` raises its `Tick` event, the following code displays the times:

```
// Display the time in the various time zones.
private void clockTimer_Tick(object sender, EventArgs e)
{
    // Get the current time.
    DateTime utcTime = DateTime.UtcNow;

    // Display the times.
    for (int i = 0; i < ClockLabels.Length; i++)
    {
        DateTime time = TimeZoneInfo.ConvertTimeFromUtc(utcTime,
            TimeZoneInfos[i]);
        ClockLabels[i].Text = time.ToLongTimeString();
    }
}
```

This code gets the current UTC time. It then loops through the `TimeZoneInfo` objects, converts the time into that time zone, and displays the result in the appropriate label.

Download the `TimeZoneClocks` example solution to see additional details.

46. Local time zone clocks

This example solution uses an approach similar to the one used by the preceding solution to store `TimeZoneInfo` objects for cities. It also uses the following code to declare an array to hold the cities' `CultureInfo` objects:

```
private CultureInfo[] CultureInfos;
```

The form's `Load` event handler initializes the arrays holding the clock labels and city `TimeZoneInfo` objects as before. It also includes the following code to initialize the cities' `CultureInfo` objects:

```
// Get the corresponding CultureInfo objects.
string[] cultureNames = { "en-US", "fr-FR", "en-GB", "JP-jp", "en-AU",
};
CultureInfos = new CultureInfo[cultureNames.Length];
for (int i = 0; i < cultureNames.Length; i++)
    CultureInfos[i] = new CultureInfo(cultureNames[i]);
```

This code creates an array holding the cities' culture codes. It then loops through those codes to create the corresponding `CultureInfo` objects.

Finally, the program uses the following code to update the clock labels:

```
// Display the time in the various time zones.
private void clockTimer_Tick(object sender, EventArgs e)
{
    // Get the current time.
    DateTime utcTime = DateTime.UtcNow;

    // Display the times.
    for (int i = 0; i < ClockLabels.Length; i++)
    {
        DateTime time = TimeZoneInfo.ConvertTimeFromUtc(utcTime,
            TimeZoneInfos[i]);
        ClockLabels[i].Text = time.ToString(
            CultureInfos[i].DateTimeFormat.LongTimePattern);
    }
}
```

This is similar to the previous program's code. The only difference is in the statement that sets the labels' text. In this version, the code calls the time structure's `ToString` method, passing that method the long time pattern for the city's locale.

Download the `LocalTimeZoneClocks` example solution to see additional details.

47. Calculating duration

The example solution uses the techniques described in Solution *42. Date and time picker*, to allow the user to select dates and times. When you click **Find Duration**, the program uses the following code to display the elapsed time:

```
// Display the duration between the two dates and times.
private void findDurationButton_Click(object sender, EventArgs e)
{
    DateTime localStart = startDatePicker.Value;
    DateTime localStop = stopDatePicker.Value;
    TimeSpan localInterval = localStop - localStart;
    localIntervalLabel.Text =
        localInterval.TotalHours.ToString() + " hours";

    DateTime utcStart = localStart.ToUniversalTime();
    DateTime utcStop = localStop.ToUniversalTime();
    TimeSpan utcInterval = utcStop - utcStart;
    utcIntervalLabel.Text =
        utcInterval.TotalHours.ToString() + " hours";
}
```

The code gets the selected date/time values, uses them to calculate a `TimeSpan` representing the interval between them, and then displays the total number of hours in the `TimeSpan`.

The program then converts the dates into UTC dates, calculates the new interval, and displays the elapsed time again.

In my test, the interval between the local times was 24 hours, but the interval between the UTC times was 23 hours. The local times do not correctly take into account the fact that Daylight Saving Time started between the two times.

The moral is that you should always use UTC times when you are calculating the interval between two times that may span the start or end of Daylight Saving Time.

 When you subtract two `DateTime` values, the program does not take into account the values' `Kind` properties. For example, if you subtract a local time from a UTC time, you will get a result that is off by the local time zone's UTC offset.

Download the `CalculateDuration` example solution to see additional details.

48. Calculating age

This seems like a simple problem, but it's harder than you might initially imagine. The obvious approach would be to subtract the birthdate from the current date to get a `TimeSpan` representing the elapsed time interval. You would then use the `TimeSpan` structure's properties to see how many years, months, and days have passed.

Unfortunately, the `TimeSpan` structure doesn't have properties that deal with elapsed years and months. The problem is that months and years don't always have the same number of days. You could use a `TimeSpan` to get the number of days between the current date and the birthdate and then divide that by 365.25 to get the approximate number of years that have passed, but the result won't be exact.

Still, it's not too hard to define an age intuitively, although even then different cultures may handle this differently. For this problem, I'll assume that a year has passed when the current date has reached the same month and day of the month as the birthdate. Similarly, a month has passed when the current day of the month has reached the same day of the month as the birthdate.

The example solution uses the following method to calculate the number of years, months, and days between two dates:

```
// Calculate the years, months, and days between the two dates.
private void CalculateElapsedYMD(DateTime startDate, DateTime endDate,
    out int years, out int months, out int days)
{
    // Years.
    years = endDate.Year - startDate.Year;
    if (startDate.AddYears(years) > endDate) years--;
    startDate = startDate.AddYears(years);

    // Months.
    months = endDate.Month - startDate.Month;
    if (endDate.Year > startDate.Year) months += 12;
    if (startDate.AddMonths(months) > endDate) months--;
    startDate = startDate.AddMonths(months);

    // Days.
    days = (endDate - startDate).Days;
}
```

The method subtracts the end and start dates' years to get the number of years that have elapsed. However, if the end date's month and day comes before the start date's month and date, then the number of years is too big, so the code subtracts one year. The method updates the start date by adding that number of years.

Next, the code performs similar steps with the month. It subtracts the start date's month from the end date's month. If the two dates are in different years, the code adds 12 months. However, if the end date's day number is smaller than the start date's day number, then this is too big, so the program subtracts one month. The method updates the start date by adding that number of months.

The code finishes by subtracting the two dates and getting the number of days between them.

For example, suppose the start date is February 10, 2000 and the end date is January 7, 2010. In this case, the years variable is initially 2010 – 2000 = 10. If we add 10 years to the start date, we get February 10, 2010. This is after the end date January 7, 2010, so the code subtracts one year to get nine years. It then updates the start date by adding nine years to get February 10, 2009.

Next, the code subtracts the dates' month numbers. In this example, that's January –
February = 1 – 2 = -1. The two dates are in different years, so the program adds 12 to get 11.
If we add 11 months to the start date, we get January 10, 2010. Again, this is after the end
date, January 7, 2010, so the program subtracts one month to get 10 months. It then updates
the start date by adding 10 months to get December 10, 2009.

Finally, the code calculates January 7, 2010 - December 10, 2009 and gets 28 days.

The final result is 9 years, 10 months, and 28 days.

Download the `CalculateAge` example program to see additional details.

4
Randomization

This chapter deals with generating random numbers and other randomization tasks. Many other applications require random numbers or random selections. You've already seen some, such as the Monte Carlo simulations in Chapter 2, *Geometry*. Some of the solutions described in this chapter make generating and working with random numbers easier.

Problems

Use the following problems to test your skills at working with random numbers and randomization. Give each problem a try before you turn to the solutions and download the example programs.

49. Random doubles

The Random class provides three overloaded versions of its Next method; one that returns a random integer, one that returns an integer between zero and an upper limit, and one that returns an integer between lower and upper limits.

Strangely, the Random class provides only one version of its NextDouble method. That version returns a double value between 0.0 and 1.0.

Add a NextDouble extension method to the Random class to return a random double value between lower and upper bounds.

50. Random items

Add a RandomItem extension method to a generic array to return a randomly selected item from the array. Write a second extension method to do the same for a generic list of items.

51. Randomize items

Write `Randomize` extension methods to randomize the items in a generic array or list.

52. Random groups

Write `ChooseGroup` extension methods that pick a specified number of random items (without duplicates) from a generic array or list without modifying the original array or list.

53. Choose items with probabilities

Write extension methods that choose items from an array or list with given probabilities passed into the method in an array. For example, if the first item's probability is 0.1, then it should be picked roughly 10% of the time.

Write a program to test your methods by performing a large number of trials and displaying the percentage of times the different items were selected.

54. Random passwords

Write an extension method that generates random passwords. Parameters should indicate the minimum and maximum password length, and whether to allow or require lowercase letters, uppercase letters, numbers, special characters, or other, which includes characters entered by the user. Write a program similar to the one shown in the following screenshot to test your method:

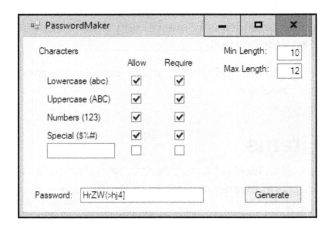

55. Random walks

A random walk is a path consisting of a series of random steps. Build a program that draws random walks similar to the one shown in the following screenshot:

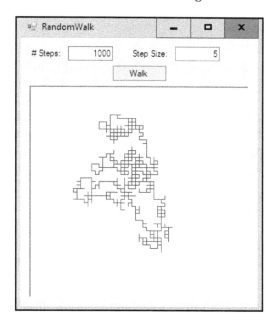

Solutions

You can download the example solutions to see additional details and to experiment with the programs at https://github.com/PacktPublishing/The-Modern-CSharp-Challenge/tree/master/Chapter04.

49. Random doubles

The following NextDouble extension method uses the Random class's existing NextDouble method to generate a double value within a range:

```
public static class RandomExtensions
{
    // A Random objects shared by all extensions.
    private static Random Rand = new Random();
```

```
// Return a double between minValue and maxValue.
public static double NextDouble(this Random rand,
    double minValue, double maxValue)
{
    return minValue + Rand.NextDouble() * (maxValue - minValue);
}
}
```

The `RandomExtensions` class creates a `Random` object at the class level. That object is `static`, so it is available to all extension methods defined in this class.

If you create a new `Random` object without passing its constructor a seed value, the class uses the system's time to initialize the new object. If a method creates its own `Random` object and the main program calls that method many times very quickly, then some of the method calls' `Random` objects may be initialized with the same system time. That would make them all return the same sequence of *random* numbers, and that wouldn't be very random at all! That's why the `RandomExtensions` class uses a single static `Random` object for all of its methods.

The new version of the `NextDouble` method returns `minValue` plus a random value times `maxValue - minValue`. The random value lies between `0.0` and `1.0`, so the result lies between `minValue` and `maxValue`.

Download the `RandomDoubles` example solution to see additional details.

50. Random items

The following extension method returns a random object from a generic array:

```
// Return a random object selected from the array.
public static T Random<T>(this T[] values)
{
    return values[Rand.Next(0, values.Length)];
}
```

The method uses the static `Random` object of the `RandomExtensions` class to pick a random index in the array.

The `Random` class's `Next` method returns an integer between an inclusive lower limit and an exclusive upper limit. In other words, the method returns a value, *R*, where *[lower limit]* ≤ *R* < *[upper limit]*. In this example, the call to `Next` returns a valid array index between zero and one less than the array's length.

The following code shows a similar method for picking a random item from a generic list:

```
// Return a random object selected from the list.
public static T Random<T>(this List<T> values)
{
    return values[Rand.Next(0, values.Count)];
}
```

Using these methods is easy. The `RandomItems` example solution uses the following two lines to pick random items from its `Animals` array and `Foods` list:

```
arrayItemTextBox.Text = Animals.Random();
listItemTextBox.Text = Foods.Random();
```

Download the `RandomItems` example solution to see additional details.

51. Randomize items

To randomize the items in an array, loop through the items. For each position i, pick a random position j with j ≥ i and swap items i and j.

After you swap an item into position i, you don't need to consider moving that item again later. This algorithm puts each item in any given position with an equal probability, at least as long as the random number generator is reasonably random.

The following code shows this algorithm implemented as a generic array extension method:

```
// Randomize the array in place.
public static void Randomize<T>(this T[] values)
{
    int numItems = values.Length;

    // Pick a random item for each position.
    for (int i = 0; i < numItems - 1; i++)
    {
        // Pick a later item to swap into position i.
        int j = Rand.Next(i, numItems);
```

```
                    // Swap items i and j.
                    T temp = values[i];
                    values[i] = values[j];
                    values[j] = temp;
            }
    }
```

This code simply follows the algorithm. The exact same code also works for a generic list of items. The only difference is that the array method uses the array's `Length` property to get the number of items while the list version uses the list's `Count` property.

Using the extension methods is easy. The following code shows how the `RandomizeItems` example solution randomizes its `FirstNames` array and `LastNames` list:

```
FirstNames.Randomize();
LastNames.Randomize();
```

Download the `RandomizeItems` example solution to see additional details.

52. Random groups

This is slightly more complicated than it might initially appear, largely due to the requirement that we leave the original array or list unmodified. If it weren't for that requirement, you could simply randomize the array or list and then return the required number of items from the randomized values.

That won't work in this case, but it does suggest a simple workaround. Copy the original array or list, randomize the copy, and return the desired number of items. If the items are small, such as integers or references to objects, then that would be reasonable. However, if the items are large, such as large structures, then that would use a lot of memory.

The approach that I use is to make an array of indices. You can then randomize the indices and use them to pick the values to return. The following method demonstrates that approach:

```
// Pick the indicated number of random items.
public static T[] ChooseGroup<T>(this T[] values, int number)
{
    // Make an array holding indices 0, 1, 2, ..., numValues - 1.
    int numItems = values.Length;
    int[] indices = Enumerable.Range(0, numItems).ToArray();

    // Partly randomize the indices array.
    if (number > numItems) number = numItems;
```

```
for (int i = 0; i < number; i++)
{
    // Pick a later item to swap into position i.
    int j = Rand.Next(i, numItems);

    // Swap items i and j.
    int temp = indices[i];
    indices[i] = indices[j];
    indices[j] = temp;
}

// Build the result array.
T[] results = new T[number];
for (int i = 0; i < number; i++) results[i] = values[indices[i]];
return results;
}
```

The method gets the number of items in the array and then uses Enumerable.Range to make an array holding the values 0, 1, 2, and so on up to the array's last index.

The method then uses code similar to the code used by Solution 51, *Randomize items,* to randomize the beginning of the array of vertices. You could simply call the index array's Randomize extension method, but we don't need to randomize the entire array. This code only randomizes enough indices to return the desired number of items.

Next, the code creates a results array. It loops through the desired number of items, uses the corresponding indices to find the randomly selected items, and inserts them into the new array. When it has filled the results array, the method returns it.

The code to choose a group of random items from a list is very similar. The main difference is that you need to use the list's Count property to determine the number of items in the list.

In the example solution, I also made the list version of the method return a list of items instead of an array of items, mostly to show how you could do that.

Download the RandomGroups example solution to see additional details.

53. Choose items with probabilities

The following surprisingly simple method picks items from an array with given probabilities:

```
// Return a random value where the values have the indicated
// probabilities.
// The probabilities must add up to 1.0.
public static T PickWithProbability<T>(this T[] values,
    double[] probabilities)
{
    // Pick a random probability.
    double prob = Rand.NextDouble();

    // Find the selected item.
    for (int i = 0; i < values.Length; i++)
    {
        prob -= probabilities[i];
        if (prob <= 0) return values[i];
    }

    throw new Exception("Probabilities do not add up to 1.0");
}
```

The method uses the `Rand` object's `NextDouble` method to pick a `prob` value between `0.0` and `1.0`. It then loops through the probabilities, subtracting each from `prob`. When `prob` is less than or equal to zero, the method returns the item with the most recently subtracted probability.

Download the `ChooseItemsWithProbabilities` example solution to see additional details.

54. Random passwords

Handling all of this problem's requirements takes some time but is actually fairly easy if you use the randomization tools we've already built in this chapter. The following `RandomPassword` method generates a password:

```
// Make a random password.
private Random Rand = new Random();
private string RandomPassword(
    int minLength, int maxLength,
    bool allowLowercase, bool requireLowercase,
    bool allowUppercase, bool requireUppercase,
    bool allowDigit, bool requireDigit,
```

```
        bool allowSpecial, bool requireSpecial,
        bool allowOther, bool requireOther, string other)
{
        const string lowers = "abcdefghijklmnopqrstuvwxyz";
        const string uppers = "ABCDEFGHIJKLMNOPQRSTUVWXYZ";
        const string digits = "0123456789";
        const string specials = @"~!@#$%^&*():;[]{}<>,.?/\|";

        // Make a string containing all allowed characters.
        string allowed = "";
        if (allowLowercase) allowed += lowers;
        if (allowUppercase) allowed += uppers;
        if (allowDigit) allowed += digits;
        if (allowSpecial) allowed += specials
        if (allowOther) allowed += other;

        // Pick the number of characters.
        int passwordLength = Rand.Next(minLength, maxLength + 1);

        // Satisfy the requirements.
        string password = "";
        if (requireLowercase) password += lowers.ToCharArray().Random();
        if (requireUppercase) password += uppers.ToCharArray().Random();
        if (requireDigit) password += digits.ToCharArray().Random();
        if (requireSpecial) password += specials.ToCharArray().Random();
        if (requireOther) password += other.ToCharArray().Random();

        // Add the remaining characters randomly.
        while (password.Length < passwordLength)
            password += allowed.ToCharArray().Random();

        // Randomize so the required characters don't all appear at the
        // front.
        char[] chars = password.ToCharArray();
        chars.Randomize();

        return new string(chars);
}
```

The method begins with some strings that define lowercase letters, uppercase letters, digits, and special characters. It then uses its `allowed` Boolean parameters to build a single string that contains all of the allowed characters.

Next, the method uses the `Rand` object to pick a length for the password between `minLength` and `maxLength`. It then satisfies the character requirements.

If a type of character is required, the code calls the appropriate string's `ToCharArray` method, uses the `Random` extension method to randomly pick a character from the array, and adds it to the password.

After it has picked one character from each of the required character categories, the method picks random characters from the `allowed` string to fill out the password to its desired length.

At this point, the password satisfies the requirements and uses only allowed characters, but one of each of the required characters is at the beginning of the string so the password isn't truly random. In fact, if all of the character types are required, then you know that the password begins with the sequence—lowercase, uppercase, digit, special, and other.

To avoid that kind of pattern, the code converts the password into an array of characters and randomizes the array. It then uses the randomized characters to create a new string and returns that as the password.

Download the `PasswordMaker` example solution to see additional details.

55. Random walks

This problem is relatively straightforward. The example solution uses the following code to generate a random walk:

```
Random Rand = new Random();
Point[] Points = null;

// Generate a random walk.
private void walkButton_Click(object sender, EventArgs e)
{
    // Get parameters.
    int numSteps = int.Parse(numStepsTextBox.Text);
    int stepSize = int.Parse(stepSizeTextBox.Text);

    // Start in the center of the PictureBox.
    int x = walkPictureBox.ClientSize.Width / 2;
    int y = walkPictureBox.ClientSize.Height / 2;

    // Build the points.
    Points = new Point[numSteps];
    for (int i = 0; i < numSteps; i++)
    {
        Points[i] = new Point(x, y);
        switch (Rand.Next(0, 4))
```

```
        {
            case 0: // Up.
                y -= stepSize;
                break;
            case 1: // Right.
                x += stepSize;
                break;
            case 2: // Down.
                y += stepSize;
                break;
            case 3: // Left.
                x -= stepSize;
                break;
        }
    }

    // Redraw.
    walkPictureBox.Refresh();
}
```

The code first creates a form-level `Random` object. It also defines a `Points` array and sets it to `null`.

When you click the **Walk** button, its event handler gets the number of steps and the size of each step that you entered in the text boxes. It positions the point (`x`, `y`) in the center of the `PictureBox` and then loops through the desired number of steps.

For each step, the code saves the point (`x`, `y`) in the `Points` array. It then uses the `Rand` object to randomly move (`x`, `y`) up, down, left, or right for the next point in the walk.

The method finishes by refreshing the `PictureBox`, which makes the following `Paint` event handler execute:

```
// Draw the walk.
private void walkPictureBox_Paint(object sender, PaintEventArgs e)
{
    if (Points == null) return;

    e.Graphics.Clear(walkPictureBox.BackColor);
    e.Graphics.DrawLines(Pens.Blue, Points);
}
```

If the `Points` array has not yet been created, the method simply exits. Otherwise, it clears the `PictureBox` and uses the `Graphics` object's `DrawLines` method to draw lines connecting the points that define the random walk.

5 Strings

This chapter describes several problems that ask you to manipulate strings. Some are just exercises in performing string operations. Others, such as finding palindromic substrings and longest common substrings, use interesting algorithms. The remaining exercises may actually be useful for some programs.

Problems

Use the following problems to test your skills at working with strings. Give each problem a try before you turn to the solutions and download the example programs.

56. Roman numerals

Write `string` and `long` extension methods that convert between Roman and Arabic numerals. Use the usual Roman digits, I = 1, V = 5, X = 10, L = 50, C = 100, D = 500, and M = 1,000. Also use the usual rules so that digits add unless a digit precedes a larger digit. For example, IX means subtract I from X to get 10 – 1 = 9.

Finally, support one extra rule that the Romans sometimes used to represent large numbers. That rule uses parentheses to represent multiplication by 1,000. For example, (IV)XIV means 4,014. Parentheses can be nested, as in ((XX)III)IV for 20,003,004, but won't appear in two places not nested, as in ((X))(III)IV.

For more information about Roman numerals, including some interesting history and a fascinating story about inheritance, go to `http://www.web40571.clarahost.co.uk/roman/howtheywork.htm`.

57. Bytes to hex

The goal of this problem is to write a program similar to the one shown in the following screenshot:

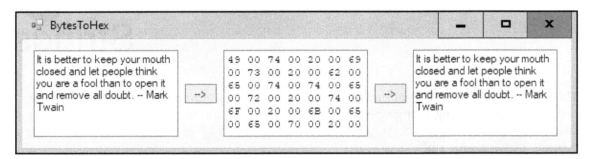

To build this program, create the following four extension methods:

- `StringToBytes`: Converts a string into an array of bytes holding the string's Unicode data
- `BytesToString`: Converts a byte array holding Unicode data into a string
- `BytesToHex`: Converts a byte array into a hexadecimal string representing the bytes
- `HexToBytes`: Converts a hexadecimal string into a byte array

When the user clicks the button on the left, convert the entered text into a byte array and then display its hexadecimal representation. When the user clicks the button on the right, convert the hexadecimal string into a byte array and then convert that array back into the original string.

58. Removing punctuation

Write a string extension method that returns the string with punctuation characters removed.

59. Palindromic substrings

In English, a **palindrome** is a string that has the same letters when written forwards or backwards, ignoring punctuation, capitalization, and spaces. For example, *A man, a plan, a canal—Panama* and *Taco cat* are palindromes.

A **palindromic substring** is a piece of a string that is the same forwards and backwards. For example, the string ABBACAB has several palindromic substrings, including C, BB, ABBA, and BACAB. (Note that each letter in the string is a trivial palindrome of length 1.)

Write a program that finds the longest palindromic substring in a given string.

60. Validating passwords

The purpose of this exercise isn't to see if a password is correct for a particular user. Problem *54. Random passwords*, asked you to write a program to generate random passwords that meet certain criteria. This problem assumes that the user will pick a password, and you need to verify that it meets those criteria.

Write a program that checks whether a password meets criteria similar to those used in Problem *54. Random passwords.* In particular, write a method that takes parameters giving the password and Boolean values, indicating whether to allow or require lowercase letters, uppercase letters, numbers, special characters, or other, which includes characters entered by the user. The method should then return `true` or `false` to indicate whether the password meets the requirements.

61. Edit distance

In order to make autocorrect suggestions, a program needs to be able to tell how close two words are to each other. The **edit distance** between two words is the number of changes that you would need to make to convert one word into the other. For example, to convert *dungeons* into *dragons*, you could use the following steps:

1. Remove u to get dngeons
2. Insert r to get drngeons
3. Remove the first n to get drgeons
4. Remove e to get drgons
5. Insert a to get dragons

This route gives an edit distance of five because it uses five steps, but for some words it may not be obvious that you have found the shortest path between the two words.

For this problem, write a program similar to the one shown in the following screenshot, which finds the edit distance between two words:

If you don't know how to get started, the first part of the solution describes an approach that you can take.

62. Soundex

The edit distance algorithm lets you determine how similarly two words are spelled. A **Soundex algorithm** gives you an idea about how similarly two names are pronounced. That is particularly useful for customer service applications where you might need to enter a customer's name without knowing how it is spelled.

For example, suppose you order a Lord of the Rings litter box for your cat, but it arrives with the Great Eye broken. When you call customer service, they ask for your name and you tell them it's *Emily Smith*. Unfortunately, your name is spelled *Emmalee Smythe*. If the rep types *Emily Smith* into the order tracking system, you won't be there.

That's where Soundex comes in. Soundex uses a set of rules to encode a word to make similarly pronounced words easier to find. A program can then look up your name's code and hopefully find orders placed by Emmalee Smythe.

The American Soundex algorithm encodes a name as a letter, followed by three digits. It uses the following rules to encode a name:

1. Keep the first letter of the name.
2. Drop all other occurrences of A, E, I, O, U, Y, H, and W.
3. Replace consonants (other than the first letter) with digits, as shown in the following table:

Replace Letter	With Digit
B, F, P, V	1
C, G, J, K, Q, S, X, Z	2
D, T	3
L	4
M, N	5
R	6

4. If two or more letters are adjacent in the original word or are separated by W or H, and have the same encoding digit, keep only the first one. For example, in BAMNER, the M and N both encode to 6, so you should discard the N.
5. If the result has fewer than three digits, pad it with zeros. If the result has more than three digits, truncate it.

For this problem, write a program that calculates the American Soundex encoding for names. Use your program to verify the values in the following table:

Name	Stephens	Robert	Rubin	Ashcroft	Tymczak	Pfister	Honeyman
Encoding	S315	R163	R150	A261	T522	P236	H555

Also verify that Smith, Smithe, and Smythe all encode to S530.

63. Longest common substring

The **longest common substring** of two strings is, as you can probably guess, the longest substring that they have in common. For example, the longest common substring of the strings *programming is easy* and *cramming is easiest before a test* is *ramming is eas*.

Write a program that finds the longest common substring between two strings. If there are multiple longest common substrings with the same lengths, display one of them.

There are several approaches that you might take. The most obvious is to examine every possible substring of the first string and see whether it appears in the second string. You should be able to implement that approach.

The solution describes that approach and another one that demonstrates a useful dynamic programming technique.

Solutions

The following sections describe solutions to the preceding problems. You can download the example solutions, to see additional details and to experiment with the programs at https://github.com/PacktPublishing/The-Modern-CSharp-Challenge/tree/master/Chapter05.

56. Roman numerals

There are many ways that you could approach this problem. I decided to use lookup tables to make things faster and simpler.

The following code shows a string extension method that converts a Roman numeral string into a long integer:

```
// Maps letters to numbers.
private static Dictionary<char, long> LetterValues = null;

// Convert Roman numerals into an integer.
public static long ToArabic(this string roman)
{
    // Initialize the letter lookup table if
    // it hasn't been initialized yet.
    if (LetterValues == null)
    {
        LetterValues = new Dictionary<char, long>();
        LetterValues.Add('I', 1);
        LetterValues.Add('V', 5);
        LetterValues.Add('X', 10);
        LetterValues.Add('L', 50);
        LetterValues.Add('C', 100);
        LetterValues.Add('D', 500);
        LetterValues.Add('M', 1000);
    }

    // If this is a blank string, return 0.
```

```
roman = roman.Trim();
if (roman.Length == 0) return 0;
roman = roman.ToUpper();

// If the number begins with "(," break out
// the part inside the parentheses.
if (roman[0] == '(')
{
    // Find the last ")."
    int end = roman.LastIndexOf(')');

    // Get the value inside the parentheses.
    string part1 = roman.Substring(1, end - 1);
    string part2 = roman.Substring(end + 1);

    // Evaluate the part inside parentheses, multiply by 1,000,
    // and add the rest.
    return 1000L * part1.ToArabic() + part2.ToArabic();
}

// At this point, we're down to plain digits. Evaluate them.
long total = 0;
long lastValue = 0;  // The value of the last letter.

// Loop through letters right to left.
for (int i = roman.Length - 1; i >= 0; i--)
{
    // Get the next letter.
    long newValue = LetterValues[roman[i]];

    // If the new value is less than the previous one,
    // then subtract this one, as in IV.
    if (newValue < lastValue)
        total -= newValue;
    else
    {
        total += newValue;
        lastValue = newValue;
    }
}
// Return the result.
return total;
}
```

This code starts by declaring a private lookup dictionary. The `ToArabic` extension method checks that dictionary and initializes it if it hasn't yet been initialized. The dictionary's values map Roman numeral letters to their long integer equivalents. For example, `LetterValues['X']` is 10.

Next, the code removes whitespace from the beginning and end of the Roman number string. If the string is then empty, the method returns 0.

The method then checks whether the string starts with an open parenthesis. If it does, then the code locates the matching close parenthesis. Because parentheses may be nested but will not sit side-by-side, we know that the matching close parenthesis is the last one in the string.

The code then breaks the string into two pieces—the piece inside the parentheses and the piece after the parentheses. It recursively calls itself to evaluate the two pieces, multiplies the first by 1,000, adds them together, and returns the result.

If the string does not begin with an open parenthesis, then it includes only letters. The method loops through the letters from right to left and evaluates them. As it does so, the method keeps track of the value of the last letter that it examined and, if it encounters a smaller value, it subtracts the letter's value from the current total.

For example, suppose the method is reading IX and has already read the X, so the current total value is 10. When it then reads the I, the code sees that 1 is less than 10, so it subtracts 1 from the total 10 to get 9.

When it examines a letter inside the loop, if the letter is not smaller than the preceding letter, then the code simply adds the new value to the total.

After it has examined all of the letters, the method returns the result.

The extension method that converts from a long integer to a Roman numeral string also uses lookup tables. The following code shows the `ToRoman` extension method:

```
// Map digits to letters.
private static string[] roman1000s = { "", "M", "MM", "MMM" };
private static string[] roman100s =
    { "", "C", "CC", "CCC", "CD", "D", "DC", "DCC", "DCCC", "CM" };
private static string[] roman10s =
    { "", "X", "XX", "XXX", "XL", "L", "LX", "LXX", "LXXX", "XC" };
private static string[] roman1s =
    { "", "I", "II", "III", "IV", "V", "VI", "VII", "VIII", "IX" };

// Convert Arabic numerals into Roman numerals.
public static string ToRoman(this long arabic)
```

```
{
    // If it's >= 4,000, use parenthese.
    if (arabic >= 4000)
    {
        long thousands = arabic / 1000;
        arabic %= 1000;
        return "(" + thousands.ToRoman() + ")" + arabic.ToRoman();
    }

    // If it's < 4,000, process the letters.
    string result = "";

    // Thousands.
    long num;
    num = arabic / 1000;
    result += roman1000s[num];
    arabic %= 1000;

    // Hundreds.
    num = arabic / 100;
    result += roman100s[num];
    arabic %= 100;

    // Tens.
    num = arabic / 10;
    result += roman10s[num];
    arabic %= 10;

    // Ones.
    result += roman1s[arabic];
    return result;
}
```

This code begins by defining arrays to hold the Roman numeral equivalent of values in the thousands, hundreds, tens, and ones. The values are arranged so that the indices into the arrays give the corresponding Roman numeral value. For example, roman100s[2] holds CC, which is the Roman numeral representation of 200.

The ToRoman method first checks whether the value is greater than or equal to 4,000. It does that because 3,999 is the largest value that it will represent without using parentheses.

If the value is greater than or equal to 4,000, the method uses division and the modulus operator to pull out the thousands and the remainder. It then recursively calls itself to evaluate those pieces. It surrounds the thousands' string with parentheses, adds the remainder's string, and returns the result.

If the value is less than 4,000, the method processes it without parentheses. First, it extracts any thousands from the value. It uses the `roman1000s` array to look up the correct Roman numeral representation for that number of thousands. Notice that the `roman1000s` entry for 0 is an empty string, so if the value is less than 1,000, the program adds an empty string to the result.

The code then repeats the same technique for the value's hundreds, tens, and ones. After it has finished processing the value, the method returns the result.

Download the `RomanNumerals` example solution to see additional details.

57. Bytes to hex

Most of these extension methods are relatively straightforward when using .NET Framework classes. The following code shows the first three methods:

```
// Convert a string into an array of bytes.
public static byte[] StringToBytes(this string input)
{
    UnicodeEncoding encoder = new UnicodeEncoding();
    return encoder.GetBytes(input);
}

// Convert the bytes into a string and return it.
public static string BytesToString(this byte[] bytes)
{
    UnicodeEncoding encoder = new UnicodeEncoding();
    return encoder.GetString(bytes);
}

// Convert from a byte array to a hex string.
public static string BytesToHex(this byte[] bytes, char separator)
{
    return BitConverter.ToString(bytes, 0).Replace('-', separator);
}
```

The `StringToBytes` method makes a `UnicodeEncoding` object and calls its `GetBytes` method to convert the input string into a byte array.

The `ToBytesString` method reverses that operation. It makes a `UnicodeEncoding` object and calls its `GetString` method to convert the input byte array into a string.

The `BytesToHex` method calls the `BitConverter` class's static `ToString` method to convert its byte array into a hexadecimal string. (The parameter 0 tells the method to start at index 0 in the array.) The code replaces the default dash character used by the `ToString` method with the separator passed in as a parameter.

Unfortunately, the .NET Framework does not have a simple method for converting from a hexadecimal string back into a byte array. The following method performs that conversion by looping through the hexadecimal values:

```
// Convert a string of hexadecimal values into a byte array.
public static byte[] HexToBytes(this string theString)
{
    // Get the separator character.
    char separator = theString[2];

    // Split at the separators.
    string[] pairs = theString.Split(separator);
    byte[] bytes = new byte[pairs.Length];
    for (int i = 0; i < pairs.Length; i++)
        bytes[i] = Convert.ToByte(pairs[i], 16);
    return bytes;
}
```

This method gets the string's separator character from its third character. It then uses the string's `Split` method to break the string into its hexadecimal pieces, delimited by that separator, and stores the pieces in the `pairs` array.

Next, the code uses the length of the `pairs` array to create a new `bytes` array. It then loops through the hexadecimal pairs and uses `Convert.ToByte` to convert the hexadecimal values into bytes. The parameter 16 tells `ToByte` that the input strings are in hexadecimal (base 16).

After it finishes converting all of the values, the method returns the `bytes` array.

Download the `BytesToHex` example solution to see additional details.

58. Removing punctuation

There are several approaches to this problem that you can take, including using LINQ or regular expressions. The following code simply loops through the string's characters to find those that are not punctuation:

```
// Return the string with punctuation removed.
public static string RemovePunctuation(this string input)
```

```
    {
        StringBuilder sb = new StringBuilder();
        foreach (char ch in input)
            if (!char.IsPunctuation(ch))
                sb.Append(ch);
        return sb.ToString();
    }
```

The code loops through the characters, uses `char.IsPunctuation` to see which are punctuation, and adds those that are not punctuation to a `StringBuilder`. After it finishes its loop, the method returns the `StringBuilder` object's contents.

Download the `RemovePunctuation` example solution to see additional details.

59. Palindromic substrings

One way to search for palindromic substrings is to consider strings with odd and even lengths separately.

A string may contain palindromes with either odd or even lengths. For example, the string CATTACAT includes the odd-length palindrome TACAT and the even-length palindrome CATTAC. In both cases, the palindrome is symmetric around its center, and the pieces on the two sides of the center are reverses of each other.

For an odd-length palindrome, the center is the middle letter. In the palindrome TACAT, the center is the C, the left side is TA, and the right side is AT.

For an even-length palindrome, the center is the border between two letters. In the palindrome CATTAC, the center is the border between the two Ts, the left side is CAT, and the right side is TAC.

All of this suggests a method for finding palindromes. To find odd-length palindromes, start at the center letter. Then, consider the letters one position to the left and right of the center. If they are the same, consider the letters two positions to the left and right of the center. Continue expanding out from the center until the corresponding letters do not match or you reach one of the ends of the string.

The method for finding an even-length palindrome is similar, except the center is between letters instead of on a letter.

The following code shows a helper method that uses this technique to return the longest palindrome with a given center position:

```
// Return the longest palindromic substring with center
// between start and end.
private static string LongestPalAt(string input, int start, int end)
{
    while ((start >= 0) && (end < input.Length) &&
        (input[start] == input[end]))
    {
        start--;
        end++;
    }
    return input.Substring(start + 1, end - start - 1);
}
```

The parameters `start` and `end` indicate the first letters on the left and right sides of the center, whether that center is on a letter or a border between letters.

As long as the `start` and `end` indices lie within the string, and as long as the characters at those positions match, the code expands the search.

After the loop ends, the `start` and `end` values point one position beyond the ends of the longest palindrome at this position. The method uses the string's `Substring` method to pull out the palindrome and returns it.

The following method uses the `LongestPalAt` helper method to find the longest palindromic substring within a string:

```
// Return the longest palindromic substring in this string.
public static string LongestPalindromicSubstring(this string input)
{
    // Remove punctuation and spaces and convert to uppercase.
    input = input.RemovePunctuation().Replace(" ", "").ToUpper();

    // Start with the first character as the longest palindromic
    // substring.
    string bestPal = input.Substring(0, 1);
    int bestLength = 1;

    // Look for odd-length palindromes.
    int inputLength = input.Length;
    for (int i = 1; i < inputLength; i++)
    {
        string testPal = LongestPalAt(input, i, i);
        if (testPal.Length > bestLength)
        {
```

```
                    bestPal = testPal;
                    bestLength = bestPal.Length;
            }
    }

    // Look for even-length palindromes.
    for (int i = 1; i < inputLength; i++)
    {
        string testPal = LongestPalAt(input, i - 1, i);
        if (testPal.Length > bestLength)
        {
            bestPal = testPal;
            bestLength = bestPal.Length;
        }
    }

    return bestPal;
}
```

The method first uses the RemovePunctuation method that was created in the preceding solution to remove punctuation characters from the input. It also removes spaces and converts the string into uppercase.

Next, the code saves the string's first letter as the best palindrome it has found so far. (Any single character is a palindrome.)

The code then loops over the string's character positions and uses LongestPalAt to get the longest palindrome centered around each letter's position. If that palindrome is longer than the longest one found so far, the method saves the new palindrome.

Next, the code repeats those steps to look for even-length palindromes.

After it finishes checking for palindromes at each letter's position and between each pair of letters, the method returns the longest palindrome that it found.

Download the PalindromicSubstrings example solution to see additional details.

60. Validating passwords

You could solve this problem in several ways. For example, you could examine each character individually or you could use regular expressions. The approach I decided to take uses simple string methods. The following code uses those methods to validate passwords:

```
// See if the password satisfies the indicated criteria.
public static bool PasswordIsValid(this string password,
    int minLength, int maxLength,
    bool allowLowercase, bool requireLowercase,
    bool allowUppercase, bool requireUppercase,
    bool allowDigit, bool requireDigit,
    bool allowSpecial, bool requireSpecial,
    bool allowOther, bool requireOther, string other)
{
    // See if the password has an allowed length.
    if ((password.Length < minLength) || (password.Length > maxLength))
        return false;

    const string lowers = "abcdefghijklmnopqrstuvwxyz";
    const string uppers = "ABCDEFGHIJKLMNOPQRSTUVWXYZ";
    const string digits = "0123456789";
    const string specials = @"~!@#$%^&*():;[]{}<>,.?/\|";

    // Check requirements.
    if (requireLowercase &&
        (password.IndexOfAny(lowers.ToCharArray()) < 0))
            return false;
    if (requireUppercase &&
        (password.IndexOfAny(uppers.ToCharArray()) < 0))
            return false;
    if (requireDigit &&
        (password.IndexOfAny(digits.ToCharArray()) < 0))
            return false;
    if (requireSpecial &&
        (password.IndexOfAny(specials.ToCharArray()) < 0))
            return false;
    if (requireOther &&
        (password.IndexOfAny(other.ToCharArray()) < 0))
            return false;

    // Make a string containing all allowed characters.
    string allowed = "";
    if (allowLowercase) allowed += lowers;
    if (allowUppercase) allowed += uppers;
    if (allowDigit) allowed += digits;
    if (allowSpecial) allowed += specials;
```

```
        if (allowOther) allowed += other;

        // Make sure all characters in the password are allowed.
        password = password.Trim(allowed.ToCharArray());
        if (password.Length > 0) return false;

        return true;
    }
```

The method first checks the password's length and returns `false` if the length is invalid.

Next, the code determines whether the password includes required characters. For example, if a lowercase letter is required, the code uses the `IndexOfAny` method to get the first index of any lowercase letter in the password. If there is no such character, the `IndexOfAny` method returns -1 and the code returns `false` to indicate that the password is invalid.

After checking for required characters, the method builds a string containing all of the allowed characters. It then uses the `Trim` method to remove those characters from the password. If the result is non-blank, then the password contains some characters that are not in the allowed string, so the method returns `false`.

Finally, if the password passes all of those checks, the method returns `true` to indicate that the password is valid.

Download the `ValidatePasswords` example solution to see additional details.

61. Edit distance

This is a fairly advanced problem, so I'll outline a solution before I present any code. You may want to stop reading after the outline and try to implement the algorithm on your own.

The approach I'm going to describe uses an edit graph. The **edit graph** is a network of nodes that represents possible changes that you can make to change the start string into the end string.

The following diagram shows an edit graph that represents changing the word *Dungeon* into the word *Dragon*:

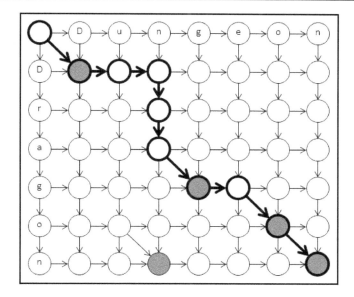

The starting word's letters fill the top row of nodes, not counting the node in the upper left corner. The end word's letters fill the left column of the nodes, also not counting the upper left corner.

Each horizontal arrow represents removing one of the starting word's letters. For example, the arrow in the top row between the **n** and the **g** represents removing the g from the string.

Each vertical arrow represents adding a letter that belongs in the end word. For example, the arrow in the left column between the **D** and the **r** represents adding the r to the word.

The shaded nodes have the same letter in their leftmost columns and topmost rows. Those nodes, which are called **match points**, represent leaving a letter unchanged. For example, the shaded node near the middle of the bottom row represents using the first **n** in Dungeon as the **n** in Dragon. The match points get additional arrows pointing from their upper left to indicate that we have skipped two steps that remove and re-add the same letter.

Any path through this graph represents a way to change the starting word into the end word. For example, you could move horizontally across the top row, removing all of the starting word's letters. Then, you could move down the rightmost column, adding all of the end word's letters. That would give a valid transformation, although generally not the shortest one.

Alternatively, you could move down the leftmost column, adding all of the end word's letters, and then move horizontally across the bottom row, removing all of the starting word's letters. Again, this probably isn't the shortest path.

To find the shortest path, assign a cost of 1 to all of the horizontal and vertical links. Give the match points' diagonal links the cost zero. Now, to find the smallest edit distance, you need to find the shortest path from the upper left node to the lower right node, following the links.

The preceding diagram shows the shortest path in bold. Because the match point links have zero cost, and because each of those links replaces a horizontal move plus a vertical move, the shortest path is also the one that uses the most diagonal links.

If you want to try implementing the algorithm on your own, stop reading and do so now.

The program must perform two main tasks. First, it must build the edit graph. Second, it needs to use the graph to find the shortest way to modify the first string into the second.

To perform the second task, the code needs to keep track of how it travels through the edit graph. To store information about a position within the graph, the example solution uses the following Direction enumeration and Node structure:

```
private enum Direction
{
    FromAbove,
    FromLeft,
    FromDiagonal
}

private struct Node
{
    public int Distance;
    public Direction Direction;
}
```

The Direction enumeration indicates how you reached a node, whether from the node above, to the left, or diagonally to the left and above (for match points). The Node structure keeps track of the distance traveled to a spot in the edit graph and the link that we used to get to that node.

The following method builds the example solution's edit graph:

```
// Fill in the edit graph for two strings.
private Node[,] MakeEditGraph(string string1, string string2)
{
    // Make the edit graph array.
    int numCols = string1.Length + 1;
    int numRows = string2.Length + 1;
    Node[,] nodes = new Node[numRows, numCols];
```

```
// Initialize the leftmost column.
for (int r = 0; r < numRows; r++)
{
    nodes[r, 0].Distance = r;
    nodes[r, 0].Direction = Direction.FromAbove;
}

// Initialize the top row.
for (int c = 0; c < numCols; c++)
{
    nodes[0, c].Distance = c;
    nodes[0, c].Direction = Direction.FromLeft;
}

// Fill in the rest of the array.
char[] chars1 = string1.ToCharArray();
char[] chars2 = string2.ToCharArray();
for (int c = 1; c < numCols; c++)
{
    // Fill in column c.
    for (int r = 1; r < numRows; r++)
    {
        // Fill in entry [r, c].
        // Check the three possible paths to here.
        int distance1 = nodes[r - 1, c].Distance + 1;
        int distance2 = nodes[r, c - 1].Distance + 1;
        int distance3 = int.MaxValue;
        if (chars1[c - 1] == chars2[r - 1])
        {
            // There is a diagonal link.
            distance3 = nodes[r - 1, c - 1].Distance;
        }

        // See which is cheapest.
        if ((distance1 <= distance2) && (distance1 <= distance3))
        {
            // Come from above.
            nodes[r, c].Distance = distance1;
            nodes[r, c].Direction = Direction.FromAbove;
        }
        else if (distance2 <= distance3)
        {
            // Come from the left.
            nodes[r, c].Distance = distance2;
            nodes[r, c].Direction = Direction.FromLeft;
        }
        else
        {
```

```
                // Come from the diagonal.
                nodes[r, c].Distance = distance3;
                nodes[r, c].Direction = Direction.FromDiagonal;
            }
        }
    }
    return nodes;
}
```

The method first builds an array of nodes big enough to hold all of the nodes shown in the earlier diagram. It then sets the `Distance` value in node `i` in the leftmost column to `i`. For example, it takes three steps to move from the upper left corner node to the third node below it. The code also sets each of those nodes' `Direction` values to `FromAbove` because the only way to get to those nodes is from the nodes above.

The code then uses a similar process to initialize the `Distance` and `Direction` values in the topmost row.

Next, the method loops through the rest of the array. There are three ways that you might be able to reach any given node, other than those in the top row and left column.

First, the cost to reach a node from the left is the cost to get to its left neighbor, plus 1 to move across the horizontal link. Similarly, the cost to reach a node from above is the cost to get to its upper neighbor, plus 1 to move down the vertical link.

The cost to move across a diagonal link is zero, so the total distance to a node via its diagonal link is the cost to get to its upper left neighbor plus zero. Note that the diagonal link only exists if the corresponding characters in the two words match, so this is a match point.

After calculating the distance to a node via each of the three possible methods, the code picks the cheapest route for that node and records it in the node's `Distance` and `Direction` values.

After initializing the edit graph, the `MakeEditGraph` method returns its array of nodes.

The second main task that the program must perform is to read the shortest sequence of edits out of the edit graph.

Learning the shortest edit distance is easy. It's stored in the `Distance` value of the node in the lower right corner of the graph. Each increment in the distance represents adding or removing a letter, so that node's `Distance` value tells you the number of moves it took to make the full conversion.

Retracing the steps used is also relatively easy. Start at the lower right node and follow the nodes' `Direction` values back through the graph until you reach the start node. This gives you the path backwards, but you can simply reverse it to get the path forward from the start node to the end node.

Understanding exactly what each move means is a bit more confusing. The example solution uses the following method to generate a list of steps taken during the transformation:

```
// Make a list showing the transformation from word1 to word2.
private List<string> DescribePath(Node[,] graph,
    string word1, string word2)
{
    //  Build the path backward.
    int numRows = graph.GetUpperBound(0) + 1;
    int numCols = graph.GetUpperBound(1) + 1;
    int r = numRows - 1;
    int c = numCols - 1;

    List<string> moves = new List<string>();
    string word = word2;
    moves.Add("End with:\t" + word);

    while ((r > 0) || (c > 0))
    {
        switch (graph[r, c].Direction)
        {
            case Direction.FromAbove:
                // We added letter r. Remove it.
                moves.Add("Add " + word2.Substring(r - 1, 1) +
                    " to get:\t" + word);
                word = word.Remove(r - 1, 1);
                r--;
                break;
            case Direction.FromLeft:
                // We removed letter c. Re-add it.
                moves.Add("Remove " + word1.Substring(c - 1, 1) +
                    " to get:\t" + word);
                word = word.Insert(r, word1.Substring(c - 1, 1));
                c--;
                break;
            case Direction.FromDiagonal:
```

```
                            // We did nothing.
                            //moves.Add("Keep " + word1.Substring(c - 1, 1) +
                            //      " to get:\t" + word);
                            r--;
                            c--;
                            break;
                    }
            }
            moves.Add("Start with word:\t" + word1);

            // Reverse the moves.
            moves.Reverse();
            return moves;
    }
```

This method sets the variables r and c to the row and column of the lower right node. It creates a list to hold the transformation's steps and sets the word variable equal to the end word.

The code then enters a loop that continues until r and c reach the upper left corner node. Inside the loop, the code checks the current node's Direction value and takes one of three actions.

If the Direction value is FromAbove, then we got to this node from the node above by adding the letter in position r – 1 in the end word. The code adds a statement indicating what it is doing to the moves list and removes the letter. It then decrements r to move to the node above.

If the Direction value is FromLeft, then we got to this node from the node to the left by removing the original word's letter in position r from position c – 1. The code adds a statement indicating what it is doing to the moves list and inserts the letter. It then decrements c to move to the node on the left.

Finally, if the Direction value is FromDiagonal, then we got to this node by following a match point link. The program did not make a change to the word at this step, so the method adds nothing to the moves list. It then decrements both r and c to move to the node above and to the left.

After it finishes following nodes through the edit graph, the method adds a message, indicating its starting word. It then reverses the `moves` list to put the moves in their proper order and returns the reordered list of moves.

Download the `EditDistance` example solution to see additional details.

62. Soundex

The following code shows an extension method that returns a string's Soundex encoding:

```
// Digits for characters.
private static string LetterCodes =
    "01230120022455012623010202";

// Return an American Soundex encoding.
public static string ToSoundex(this string name)
{
    if (name == "") return "";

    // Convert to all caps.
    name = name.ToUpper();

    // Remove H and W after the first letter.
    name = name[0] + name.Substring(1)
        .Replace("H", "").Replace("W",
      "");

    // Encode the letters.
    char lastDigit = 'x';
    string encoding = "";
    foreach (char ch in name)
    {
        // Get the encoding for this letter.
        char newDigit = LetterCodes[ch - 'A'];

        // If this is the same as the previous code, ignore it.
        if (lastDigit != newDigit)
        {
            encoding += newDigit;
            lastDigit = newDigit;
        }
    }

    // Remove the first digit from the encoding.
    encoding = encoding.Substring(1);
```

```
        // Remove the vowels from the encoding.
        encoding = encoding.Replace("0", "");

        // Pad or truncate if necessary.
        if (encoding.Length < 3)
                encoding = encoding.PadRight(3, '0');
        else if (encoding.Length > 3)
                encoding = encoding.Substring(0, 3);

        // Add the original name's letter at the beginning and return.
        return name[0] + encoding;
    }
```

This code begins by defining the `LetterCodes` string. That string contains digits to encode each of the letters, from A through Z. For example, D is the fourth letter in the alphabet and the `LetterCodes` string's fourth character is 3, which is the encoding for D. Vowels, H, and W are encoded as 0.

The `ToSoundex` method returns if its input string is blank. If the name is not blank, it converts the name into uppercase and removes any H or W characters that come after the name's first letter.

Next, the code loops through the name's remaining characters. It subtracts A from each character to find the character's position in the alphabet and uses that as an index into the `LetterCodes` string. If the current letter's encoding is different from the preceding letter's encoding, the method adds it to the name's encoding.

The code then removes the first letter from the encoding because that letter will be represented by the original name's first letter rather than a number. The code removes the vowel codes, which are 0s, from the rest of the encoding, and pads or truncates the encoding so that it contains three digits.

Finally, the code adds the name's first letter to the beginning of the encoding and returns the result.

Download the `Soundex` example solution to see additional details.

63. Longest common substring

The following code uses the obvious approach described in the problem statement that examines all of the first string's possible substrings:

```
        // Find the longest substring by examining every possible
        // substring in string1.
```

```
private string FindLongestSubstring1(string string1, string string2)
{
    string bestSubstring = "";
    int bestLength = 0;

    // Loop over all possible starting positions.
    for (int startPos = 0; startPos < string1.Length - 1; startPos++)
    {
        // Loop over possible lengths starting at this position.
        for (int length = bestLength + 1;
            length <= string1.Length - startPos;
            length++)
        {
            string testSubstring = string1.Substring(startPos, length);
            int testPos = string2.IndexOf(testSubstring);
            if (testPos >= 0)
            {
                bestLength = length;
                bestSubstring = testSubstring;
            }
        }
    }

    return bestSubstring;
}
```

This method initializes the `bestSubstring` and `bestLength` variables to indicate that it hasn't found a solution.

The code then enters two nested loops. First, the code loops over all possible starting positions in the first string.

For each starting position, the code loops over all possible lengths that are greater than the longest length found so far and that a substring can have starting at that position. There's no point looking at shorter lengths because they would be shorter than the best one found so far. There's also no point looking at a string of length 10 if the position is 2 characters from the end of the string.

Within the inner loop, the code uses the second string's `IndexOf` method to see if the test substring appears in the second string. If the test substring is present then the code updates the best solution it has found.

After it finishes examining every possible substring, the method returns the longest substring that it found.

There's actually an easy way to make this method much faster. You may want to stop reading for a minute and try to figure it out on your own.

Suppose the inner loop is examining substrings that start at position `startPos`, and `string2` does not contain a substring of a given length. In that case, it cannot contain any longer substrings starting at position `startPos` either.

For example, suppose `string1` is MAYBE and `string2` is ALWAYS. Now, suppose the outer loop is considering position 1 in `string1`. The possible substrings at that position are A, AY, AYB, and AYBE.

The inner loop checks to see if substring A appears in `string2` and finds it. It then looks for substring AY and finds that one, too. The loop then looks for substring AYB, but that substring isn't in `string2`. Because AYB isn't present, that means the longer substring, AYBE, also must not be present. When the inner loop fails to find AYB, it can exit the loop without finishing it. This test saves a lot of time because, unless the strings have a really strange structure, most common substring tests will fail for relatively short substrings.

The following code shows the modified method with the new test highlighted in bold:

```
// Find the longest substring by examining every possible
// substring in string1.
private string FindLongestSubstring1(string string1, string string2)
{
    string bestSubstring = "";
    int bestLength = 0;

    // Loop over all possible starting positions.
    for (int startPos = 0; startPos < string1.Length - 1; startPos++)
    {
        // Loop over possible lengths starting at this position.
        for (int length = bestLength + 1;
            length <= string1.Length - startPos;
            length++)
        {
            string testSubstring = string1.Substring(startPos, length);
            int testPos = string2.IndexOf(testSubstring);
            if (testPos < 0) break;

            bestLength = length;
            bestSubstring = testSubstring;
        }
    }

    return bestSubstring;
}
```

This method is much faster than the original version, particularly for long strings.

This version is fast enough to be practical, but I want to describe another method, mostly because it demonstrates a useful dynamic programming technique. *Dynamic programming* is any technique that uses known information to calculate new information. Solution 5. *Fibonacci numbers*, provides a good example. One of the approaches for finding Fibonacci numbers used a table of previously calculated values to find new values.

For the longest substring problem, you can build an array that gives the lengths of the longest substrings that end at a particular letter in each word. For example, if the array is called num, then num[i, j] is the length of the longest substring that ends at position i in the first string and position j in the second string.

The following diagram shows the array for the strings IGUANA and BANANA. The bold entries show the places where the two strings have common substrings. For example, num[6, 4] holds the value 3, indicating that the substring ANA with length 3 ends at that position. (When numbering the rows and columns, ignore the picture's first row and column, which show the words' letters and are not really part of the array.):

		B	A	N	A	N	A
	0	0	0	0	0	0	0
I	0	0	0	0	0	0	0
G	0	0	0	0	0	0	0
U	0	0	0	0	0	0	0
A	0	0	**1**	0	**1**	0	**1**
N	0	0	0	**2**	0	**2**	0
A	0	0	**1**	0	**3**	0	**3**

After you build this table, you can find the longest substring by finding the biggest value and then looking backwards through the strings. The real trick is building the table, and that turns out to be easier than you might imagine.

The first row and column in the table are filled with 0s to make later bookkeeping easier.

Suppose you've filled in the table's rows up to row R - 1 and now you're considering row R, column C. You need to figure out the longest substring that ends with the letter at position C in the first string and the letter at position R in the second. There are two possible cases.

First, suppose the two strings' letters at those positions are different. In that case, there is no matching substring here, so the table's entry num[R, C] should be 0.

Second, suppose the two strings' letters at those positions are the same. In that case, this will be num[R, C] should be num[R – 1, C – 1] + 1. In other words, the longest substring at position [R, C] is the same as the longest substring at position [R – 1, C – 1], with the new character at position [R, C] added at the end.

For example, look again at the previous table and suppose you're looking at num[7, 7] in the lower right corner. That position corresponds to the second A in IGUAN**A** and the third A in BANAN**A**. The letters match, so you look one row up and one column left at num[6, 6]. That value is 2, so num[7, 7] = 2 + 1 = 3.

If you think about the substrings, this means we're adding A to the end of the previously found matching substring, AN, to get ANA.

You might want to stop reading at this point and try to implement this new algorithm. The following code shows the implementation used by the example solution:

```
// Use a dynamic table to find the longest substring.
private string FindLongestSubstring3(string string1, string string2)
{
    int[,] num = new int[string1.Length + 1, string2.Length + 1];
    int bestLength = 0;
    int bestEnd = -1;

    for (int i = 1; i < string1.Length + 1; i++)
    {
        char ch1 = string1[i - 1];
        for (int j = 1; j < string2.Length + 1; j++)
        {
            char ch2 = string2[j - 1];

            // Compare the characters.
            if (ch1 != ch2)
                // They don't match. No matching substring here.
                num[i, j] = 0;
            else
            {
                // They match.
                num[i, j] = num[i - 1, j - 1] + 1;
```

```
            // See if this is better than the best found so far.
            if (num[i, j] > bestLength)
            {
                bestLength = num[i, j];
                bestEnd = i;
            }
        }
    }
}
int bestStart = bestEnd - bestLength + 1;
return string1.Substring(bestStart - 1, bestLength);
}
```

In theory, this last approach is probably the fastest of the three described here. In practice, however, the second approach is slightly faster. I suspect that's because it takes advantage of the string class's `IndexOf` method, which is remarkably fast.

Download the `LongestCommonSubstring` example solution to see additional details.

6

Files and Directories

This chapter describes problems that work with files and directories. Some merely provide practice on working with files and the filesystem. You may find others to be a welcome addition to your programming toolkit. For example, some examples show how to search for duplicate files, load an image file without locking it, and save JPG images with different levels of compression.

Note that working with files and directories can be particularly dangerous for a program because that are many ways those operations can fail. For example, a directory might not exist, a file might be locked, a program might not have permission to read or write in a particular directory, or a disk drive may be corrupted. The examples in this chapter use `try...catch` blocks to protect themselves from unexpected file and directory errors but, to save space, I have not included that error handling code in the text shown here. To see all of the programs' details, download the example solutions from this book's web page.

Also note that some example solutions may take a long time to run depending on your system. For example, it may take a while to to recursively search an entire 1 TB hard drive for files containing target text.

Problems

Use the following problems to test your skills at working with files and directories. Give each problem a try before you turn to the solutions and download the example programs.

64. Removing blank lines

Write a method that removes the blank lines from a file and returns the number of blank and nonblank lines in the original file. Write a program to test your method.

65. Directory size

Add an extension method to the `DirectoryInfo` class that returns the total size of the directory's files. Give the method an optional parameter indicating whether the method should include subdirectories. Write a program that uses your method to display a directory's size in bytes and file units, as in 24.1 KB.

66. Finding duplicate files

Write a program that searches a directory for duplicate files and displays any duplicates within the same branches of a `TreeView` control, as shown in the following screenshot:

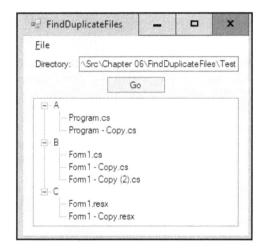

67. Thumbnails

Write a `MakeThumbnail` method that creates a thumbnail bitmap for an image file. Give it `maxWidth` and `maxHeight` parameters to indicate the thumbnail's size.

Use this method to write a program that searches a directory for image files and makes thumbnails for them all, saving the results in a `Thumbnails` subdirectory. Give the thumbnail files the same names as the original files with `thumbnail` added at the end, as in `MyPhoto thumbnail.bmp`.

68. Thumbnail web page

Modify the program you wrote for Problem 67. *Thumbnails*, so that it also generates an HTML web page to display the thumbnail images. The page should use relative paths for the thumbnails and images. Clicking a thumbnail on the page should open the original image at full scale.

After it finishes building the thumbnails and web page, the program should display the page in the system's default web browser.

69. Find files

Add an extension method to the `DirectoryInfo` class that searches the directory for files. This method should take an `IEnumerable<string>` parameter, listing patterns that the files should match (such as `*.*` or `*.cs`), optional target text that the files should contain, and a parameter indicating whether the search should include subdirectories.

Write a program to test your method. It should use a `ComboBox` control to allow the user to enter or select a sequence of file-matching patterns separated by semi-colons. Make the program allow the user to enter a multiline target string.

70. Find and Replace

Modify the program you wrote for Problem 69. *Find files*, so that it lets the user find and replace strings in files. When the user enters file-matching patterns and a target string and clicks **Find**, the program should display the matching files in a `CheckedListBox` control. If the user checks files and clicks **Replace**, the program should replace the target text with text entered in another text box in the selected files.

 This is a dangerous operation because it modifies the selected files. Making the user select specific files for replacement helps prevent the program from modifying files that the user didn't know would be selected.

 Because this is a potentially dangerous program, make sure to test it in a directory containing files that you don't mind losing, just in case, until you get the program working correctly.

71. Saving images

Write an extension method for the Image class named SaveImage that saves the image with an appropriate file format. For example, if the method's filename parameter has a .png extension, the method should save the image with the PNG format.

Write a program to test this method.

72. Compressing images

Write an extension method for the Image class named SaveCompressed that saves a JPG image with a specified level of compression. (Hint: Use an ImageCodecInfo object)

To test your method, write a program that lets the user open an image and then use a scrollbar to view the image at different compression levels. When the user changes the compression level, the program should display the compressed image, the compression level, and the compressed file's size. Let the user save the image into a new file at the currently selected compression level.

Solutions

The following sections describe solutions to the preceding problems. You can download the example solutions to see additional details and to experiment with the programs at https:/
/github.com/PacktPublishing/The-Modern-CSharp-Challenge/tree/master/Chapter06.

64. Removing blank lines

The following RemoveBlankLines method removes the blank lines from a file:

```
// Remove the empty lines from the indicated file.
private void RemoveBlankLines(string filename, out int numBlankLines,
    out int numNonBlankLines)
{
    // Read the file.
    string[] lines = File.ReadAllLines(filename);
    int totalLines = lines.Length;

    // Remove blank lines.
    List<string> nonblankLines = new List<string>();
    foreach (string line in lines)
```

```
        if (line.Trim().Length > 0)
            nonblankLines.Add(line);

    // Write the processed file.
    numNonBlankLines = nonblankLines.Count;
    numBlankLines = totalLines - numNonBlankLines;
    File.WriteAllLines(filename, nonblankLines.ToArray());
}
```

This method uses the `File` class's `ReadAllLines` method to read the file's lines into an array of strings. It then creates a list to hold nonblank lines and loops through the array of lines.

The code calls each line's `Trim` method to remove whitespace from the line's ends. If the result is not blank, the code adds the original, non-trimmed line to the nonblank line list.

> The `Trim` method returns a copy of a string with whitespace removed from its ends; it does not modify the original string. That's important in this example so that the trimmed line isn't added to the nonblank lines list.

After it has processed all of the file's lines, the method calculates the number of blank and nonblank lines in the original file and writes the nonblank lines back into the original file.

Download the `RemoveBlankLines` example solution to see additional details.

65. Directory size

The following extension method returns the size of a directory's contents:

```
    // Calculate the directory's size.
    public static long Size(this DirectoryInfo dirinfo,
        bool includeSubdirs = false)
    {
        // Get the files within the directory.
        FileInfo[] fileinfos;
        if (includeSubdirs)
            fileinfos = dirinfo.GetFiles("*", SearchOption.AllDirectories);
        else
            fileinfos = dirinfo.GetFiles("*",
              SearchOption.TopDirectoryOnly);
```

```
// Add the file sizes.
long size = 0;
foreach (FileInfo fileinfo in fileinfos) size += fileinfo.Length;

return size;
}
```

This method calls the `DirectoryInfo` object's `GetFiles` method to get information on the files contained within the directory. Depending on the value of its `includeSubdirs` parameter, the method either tells `GetFiles` to consider only files directly contained in the directory or to consider files in the directory's subdirectories.

The method then simply loops through the returned files and adds their sizes. It finishes by returning the total file size.

Download the `DirectorySize` example solution to see additional details.

The program uses the following `ToFileSize` extension method to format a value in file units as in 24.1 KB:

```
[DllImport("Shlwapi.dll", CharSet = CharSet.Auto)]
public static extern Int32 StrFormatByteSize(long fileSize,
    [MarshalAs(UnmanagedType.LPTStr)]
    StringBuilder buffer, int bufferSize);

// Use the StrFormatByteSize API function to convert
// a number of bytes into a file size.
public static string ToFileSize(this long fileSize)
{
    StringBuilder sb = new StringBuilder(20);
    StrFormatByteSize(fileSize, sb, 20);
    return sb.ToString();
}
```

This code imports the Windows `StrFormatByteSize` API function. The `ToFileSize` method simply uses that function to format a long value in file units and returns the result.

66. Finding duplicate files

One way to determine whether two files are identical is to compare the files byte-by-byte. The following method uses this approach to determine whether two files are identical:

```
// Return true if the files are identical.
public static bool FilesAreIdentical(FileInfo fileinfo1,
    FileInfo fileinfo2)
{
    byte[] bytes1 = File.ReadAllBytes(fileinfo1.FullName);
    byte[] bytes2 = File.ReadAllBytes(fileinfo2.FullName);
    if (bytes1.Length != bytes2.Length) return false;
    for (int i = 0; i < bytes1.Length; i++)
        if (bytes1[i] != bytes2[i]) return false;
    return true;
}
```

This method uses the `File` class's `ReadAllBytes` method to read the two files into byte arrays. If the arrays have different lengths, then the files are not identical, so the method returns `false`.

If the arrays have the same lengths, then the method loops through the arrays' bytes. If two corresponding bytes are different, the method again returns `false`.

If the method finishes its loop, all of the arrays' bytes are the same, so the method returns `true`.

Unfortunately, this method could be relatively slow, particularly if the files are large or if the directory holds many files. If the directory holds N files, then the program would have to use the method to compare N × (N - 1) pairs of files. For example, if N is 1,000, then the program would have to make 999,000 comparisons. If each of the comparisons is slow, this could take a while.

Fortunately, you can reduce the number of comparisons that you need to make by first comparing the files' sizes. If two files have the same size, they may not be identical, so you still need to compare them byte-by-byte, but if two files have different sizes, then you know for certain that they are different.

That's the approach taken by the example solution. It finds the files in the directory, sorts them by size, finds groups of files with matching sizes, and then examines those groups more closely to see which files are identical.

The following `GetSameSizedFiles` method searches a directory for groups of files that have the same sizes:

```
// Return lists of files with the same sizes.
// If a file is the only one of its size, do not include it.
public static List<List<FileInfo>> GetSameSizedFiles(
    this DirectoryInfo dirinfo)
{
    // Get the directory's files.
    FileInfo[] fileinfos = dirinfo.GetFiles();

    // Get the file sizes.
    long[] filesizes = new long[fileinfos.Length];
    for (int i = 0; i < fileinfos.Length; i++)
        filesizes[i] = fileinfos[i].Length;

    // Sort by file size.
    Array.Sort(filesizes, fileinfos);

    // Find groups of files with the same sizes.
    List<List<FileInfo>> groups = new List<List<FileInfo>>();
    int num = 1;
    while (num < fileinfos.Length)
    {
        if (fileinfos[num].Length != fileinfos[num - 1].Length)
            // No match. Move on to the next size.
            num++;
        else
        {
            // We have a match. Make a list of files with this size.
            List<FileInfo> files = new List<FileInfo>();
            groups.Add(files);
            files.Add(fileinfos[num - 1]);
            long length = fileinfos[num - 1].Length;
            while ((num < fileinfos.Length) &&
                    (fileinfos[num].Length == length))
            {
                files.Add(fileinfos[num++]);
            }
        }
    }
    return groups;
}
```

The method uses the `DirectoryInfo` class's `GetFiles` method to get the directory's files. It then creates an array holding the files' lengths and uses `Array.Sort` to sort the files by their sizes.

Next, the code creates a list of lists of `FileInfo` objects named `groups`. It then loops through the files looking for files that have the same size. Because the files are sorted by their sizes, any files with matching sizes will be adjacent in the `fileinfos` array.

When the code finds two files that have the same size, it creates a list named `files` and adds it to the list of lists named `groups`. It adds the files with the matching size and any other files that have the same size to the `files` list.

When it has finished examining all of the files, the method returns the `groups` list.

After calling the `GetSameSizedFiles` method, the program has lists of files with matching sizes. It still needs to examine files with matching sizes to see which are truly identical. The following `GetIdenticalFiles` method does that:

```
// Return lists of identical files.
public static List<List<FileInfo>> GetIdenticalFiles(
    this DirectoryInfo dirinfo)
{
    // Get lists of files that have the same sizes.
    List<List<FileInfo>> sameSizedFiles = dirinfo.GetSameSizedFiles();

    // Make a list to hold identical file lists.
    List<List<FileInfo>> results = new List<List<FileInfo>>();
    if (sameSizedFiles.Count == 0) return results;

    foreach (List<FileInfo> sizeGroup in sameSizedFiles)
    {
        while (sizeGroup.Count > 1)
        {
            // Make a list for the first file.
            List<FileInfo> identicalGroup = new List<FileInfo>();
            FileInfo fileinfo1 = sizeGroup[0];
            identicalGroup.Add(fileinfo1);
            identicalGroup.RemoveAt(0);

            // See if any other files should be in this group.
            for (int i = sizeGroup.Count - 1; i >= 0; i--)
            {
                if (FilesAreIdentical(fileinfo1, sizeGroup[i]))
                {
                    // The files are identical.
                    // Add the new one to the identical list.
                    identicalGroup.Add(sizeGroup[i]);
                    sizeGroup.RemoveAt(i);
                }
            }
```

```
                        // See if this identical group is empty.
                        if (identicalGroup.Count > 1) results.Add(identicalGroup);
                }
        }

        // Return the identical groups.
        return results;
}
```

This method calls the `GetSameSizedFiles` method to get the same-sized file lists. It then creates a new list of lists named `results` to hold the final lists of identical files.

Next, the code loops through lists of same-sized files. For each size list, the program enters a loop that continues until that size list is empty.

Inside the loop, the code saves the first item in the `fileinfo1` variable, adds it to a new `identicalGroup` list, and removes it from the size list. The method then loops through the other files in the list and compares them byte-by-byte to the file that it just removed. If a file is identical to the removed file, then the code adds it to the `identicalGroup` list and removes it from the same size list.

After it has finished looking for files that are identical to `fileinfo1`, the code examines the identical file list. If that list contains more than one file, it adds the list to the results. If the list contains only one file, then the method ignores it and it is discarded.

When it finishes examining all of the size lists, the method returns its results.

The final interesting piece in the example solution is the following `ProcessFiles` method:

```
// Process the files.
private void ProcessFiles()
{
    DirectoryInfo dirinfo = new DirectoryInfo(directoryTextBox.Text);
    List<List<FileInfo>> groups = dirinfo.GetIdenticalFiles();

    if (groups.Count == 0)
        filesTreeView.Nodes.Add("No identical files");
    else
    {
        char label = 'A';
        foreach (List<FileInfo> group in groups)
        {
            // Create a branch for this group.
            TreeNode branch =
             filesTreeView.Nodes.Add(label++.ToString());
```

```
        // Add the files.
        foreach (FileInfo fileinfo in group)
        {
            // Display the file's name.
            TreeNode node = branch.Nodes.Add(fileinfo.Name);

            // Save the FileInfo in case we want it later.
            node.Tag = fileinfo;
        }
    }
    filesTreeView.ExpandAll();
  }
}
```

This method creates a `DirectoryInfo` object for the directory entered by the user and then calls that object's `GetIdenticalFiles` extension method. If the result contains no groups of identical files, the program displays a message inside its `TreeView` control.

Otherwise, if there are groups of identical files, the code loops through them. For each group, the method adds a branch to the `TreeView`. It then loops through the `FileInfo` objects in the group and adds their file names to the new branch.

 The code also saves the files' `FileInfo` objects in the new nodes' `Tag` properties in case the program needs them later. For example, you could modify the program to let the user right-click on a branch to delete its file. The program would use the `Tag` property to determine which file should be deleted.

Download the `FindDuplicateFiles` example solution to see additional details.

67. Thumbnails

The following `MakeThumbnail` extension method creates a thumbnail file for an image:

```
// Make a thumbnail for the file with maximum
// dimensions maxWidth x maxHeight.
private Bitmap MakeThumbnail(string filename, int maxWidth,
    int maxHeight)
{
    // Load the image.
    Bitmap bm = LoadImageWithoutLocking(filename);

    // Calculate the scale.
    float xscale = maxWidth / (float)bm.Width;
    float yscale = maxHeight / (float)bm.Height;
```

```
float scale = Math.Min(xscale, yscale);

// Make the thumbnail's bitmap.
int width = (int)Math.Round(bm.Width * scale);
int height = (int)Math.Round(bm.Height * scale);
Bitmap thumbnail = new Bitmap(width, height);
using (Graphics gr = Graphics.FromImage(thumbnail))
{
    gr.InterpolationMode = InterpolationMode.High;

    Rectangle srcRect = new Rectangle(0, 0, bm.Width, bm.Height);
    Point[] destPoints =
    {
            new Point(0, 0),
            new Point(width, 0),
            new Point(0, height),
        };
    gr.DrawImage(bm, destPoints, srcRect, GraphicsUnit.Pixel);
}

return thumbnail;
}
```

This method first calls the `LoadImageWithoutLocking` method, which is described shortly, to load the image file without locking it. The code then calculates vertical and horizontal scales that it could use to resize the image so that it has the maximum allowed thumbnail width or height. It picks the smaller of the two scales to be the one that it will use so that the resulting thumbnail fits within the allowed bounds and is not stretched out of shape.

Next, the method calculates the image's scaled dimensions and creates a `Bitmap` of that size. It creates an associated `Graphics` object and sets that object's `InterpolationMode` property so that the image is resized smoothly.

The method defines a source rectangle that covers the entire original image. It then creates a destination array of `Point` structures that cover the area of the thumbnail bitmap. Finally, the code calls the `Graphics` object's `DrawImage` method to copy the original image onto the bitmap and returns the result.

Normally, if you load a `Bitmap` object from a file, the program keeps the file locked so that it can use it if necessary to redraw the image. This can be inconvenient if you want to edit or delete the image file while your program is displaying the image.

In this program, this may seem like a non-issue because the `MakeThumbnail` method does not need to redraw the original images. When the method ends, the `Bitmap` objects that it created leave the program's so they are destroyed and they unlock their files.

Unfortunately, C# does not necessarily destroy `Bitmap` objects immediately. They may hang around, keeping their files locked, until the garbage collector runs and frees their resources.

One solution is to call the `Bitmap` objects' `Dispose` methods or to place them inside `using` blocks so that the `Dispose` method is called automatically. This example uses a different approach. It uses the following method to open the image files:

```
// Load an image file without locking it.
private Bitmap LoadImageWithoutLocking(string filename)
{
    using (Bitmap bm = new Bitmap(filename))
    {
        return new Bitmap(bm);
    }
}
```

This code opens the image file, placing the `Bitmap` in a `using` block. It then makes a new `Bitmap` from the first bitmap and returns it. The new `Bitmap` contains a copy of the original object's data, but doesn't need the original image file to draw itself.

When the `using` block ends, the original `Bitmap` is disposed, so its resources are freed and its image file is unlocked.

The next major piece in the example is the following `ProcessFiles` method:

```
// Process the files.
private void ProcessFiles()
{
    // Get the input parameters.
    string dirname = directoryTextBox.Text;
    int thumbWidth = int.Parse(widthTextBox.Text);
    int thumbHeight = int.Parse(heightTextBox.Text);

    // Graphic file name patterns.
    string[] patterns = { "*.png", "*.bmp", "*.jpg", "*.jpeg",
        "*.gif" };

    // Make a list of the directory's image files.
    List<string> filenames = new List<string>();
    foreach (string pattern in patterns)
        filenames.AddRange(Directory.GetFiles(dirname, pattern));
```

```
    // Compose the thumbnail directory's name.
    string thumbdir = Path.Combine(dirname, "Thumbnails");

    // Create an empty thumbnail directory.
    EmptyDirectory(thumbdir);
    Directory.CreateDirectory(thumbdir);

    // Process the files.
    foreach (string filename in filenames)
    {
        Bitmap bm = MakeThumbnail(filename, thumbWidth, thumbHeight);
        string thumbname = Path.Combine(thumbdir,
            Path.GetFileNameWithoutExtension(filename)) +
            " thumb.bmp";
        bm.Save(thumbname);
    }
    numCreatedLabel.Text = $"Created {filenames.Count} thumbnails";
}
```

This code gets the directory name, width, and height entered by the user. It then creates an array holding image file extensions and loops through that array.

For each extension, the method calls the `Directory` class's `GetFiles` method to get files that have the extension and adds the returned file names to the `filenames` list.

Next, the code uses `Path.Combine` to create the name of the thumbnail directory inside the image directory. The code calls the `EmptyDirectory` method, which is described shortly, to remove any files from that directory and then uses the `Directory` class's `CreateDirectory` method to create the directory if it doesn't already exist.

Now, the method loops through the image files, calls `MakeThumbnail` for each, and saves the resulting bitmaps in the thumbnail directory.

The final interesting piece of code in this example is the following `EmptyDirectory` method:

```
    // Delete the files in this directory.
    // Hide errors if the directory doesn't exist.
    private void EmptyDirectory(string dirname)
    {
        DirectoryInfo dirinfo = new DirectoryInfo(dirname);
        if (!dirinfo.Exists) return;

        foreach (FileInfo fileinfo in dirinfo.GetFiles())
    fileinfo.Delete();
    }
```

This method creates a `DirectoryInfo` object for the directory. If the directory exists, the method then loops through the directory's files and deletes them.

Download the `Thumbnails` example solution to see additional details.

68. Thumbnail web page

This solution is similar to the preceding solution. The main differences lie in the `ProcessFiles` method. The following code shows this method with the differences highlighted:

```
// Process the files.
private void ProcessFiles()
{
    // Get the input parameters.
    string dirname = directoryTextBox.Text;
    int thumbWidth = int.Parse(widthTextBox.Text);
    int thumbHeight = int.Parse(heightTextBox.Text);

    // Graphic file name patterns.
    string[] patterns = { "*.png", "*.bmp", "*.jpg", "*.jpeg",
        "*.gif" };

    // Make a list of the directory's image files.
    List<string> filenames = new List<string>();
    foreach (string pattern in patterns)
        filenames.AddRange(Directory.GetFiles(dirname, pattern));

    // Compose the thumbnail directory's name.
    string thumbdir = Path.Combine(dirname, "Thumbnails");

    // Create an empty thumbnail directory.
    EmptyDirectory(thumbdir);
    Directory.CreateDirectory(thumbdir);

    // Start the web page.
    StringBuilder sb = new StringBuilder();
    sb.AppendLine("<html>");
    sb.AppendLine("<body>");

    // Process the files.
    foreach (string filename in filenames)
    {
        // Create the thumbnail.
        Bitmap bm = MakeThumbnail(filename, thumbWidth, thumbHeight);
        string thumbname = Path.Combine(thumbdir,
```

```
            Path.GetFileNameWithoutExtension(filename)) +
            " thumb.bmp";
        bm.Save(thumbname);

        // Add an entry to the web page.
        FileInfo fileinfo = new FileInfo(filename);
        string bigFilename = Path.Combine("..", fileinfo.Name);
        FileInfo thumbinfo = new FileInfo(thumbname);
        string thumbFilename = thumbinfo.Name;
        sb.AppendLine("  <a href=\"" + bigFilename + "\">" +
            "<img src=\"" + thumbFilename + "\">" +
            "</a>");
    }
    sb.AppendLine("</body>");
    sb.AppendLine("</html>");

    // Write the web page.
    string webFilename = Path.Combine(thumbdir, "Thumbnails.html");
    File.WriteAllText(webFilename, sb.ToString());

    // Display the web page in the system's default browser.
    System.Diagnostics.Process.Start(webFilename);

    numCreatedLabel.Text = $"Created {filenames.Count} thumbnails";
}
```

The method begins as the previous version did. It then creates a StringBuilder to hold the web page and adds <html> and <body> elements to it.

The code then creates the thumbnails as before. For each thumbnail, it also adds a new line to the web page with the following format:

```
<a href="..\banner.png"><img src="banner thumb.bmp"></a>
```

This is a link to the banner.png file in the current directory's parent directory. The link displays the picture in the banner thumb.bmp file inside the current directory.

After it processes all of the files, the method adds the closing </body> and </html> elements and writes the StringBuilder contents into the web page file.

The final new piece of the method is the following statement:

```
System.Diagnostics.Process.Start(webFilename);
```

This statement makes the system open the file named webFilename. The system opens the file with the default program associated with that type of file. This file's name ends with the .html extension, so the system opens it with its default web browser.

You might prefer to display the new web page within the program in a `WebBrowser` control. Unfortunately, that control seems to be unable to work with relative image paths such as `banner thumb.bmp`, so it cannot correctly display this web page. You could modify the code to use absolute paths to the image files, but then the web page would be less useful on an actual website.

Download the `ThumbnailWebPage` example solution to see additional details.

69. Find files

The following extension method searches a directory for files that match a list of patterns:

```
// Find files that match any of the indicated patterns.
// Do not include duplicates and return the files sorted.
public static FileInfo[] GetFiles(this DirectoryInfo dirinfo,
    IEnumerable<string> patterns,
    SearchOption option = SearchOption.TopDirectoryOnly)
{
    // Find files matching the patterns.
    Dictionary<string, FileInfo> fileDict =
        new Dictionary<string, FileInfo>()

    foreach (string pattern in patterns)
    {
        foreach (FileInfo fileinfo in dirinfo.GetFiles(pattern,
         option))
        {
            if (!fileDict.ContainsKey(fileinfo.FullName))
                fileDict.Add(fileinfo.FullName, fileinfo);
        }
    }

    // Sort and return.
    FileInfo[] fileinfos = fileDict.Values.ToArray();
    string[] filenames = fileDict.Keys.ToArray();
    Array.Sort(filenames, fileinfos);
    return fileinfos;
}
```

The method starts by making a dictionary to hold the files that it finds. Dictionaries are handy for quickly determining whether you have already found something that should be saved only once.

The code then loops through the patterns and calls the `DirectoryInfo` object's `GetFiles` method to find files that match each pattern. It loops through the returned files and adds those that have not already been found to the dictionary. This prevents the method from listing the same file twice case it matches more than one pattern.

After it finishes gathering the files, the code extracts the dictionary's values (the `FileInfo` objects) and keys (the filenames) into arrays. The items in a dictionary are not stored in any particular order, but its `Values` and `Keys` collections do return their contents in the same order, so corresponding items in the arrays go together.

The method sorts the `FileInfo` objects using the filenames as keys and returns the result.

The following method uses the `GetFiles` method to search for files that match patterns and that contain target text:

```
// Find files that match any of the indicated patterns and
// that contain the target string. Do not include duplicates
// and return the files sorted.
public static FileInfo[] FindFiles(this DirectoryInfo dirinfo,
    IEnumerable<string> patterns, string target = "",
    SearchOption option = SearchOption.TopDirectoryOnly)
{
    // Find files matching the patterns.
    FileInfo[] fileinfos = dirinfo.GetFiles(patterns, option);

    // See if we should examine the files' contents.
    if ((target != null) && (target.Length > 0))
    {
        // See which files contain the required contents.
        List<FileInfo> newFiles = new List<FileInfo>();
        foreach (FileInfo fileinfo in fileinfos)
        {
            string text = File.ReadAllText(fileinfo.FullName);
            if (text.Contains(target)) newFiles.Add(fileinfo);
        }
        fileinfos = newFiles.ToArray();
    }

    return fileinfos;
}
```

This method calls the previous `GetFiles` method to get an array of `FileInfo` objects representing files that match the indicated patterns.

Then, if `target` is nonblank, the method loops through the files. For each file, the code uses `File.ReadAllText` to get the file's contents and uses `IndexOf` to see if the text contains the target string. If the file contains `target`, the code adds the file to its result list.

After it has checked every file, the method returns the files that it found.

The only remaining code of any real interest in this program is the following snippet, which converts patterns entered by the user into an array of pattern strings:

```
// Get the patterns.
string patternsString = patternsComboBox.Text;
if (patternsString.Contains(':'))
    patternsString =
        patternsString.Substring(
            patternsString.IndexOf(':') + 1).Trim();
string[] patterns = patternsString.Trim().Split(
    new char[] { ';' }, StringSplitOptions.RemoveEmptyEntries);
for (int i = 0; i < patterns.Length; i++)
    patterns[i] = patterns[i].Trim();
```

This code assumes that the pattern has a format similar to the following:

```
C# Files: *.cs; *.sln; *.resx; *.config
```

If the string contains a colon, the code takes only the characters following it, so it removes the `C# Files:` part of the preceding example. The code then uses the string class's `Split` method to separate the string at the semi-colon characters. It finishes by looping through the patterns and calling their `Trim` methods to remove whitespace from their ends.

The rest of the example solution is relatively straightforward. Download the `FindFiles` example solution to see additional details.

70. Find and Replace

The parts of this program that actually find files and make replacements are relatively straightforward. The following code shows how the example solution searches for files:

```
// Search the directory.
private void findButton_Click(object sender, EventArgs e)
{
    Cursor = Cursors.WaitCursor;
    filesCheckedListBox.DataSource = null;
    Refresh();

    // Get the patterns.
```

```
        string patternsString = patternsComboBox.Text;
        if (patternsString.Contains(':'))
            patternsString =
                patternsString.Substring(
                    patternsString.IndexOf(':') + 1).Trim();

        string[] patterns = patternsString.Trim().Split(
            new char[] { ';' }, StringSplitOptions.RemoveEmptyEntries);

        // Find files matching the patterns and containing the target text.
        DirectoryInfo dirinfo = new DirectoryInfo(directoryTextBox.Text);
        FileInfo[] fileinfos = dirinfo.FindFiles(patterns,
            targetTextBox.Text, SearchOption.AllDirectories);

        // List the files.
        filesCheckedListBox.DataSource = fileinfos;

        Cursor = Cursors.Default;
    }
```

This code separates the user's selected file patterns, as in the preceding solution. Next, it creates a `DirectoryInfo` object and calls its `FindFiles` extension method to find matching files. It then simply displays the results in the `CheckedListBox` named `filesCheckedListBox`.

The following code shows how the program makes replacements in the files that are checked in the `CheckedListBox`:

```
        // Replace the target text with the replacement text in
        // the selected files.
        private void replaceButton_Click(object sender, EventArgs e)
        {
            string changeFrom = targetTextBox.Text;
            string changeTo = replaceWithTextBox.Text;
            int numReplacements = 0;
            foreach (FileInfo fileinfo in filesCheckedListBox.CheckedItems)
            {
                MakeReplacement(fileinfo, changeFrom, changeTo);
                numReplacements++;
            }
            MessageBox.Show("Made replacements in " +
                numReplacements.ToString() + " files.");

            // Clear the file list.
            filesCheckedListBox.DataSource = null;
        }
```

This code gets the target and replacement strings. It then loops through the checked files and calls the `MakeReplacement` method, which is described shortly, for each. The code finishes by displaying the number of files that were modified.

The following code shows the `MakeReplacement` method:

```
// Replace changeFrom to changedTo in the file.
private void MakeReplacement(FileInfo fileinfo, string changeFrom,
    string changeTo)
{
    string file = File.ReadAllText(fileinfo.FullName);
    file = file.Replace(changeFrom, changeTo);
    File.WriteAllText(fileinfo.FullName, file);
}
```

This method uses `File.ReadAllText` to read the file's contents. It uses the string class's `Replace` method to make the replacement and then uses `File.WriteAllText` to save the result back into the file.

Download the `FindAndReplace` example solution to see additional details.

71. Saving images

The following extension method saves an image with an appropriate file format:

```
// Save an image in a file with format determined by its extension.
public static void SaveImage(this Image image, string filename)
{
    // Check the extension to see what kind of file this should be.
    string extension = Path.GetExtension(filename);
    switch (extension.ToLower())
    {
        case ".bmp":
            image.Save(filename, ImageFormat.Bmp);
            break;
        case ".exif":
            image.Save(filename, ImageFormat.Exif);
            break;
        case ".gif":
            image.Save(filename, ImageFormat.Gif);
            break;
        case ".jpg":
        case ".jpeg":
            image.Save(filename, ImageFormat.Jpeg);
            break;
```

```
        case ".png":
            image.Save(filename, ImageFormat.Png);
            break;
        case ".tif":
        case ".tiff":
            image.Save(filename, ImageFormat.Tiff);
            break;
        default:
            throw new NotSupportedException(
                "Unsupported file extension " + extension);
    }
}
```

This method uses the `Path.GetExtension` method to get the filename's extension. It then uses a `switch` statement to take different actions depending on the extension.

The `switch` statement's `case` blocks call the image's `Save` method, passing it the filename and a parameter, indicating the correct file format for the extension.

The example solution displays an image, text box, and **Save** button. When you enter a filename and click the button, the following code saves the image with the filename that you entered:

```
// Save the image in the appropriate format.
private void saveButton_Click(object sender, EventArgs e)
{
    pictureBox1.Image.SaveImage(filenameTextBox.Text);
    filenameTextBox.Clear();
    filenameTextBox.Focus();
}
```

This code simply calls the `SaveImage` extension method to save the image with the desired filename.

If you open the files in MS Paint or some other image editor, you should be able to see the characteristics of the desired formats. For example, PNG files use lossless compression, JPG files use lossy compression, and GIF files use dithering. You can also use File Explorer to see that some formats are compressed more effectively than others.

This method can be a handy part of your image processing toolkit because it prevents you from saving an image in the wrong format. For example, it prevents you from accidentally saving an image in the `Smiley.bmp` file with the PNG file format.

Download the example solution to see additional details.

72. Compressing images

One of the key pieces of this solution is the following extension method, which saves an
image in JPG format with a specified compression level:

```
// Save a JPG file with the indicated compression level.
public static void SaveCompressed(this Image image, string filename,
    int compressionLevel)
{
    // Make an object to hold one encoder parameter.
    EncoderParameters parameters = new EncoderParameters(1);

    // Place the compression level in that parameter.
    parameters.Param[0] = new EncoderParameter(
        System.Drawing.Imaging.Encoder.Quality, compressionLevel);

    // Get the JPG codec.
    ImageCodecInfo codecInfo = GetEncoderInfo("image/jpeg");

    // Create the file, deleting it if it already exists.
    if (File.Exists(filename)) File.Delete(filename);
    image.Save(filename, codecInfo, parameters);
}
```

This method first creates an `EncoderParameters` object to hold a single parameter, which
will be used by an image encoder. It sets that parameter's category to `Quality` and sets its
value to the desired compression level.

The `Quality` parameter uses a fully qualified namespace because without
that there would be ambiguity between
`System.Drawing.Imaging.Encoder` and `System.Text.Encoder`.

The `Quality` parameter's value should be between 0 (the most
compression) and 100 (the least compression).

Next, the code creates codec information for the `image/jpeg` mime type.

A **codec**, which is short for **coder decoder**, is a program or object that
encodes and decodes a stream of data. In this example, it encodes and
decodes JPG files.

MIME stands for **Multipurpose Internet Mail Extensions**. As I'm sure
you can guess, `image/jpg` is the mime type for image files in the JPG
format.

If the file already exists, the method deletes it. It then calls the image's `Save` method, passing it the `ImageCodecInfo` object and `EncoderParameter` to tell it the compression level.

The following code fragment shows how the program uses the `SaveCompressed` method:

```
// The name of the temporary file.
private static string tempfile = "__temp.jpg";
...
// Process a newly loaded file.
private void ProcessFile(Image image)
{
    if (image == null) return;

    // Save the original image.
    OriginalImage = image;

    // Save the image in a temporary file with
    // the current compression level.
    image.SaveCompressed(tempfile, compressionScrollbar.Value);

    // Reload the file.
    compressedPictureBox.Image = LoadImageWithoutLocking(tempfile);

    // Display the file compression level.
    compressionLabel.Text = compressionScrollbar.Value.ToString();

    // Display the file's size.
    FileInfo fileinfo = new FileInfo(tempfile);
    fileSizeLabel.Text = fileinfo.Length.ToFileSize();
}
```

This method stores the image in the `OriginalImage` variable so that it can retrieve the original image later. It then calls the `SaveCompressed` method to save the image in a temporary file at the level of compression selected by the `compressionScrollbar` control. The code then reloads the image from the file and displays it in the `compressedPictureBox` control. The result shows the image in its compressed form.

The method finishes by displaying the compressed file's size in a label so that you can see how much space the file occupies.

Download the `CompressImages` example solution to see additional details.

Advanced C# and .NET Features 7

This chapter describes problems that use some of the C# language's more advanced features. Unfortunately, C# has too many capabilities, so we can't cover them all here. The particular features described here include some parts of LINQ, PLINQ, TPL, the `yield` statement, and operator overloading.

 LINQ stands for **Language Integrated Query**, **PLINQ** stands for **Parallel LINQ**, and **TPL** stands for **Task Parallel Library**.

These techniques provide new ways to simplify program structure and improve performance. Even if you don't use them on a daily basis, it's useful to know how they work so that you can understand other peoples' code when you see these techniques.

Problems

Use the following problems to test your skills at working with advanced C# language features. Give each problem a try before you turn to the solutions and download the example programs.

73. Directory size, LINQ style

Repeat Problem *65. Directory size*. This time, add a `SizeLINQ` extension method to the `DirectoryInfo` class that uses LINQ to calculate the size of the files inside the directory.

74. Directory size, PLINQ style

Repeat Problem *73. Directory size, LINQ style*, but this time use PLINQ to add file lengths in parallel. Make the test program perform the same operations using a `foreach` loop, LINQ, and PLINQ, and display the elapsed time for each. Let the user enter a number of times to repeat each operation so that you can get some meaningful times.

 Repeating each operation multiple times limits the time used by disk accesses because the file information should be cached after the first set of calculations.

75. Find files, LINQ style

Repeat Problem *69. Find files*. This time, give the `DirectoryInfo` class a `FindFilesLINQ` extension method that uses a LINQ query to search for files.

76. Parallel primes table

Repeat *Problem 12. Prime table*, using TPL to build basic, Eratosthenes, and Euler tables in parallel. Compare the speeds of the parallel and non-parallel methods.

77. Parallel prime tuples

Repeat Problem *15. Prime tuples*, using TPL to search for groups of primes in parallel. Compare the speeds of the parallel and non-parallel methods.

78. Parallel Monte Carlo π

Repeat Problem *20. Monte Carlo π*, using TPL to perform trials in parallel. Compare the speeds of the parallel and non-parallel methods.

79. Yielding primes

Write a method that uses the `yield` statement to return a specific number of prime numbers. Make the test program display those primes in a `foreach` loop.

80. Yielding Fibonacci numbers

Write a program similar to the one you built for Problem 79. *Yielding primes*, but this time make it yield Fibonacci numbers. Make the method yield all of the Fibonacci numbers that it can.

81. Complex numbers

The `System.Numerics` namespace has included the `Complex` structure to represent complex numbers since C# 4.0. Building something similar demonstrates so many useful techniques that it's still worth creating your own version. For this problem, create a `ComplexNumber` structure that has the following features:

- `Re` and `Im` properties that get and set the number's real and imaginary parts
- A `FromPolar` factory method that creates a `ComplexNumber` from a polar coordinate representation
- Static values representing 0, 1, and i
- `ToString` and `Parse` methods that translate a value to and from a string with the format x + yi
- Implementation of the `IEquatable` interface
- An overloaded `Equals` method that determines whether two values are equal with a given precision
- Read-only `Magnitude` and `Angle` properties to get the number's polar coordinate representation
- Operators that convert from a `double` implicitly and to a `double` explicitly
- Arithmetic operators that let you perform addition, subtraction, multiplication, division, and negation with `ComplexNumber` and numeric values

A **factory method** is a method that creates an instance of a class. Usually, it is a static method, so you don't need an instance of the class to invoke it. In this problem, the FromPolar method should take the polar coordinates r and θ as parameters and return an appropriate new ComplexNumber structure.

If you are unfamiliar with complex numbers or with their polar representation, see en.wikipedia.org/wiki/Complex_number or http://mathworld.wolfram.com/ComplexNumber.html, or search the web for Complex Numbers.

Hint: Use the following equation to divide two complex numbers:

$$\frac{a + bi}{c + di} = \frac{(ac + bd) + i(bc - ad)}{c^2 + d^2}$$

Write a test program that verifies the ComplexNumber class's features.

Solutions

The following sections describe solutions to the preceding problems. You can download the example solutions to see additional details and to experiment with the programs at https://github.com/PacktPublishing/The-Modern-CSharp-Challenge/tree/master/Chapter07.

73. Directory size, LINQ style

Both this solution and Solution 65. *Directory size*, use the DirectoryInfo class's GetFiles method to make an array holding FileInfo objects that represent the files contained within the directory. The previous solution then used the following code to add the files' sizes:

```
// Add the file sizes.
long size = 0;
foreach (FileInfo fileinfo in fileinfos) size += fileinfo.Length;
return size;
```

This code loops through `FileInfo` objects and adds their file lengths to the `size` variable.

The new `SizeLINQ` extension method uses the following code to perform the same task:

```
// Add the file sizes.
var sizeQuery =
    from FileInfo fileinfo in fileinfos
    select fileinfo.Length;
return sizeQuery.Sum();
```

This version creates a LINQ query that loops through the `FileInfo` objects and selects their `Length` values. The program then invokes the query's `Sum` LINQ extension method to add the selected length values.

Which version you should use is largely a matter of personal preference. LINQ programs are often slower than other methods because they don't take advantage of any special structure that's available in the data. In this example, however, the time needed to calculate a directory's size is dominated by the time it takes to access the disk, not the time needed to process the results. In one set of tests, the LINQ version of this program took only a little while longer than the non-LINQ version.

What this means is that, in cases like this where LINQ has a negligible performance impact, you should pick whichever approach makes the code easier for you to read and understand.

Download the `DirectorySizeLINQ` example solution to see additional details.

74. Directory size, PLINQ style

Turning a LINQ query into a PLINQ query is usually quite simple. The following code shows the `SizePLINQ` extension method. The difference between this version and the LINQ version is highlighted in bold:

```
// Use PLINQ to calculate the directory's size.
public static long SizePLINQ(this DirectoryInfo dirinfo,
    bool includeSubdirs = false)
{
    // Get the files within the directory.
    FileInfo[] fileinfos;
    if (includeSubdirs)
        fileinfos = dirinfo.GetFiles("*", SearchOption.AllDirectories);
    else
        fileinfos = dirinfo.GetFiles("*",
          SearchOption.TopDirectoryOnly);
```

```
        // Add the file sizes.
        var sizeQuery =
            from FileInfo fileinfo in fileinfos.AsParallel()
            select fileinfo.Length;
        return sizeQuery.Sum();
    }
```

The only difference between the PLINQ and LINQ versions is that the PLINQ version adds `.AsParallel()` to the `from` clause. That makes the query system perform loop iterations in parallel.

Unfortunately, the query simply selects the `FileInfo` objects' `Length` values. That is a relatively fast operation, so selecting those values in parallel doesn't save much time. In fact, the extra overhead needed to execute the loop in parallel and then use the `Sum` method to combine the results makes this version of the program slower.

The following screenshot shows a typical run by the example solution. If you look closely, you'll see that the LINQ version runs slightly more slowly than the `foreach` version, and the PLINQ version runs even more slowly:

The moral of the story is that PLINQ can hurt performance unless the tasks it performs are naturally parallelizable.

Download the `DirectorySizePLINQ` example solution to see additional details.

75. Find files, LINQ style

Before I describe the new example solution, let's recap how Solution *69. Find files,* handled this problem. That solution added a `GetFiles` extension method to the `DirectoryInfo` class. The method looped through a list of patterns, calling `GetFiles` for each to find the files matching each pattern. It added the returned files to a dictionary so that it could easily determine whether it had already found a file. After finding the files, the method extracted the dictionary's keys and values, sorted them, and returned the sorted files.

The `FindFiles` extension method called `GetFiles` to find files matching its patterns. It then looped through the files, read each with `File.ReadAllText`, and used the string class's `Contains` method to see if a particular file contained the target text. It added the files containing the target text to a list and, when it had checked every file, returned the list.

The following code shows the LINQ version:

```
// Find files that match any of the indicated patterns and that
// contain the target string.
// Do not include duplicates and return the files sorted.
public static FileInfo[] FindFilesLINQ(this DirectoryInfo dirinfo,
    IEnumerable<string> patterns, string target = "",
    SearchOption option = SearchOption.TopDirectoryOnly)
{
    // Find files that match the patterns.
    var fileQuery =
        from string pattern in patterns
        from FileInfo fileinfo in dirinfo.GetFiles(pattern, option)
        group fileinfo by fileinfo.FullName
        into namegroup
        select namegroup.First();

    // If target isn't blank, select files that contain it.
    if ((target != null) && (target.Length > 0))
        fileQuery =
            from FileInfo fileinfo in fileQuery
            where File.ReadAllText(fileinfo.FullName).Contains(target)
            select fileinfo;

    // Take distinct values, sort, and return as an array.
    return fileQuery.OrderBy(x => x.Name).ToArray();
}
```

This method creates a LINQ query that loops through the file patterns and calls `GetFiles` to find the files that match each of them. If a file matches more than one pattern, then the result may contain the same file multiple times. To handle this situation, the query groups `FileInfo` objects by file name. The query finishes by selecting the first `FileInfo` from each group.

Next, if the target string is nonblank, the code creates a second query that loops through the selected files, uses `File.ReadAllText` to read each file, and then uses `Contains` to see if a file contains the target string.

After setting up the query, the method invokes its `OrderBy` method to sort the results by the files' names. It converts the result into an array and returns it.

Again, the version that you should use depends on your preferences. The LINQ version is undoubtedly shorter than the two methods used by the non-LINQ version, but LINQ queries are fairly complex. You should pick the version that suits you best.

Note that you can also mix LINQ and non-LINQ operations. For example, you could use the first query without the `group` clause, use C# code to remove duplicate entries, and then feed the result into the final query.

 As was the case in Solution *74. Directory size, PLINQ style*, PLINQ is unlikely to make these queries run faster. The limiting factor will be the speed of the disk accesses, and PLINQ just adds extra overhead, which will slow things down.

Download the `FindFilesLINQ` example solution to see additional details.

76. Parallel primes table

The basic method for building a table of primes loops through odd entries in the table. It calls the `IsPrime` method for each and saves the result in the table. The `IsPrime` method simply loops through possible factors that are smaller than the square root of a number and determines whether they divide the number evenly. (Revisit Solution *12. Prime factors,* for more details).

The key feature of this method as far as parallelization is concerned is that each step looks at a single entry in the table. This means that each step can proceed without interfering with any of the other steps.

The following code shows how the example solution adapts this method to build a primes table in parallel:

```
// Use the IsPrime method to make a table of prime numbers.
private int BasicMax;
private bool[] BasicIsPrime;
private bool[] MakePrimesTable(int max)
{
    // Make the array and mark 2 and odd numbers greater than 1 as
    // prime.
    if (max % 2 == 0) max++;
    BasicIsPrime = new bool[max + 1];
    BasicIsPrime[2] = true;

    int start = 1;
    int stop = (int)(max / 2);
    Parallel.For(start, stop + 1, BasicCheck);

    return BasicIsPrime;
}
```

The method that will be executed in parallel cannot take a lot of extra parameters, so the code declares some values at the form level so that all instances of the method can use them. The BasicMax value indicates the maximum entry in the table. The BasicIsPrime array will hold the primes table.

The MakePrimesTable method builds the table of primes. Its max parameter indicates the largest value that the method should examine. If max is even, the method increments it so that it is odd. You'll see why shortly.

The method then creates the array and marks 2 and odd numbers greater than 1 as prime, much like the previous solution did.

Next, the method calculates the start and stop values to control a loop through the array's odd entries. It then uses the TPL Parallel.For method to invoke the BasicCheck method the required number of times. The first two arguments to Parallel.For give the bounds that the method should pass into the method given as the third argument. The lower bound is inclusive and the upper bound is exclusive, so they mimic the values in a typical for loop that has the following format:

```
for (int i = lowerBound; i < upperBound; i++) ...
```

After the parallel calls return, the method returns the primes table.

The following code shows the `BasicCheck` method:

```
private void BasicCheck(int i)
{
    i = 2 * i + 1;
    BasicIsPrime[i] = IsPrime(i);
}
```

This method takes a looping variable as its single parameter. For example, if the first two parameters passed into `Parallel.For` are 1 and 100, then the `BasicCheck` method is called 99 times with the parameter values 1 through 99.

We only want to examine odd-numbered entries in the primes table, however, so the method multiplies the looping value by 2 and adds 1. If the looping values run from 1 to max/2 and max is odd, then the new values run from 3 to max. (That's why the earlier code ensured that the largest index in the array was odd. This way, the final call to `BasicCheck` examines an index that fits within the array.)

After making the looping value odd, the `BasicCheck` method simply calls the same `IsPrime` method that was used by the previous solution to see if the entry is prime.

Note that it is very important that the different calls to `BasicCheck` don't interfere with each other. Each looks at a different entry in the `BasicIsPrime` array, so none of them modify a value that another instance of the method might be using simultaneously.

If you understand how the preceding code works, it'll be easier to understand how the remaining pieces of this solution build Eratosthenes and Euler sieves. The following code shows how the program builds its Eratosthenes sieve:

```
// Make a sieve of Eratosthenes.
private int EratosthenesMax;
private bool[] EratosthenesIsPrime;
private bool[] MakeSieveOfEratosthenes(int max)
{
    // Make the array and mark 2 and odd numbers greater than 1 as
    // prime.
    if (max % 2 == 0) max++;
    EratosthenesMax = max;
    EratosthenesIsPrime = new bool[max + 1];
    EratosthenesIsPrime[2] = true;
    for (int i = 3; i <= max; i += 2) EratosthenesIsPrime[i] = true;

    // Cross out multiples of odd primes.
```

```
int start = 1;
int stop = (int)(max / 2);
Parallel.For(start, stop + 1, EratosthenesCheck);

return EratosthenesIsPrime;
}
```

If you compare this method to the `MakePrimesTable` method, you'll find them practically identical. The difference is that this method calls the following `EratosthenesCheck` method in parallel:

```
private void EratosthenesCheck(int i)
{
    i = 2 * i + 1;

    // See if i is prime.
    if (EratosthenesIsPrime[i])
    {
        // Knock out multiples of i.
        for (int j = i * 2; j <= EratosthenesMax; j += i)
            EratosthenesIsPrime[j] = false;
    }
}
```

This method converts the looping value to an odd index, like the `BasicCheck` method did. It then checks the `EratosthenesIsPrime` table to see if the corresponding entry is still marked as prime. If the entry is prime, the code marks multiples of the entry as not prime.

Notice that this method is using entries in the table other than entry `i`, so we should wonder whether the different instances of the `EratosthenesCheck` method might interfere with each other.

For example, suppose one instance of the method has discovered that 13 is prime, and so marks 23, 36, and other multiples of 13 as nonprime. Now, suppose that this instance of the method has marked 36 as nonprime, and then another instance of `EratosthenesCheck` examines entry 48. This value is not yet marked as nonprime, so the new instance (incorrectly) thinks that it is prime and marks 96, 144, 192, and other multiples of 48 as nonprime.

Later, the first instance of the method resumes and continues marking multiples of 13 as nonprime. Some of that effort is wasted because the second instance of the method already marked some of those values as nonprime, but the two instances are both trying to write the same value `false` into the table so it doesn't matter which one executes first.

In contrast, suppose two parallel methods try to read and update the same variable at the same time, assigning it two different values. Depending on the exact timing of the reads and writes, each method might see a different initial value for the variable. The variable will also have a different final value depending on which method executes second.

 This kind of problem, where a result depends on the exact timing of multiple methods running in parallel, is called a **race condition**.

This solution doesn't have those problems for two reasons. First, a method might see an incorrect value in the table because it has not yet been updated by another instance of the method. If that happens, however, the second instance may do some unnecessary work, but it won't add any incorrect values to the table.

The second reason this program avoids possible problems is that all instances of the method mark table entries with the same value, `false`. If two instances try to update an array position at the same time, they both write `false` into the position so there is no race condition.

The program's `MakeEulersSieve` method is similar to the `MakeSieveOfEratosthenes` and `MakePrimesTable` methods shown earlier, except it launches parallel instances of the following `EulerCheck` method:

```
private void EulerCheck(int i)
{
    i = 2 * i + 1;
    if (EulerIsPrime[i])
    {
        // Knock out multiples of p.
        int maxQ = EulerMax / i;
        if (maxQ % 2 == 0) maxQ--;      // Make it odd.
        for (int q = maxQ; q >= i; q -= 2)
        {
            // Only use q if it is prime.
            if (EulerIsPrime[q]) EulerIsPrime[i * q] = false;
        }
    }
}
```

Like the `EratosthenesCheck` method, this code checks whether entry `i` is still marked as prime. If it is, the method marks multiples of `i` as not prime. This time, however, the method only considers multiples of `i * q`, where `q` is still marked as prime in the `EulerIsPrime` array.

There may be some values of `q` that are still marked as prime, but that will later be marked as nonprime. In that case, the method will mark those multiples as nonprime, even though they will be marked as nonprime again later. As was the case with the `EratosthenesCheck` method, this method might mark some values as nonprime multiple times unnecessarily, but that will not cause any real problems.

The following screenshots show the `PrimesTable` and `ParallelPrimesTable` example solutions:

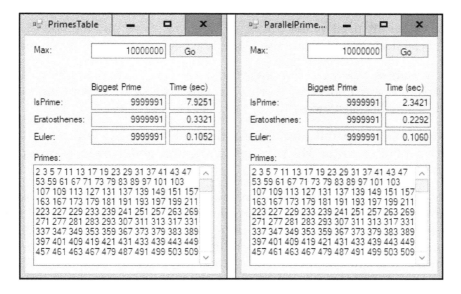

If you look at the times in the screenshots, you'll see that the parallel version builds its basic table much more quickly. It builds its Eratosthenes sieve slightly faster and its Euler sieve slightly slower. The latter two sieves are so fast to begin with that performing operations in parallel doesn't save much time and adds a bit of overhead. Download the `ParallelPrimesTable` example solution to see additional details.

77. Parallel primes tuple

The `FindPrimeGroupsInParallel` method is the heart of the `ParallelPrimesTuple` example solution. Like the preceding solution, this solution uses form-level variables to allow different instances of the parallel method to share the same values. The following code shows this example's variable declarations:

```
// Parameters used by parallel method CheckForGroupsInParallel.
private const int NumValuesPerBatch = 10000;
private object ParallelMaxLockObject = new object();
private List<List<int>> ParallelGroups = null;
private int ParallelMax = -1;
private int ParallelSpacing = -1;
private int ParallelNumPerGroup = -1;
private bool[] ParallelIsPrime = null;
```

Most of these values are used by the `CheckForGroupsInParallel` method to look for prime tuples. You'll see how they are used shortly when you read about that method.

The first two variables, `NumValuesPerBatch` and `ParallelMaxLockObject`, are more interesting. To understand how they work, you need to know a bit about coordination between parallel method instances.

In the preceding solution, parallel instances of the methods always wrote `false` into the primes table, so it didn't matter which process wrote first, and there were no race conditions.

This example needs to build a single list containing different tuples of primes, so all of the parallel instances of its methods must write different values into that same list. It would be bad if one instance were in the middle of writing to that list when another instance interrupted and wrote to the same list. Depending on the timing, it's not clear what would happen to the list. It might contain the first method's changes, the second method's changes, both sets of changes, or it might be completely corrupted and unusable.

One way to coordinate between parallel method instances is to use a lock object. A **lock object** is any object that can be seen by all instances of the method. This example simply uses a new generic `object`.

When a method needs to write to the shared list, it uses the `lock` keyword to lock that object. No other instance of the method is allowed to lock the same object until this instance unlocks it. Because only one instance of the method can lock the object at a time, only one instance can access the shared list at a time.

Unfortunately, this creates another problem—locking an object is relatively slow. For a fast search, such as the one used by this program, locking and unlocking that object many times can slow performance significantly.

One solution to this problem is to perform the work in batches. Instead of examining a single value to see if it begins a tuple of primes, each instance of the method searches a whole batch of values and builds its own list of prime tuples. After it has finished searching its batch of values, the method locks the lock object, merges its list with the program's master list, and then unlocks the lock object.

The NumValuesPerBatch constant gives the number of values that each instance of the method should search.

The following FindPrimeGroupsInParallel method starts the process of searching for prime tuples:

```
// Find groups of primes in parallel.
private List<List<int>> FindPrimeGroupsInParallel(int max, int spacing,
    int numPerGroup, bool[] isPrime)
{
    // Initialize the parallel parameters.
    ParallelGroups = new List<List<int>>();
    ParallelMax = max;
    ParallelSpacing = spacing;
    ParallelNumPerGroup = numPerGroup;
    ParallelIsPrime = isPrime;

    // Treat 2 specially.
    List<int> group = GroupAt(2, max, spacing, numPerGroup, isPrime);
    if (group != null) ParallelGroups.Add(group);

    // Look for other groups in parallel batches.
    Parallel.For(0, max / NumValuesPerBatch, CheckForGroupsInParallel);

    return ParallelGroups;
}
```

This method starts by initializing the form-level variables. For example, ParallelGroups is the list that will eventually hold all of the prime tuples.

Next, the method uses the GroupAt method to see if there is a group of primes starting at the value 2. Handling that value separately allows the rest of the code to consider only odd starting values for groups.

The GroupAt method is the same one used by Solution *15. Prime tuples* described in chapter 1, *Mathematics*. See that solution for details about how the method works.

The code then uses Parallel.For to launch several instances of the CheckForGroupsInParallel method in parallel. The number of groups is the maximum value, max, that the method should check, divided into batches of NumValuesPerBatch values.

After the parallel methods finish, the FindPrimeGroupsInParallel method returns the ParallelGroups list.

The following code shows the CheckForGroupsInParallel method, which does the real work of looking for prime tuples:

```csharp
// Check values i * ValuesPerCall through (i + 1) * ValuesPerCall.
private void CheckForGroupsInParallel(int i)
{
    // Make a list of groups found in this batch.
    List<List<int>> results = new List<List<int>>();

    // Look for prime groups.
    int start = i * NumValuesPerBatch;
    int stop = start + NumValuesPerBatch;
    if (start % 2 == 0) start++;        // Check odd values.
    if (stop == ParallelMax) stop++;    // Include the original max
    //value.
    for (int j = start; j < stop; j += 2)
    {
        List<int> group = GroupAt(j, ParallelMax, ParallelSpacing,
            ParallelNumPerGroup, ParallelIsPrime);
        if (group != null) results.Add(group);
    }

    // If we found any groups, add them to the global list.
    if (results.Count > 0)
    {
        lock (ParallelMaxLockObject)
        {
            ParallelGroups.AddRange(results);
        }
    }
}
```

The method first creates a list named `results` to hold any prime tuples that it finds. This list is not shared by other instances of the method, so it is safe for this instance to read and write into this list without risk of interference.

This method looks for prime tuples, in the ith batch of `NumValuesPerBatch` values. For example, if `i` is 14 and `NumValuesPerBatch` is 1,000, then the method considers numbers between 14,000 and 14,999 as potential starting points for prime tuples with the desired spacing and length.

The method calculates the appropriate `start` and `stop` values that it can use to cover that range, considering only odd starting numbers. (That's why we handled the special case of groups starting at 2 separately.)

The method loops through the potential starting values, calling the `GroupAt` method to see if any of the values starts a prime tuple. If `GroupAt` finds an appropriate tuple, the method adds it to its `results` list.

After it has examined all of the potential starting values, the method needs to copy its results into the master list, `ParallelGroups`. Because this might interfere with other parallel instances of the method, the code locks the `ParallelMaxLockObject`. It uses the `ParallelGroups` list's `AddRange` method to copy the newly found tuples into the master list. When the `lock` block ends, the lock on the `ParallelMaxLockObject` is automatically released, so other instances of the method can use the master list when they need to do so.

The following screenshot shows the `ParallelPrimeTuples` example program after it found sexy prime pairs (pairs of primes separated by 6) between 1 and 100 million. You can see that the parallel search was significantly faster than the single iterative search:

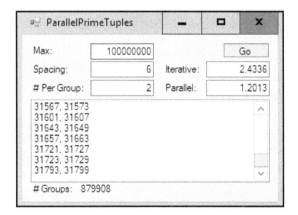

You can experiment with the `NumValuesPerBatch` constant to see how it affects performance. If you set it to 10, the program spends a lot of time coordinating many parallel method instances and locking and unlocking objects, so it is slower than the iterative search. When `NumValuesPerBatch` is large, say 10,000, the parallel search takes about half as long on my computer. My computer is a quad-core laptop, so it has four CPUs and can therefore run four method instances simultaneously. Ideally, the parallel search would take about a quarter of the time the iterative search takes, but overhead prevents you from ever actually achieving that large an improvement.

Download the `ParallelPrimeTuples` example solution to see additional details.

78. Parallel Monte Carlo π

This example solution uses the same approach used by the preceding solution. It uses form-level variables to pass information to the parallel instances of a method. Those instances perform calculations and then use locking to save their results to the form-level variables.

The following code shows the form-level variables:

```
private int NumHits = 0;
private object LockObject = new object();
private int MonteCarloWidth = 0, MonteCarloHeight = 0;
private Bitmap MonteCarloBitmap = null;
private const int PointsPerCall = 10000;
```

The following method starts the parallel execution:

```
// Use Monte Carlo simulation to estimate pi.
private double MonteCarloPi(int numPoints)
{
    // Make a bitmap to show points.
    MonteCarloWidth = pointsPictureBox.ClientSize.Width;
    MonteCarloHeight = pointsPictureBox.ClientSize.Height;
    MonteCarloBitmap = new Bitmap(MonteCarloWidth, MonteCarloWidth);
    using (Graphics gr = Graphics.FromImage(MonteCarloBitmap))
    {
        gr.Clear(Color.White);
        gr.DrawEllipse(Pens.Black, 0, 0,
            MonteCarloWidth - 1, MonteCarloWidth - 1);
    }

    // Make the random points.
    NumHits = 0;
    int numMethods = numPoints / PointsPerCall;
    Parallel.For(0, numMethods, TestPoint);
```

```
        // Display the plotted points.
        pointsPictureBox.Image = MonteCarloBitmap;

        // Get the hit fraction.
        double fraction = NumHits / (double)(numMethods * PointsPerCall);

        // Estimate pi.
        return 4.0 * fraction;
    }
```

This method creates a bitmap to show some of the test points and saves it in a form-level variable. It then uses `Parallel.For` to launch instances of the `TestPoint` method. After those parallel methods finish, the code calculates the fraction of test points that fell within the circle of radius 1, uses that to calculate an estimate for π, and returns the result.

The following code shows the `TestPoint` method:

```
    private void TestPoint(int i)
    {
        Random rand = new Random(i * DateTime.Now.Millisecond);
        int myHits = 0;
        for (int pointNum = 0; pointNum < PointsPerCall; pointNum++)
        {
            // Make a random point 0 <= x < 1.
            double x = rand.NextDouble();
            double y = rand.NextDouble();

            // See how far the point is from (0.5, 0.5).
            double dx = x - 0.5;
            double dy = y - 0.5;
            if (dx * dx + dy * dy < 0.25) myHits++;

            if (i == 0)
            {
                int ix = (int)(MonteCarloWidth * x);
                int iy = (int)(MonteCarloHeight * y);
                if (dx * dx + dy * dy < 0.25)
                    MonteCarloBitmap.SetPixel(ix, iy, Color.Gray);
                else
                    MonteCarloBitmap.SetPixel(ix, iy, Color.Black);
            }
        }

        // Slightly slower.
        //Interlocked.Add(ref NumHits, myHits);

        // Slightly faster.
```

```
        lock (LockObject)
        {
            NumHits += myHits;
        }
    }
```

This method has a problem that didn't occur in earlier examples. The Random class does not work well when it runs on multiple threads simultaneously. This means the instances of the method cannot share a form-level Random object. Instead, each instance must create its own Random object.

However, the Random class's default constructor uses the system's time to initialize new objects. Because the parallel instances of the method execute very quickly, many of them may use the same system time to initialize their Random objects. When that happens, those instances of the method will generate the same random values, so they will use the same test points. Instead of executing using many different points, the methods use the same points several times.

For example, suppose the program runs 10 instances of the method with 10,000 points each. Instead of using 100,000 points to estimate π, the program basically uses 10,000 points to estimate π 10 times. You still get an estimate, but without the precision that you would get with 100,000 different points.

To solve this dilemma, the program needs to initialize each instance's Random object differently. The example solution does that by multiplying the current time's number of milliseconds by the method instance number and passing that to the Random constructor as a seed value.

Having created a suitable Random object, the method performs its trials and counts the number of generated points that lie within the target circle. Notice that the code stores that count in a local variable. After it has finished counting hits, the method updates the form-level variable NumHits.

The code shows two ways to update NumHits. The first method, which is commented out, uses the System.Threading.Interlocked class's Add method to safely add the myHits value to NumHits. The second method, which seems to be slightly faster, explicitly locks the lock object and updates NumHits.

The following screenshot shows the iterative and parallel versions of this program after using 100 million test points to estimate π. The two programs provide roughly the same accuracy, but the parallel version only takes about 27% as long as the iterative version:

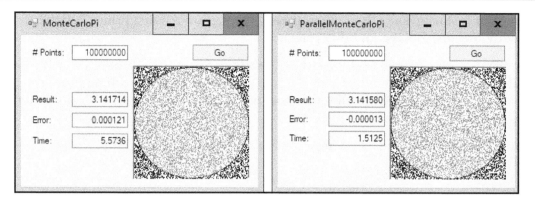

Download the `ParallelMonteCarloPi` example solution to see additional details.

79. Yielding primes

A method can use the `yield` keyword to return a value to the calling code and then resume execution later. The calling code receives the results as an `IEnumerable` and can loop through them as needed.

The following method yields primes:

```
// Yield numPrimes primes.
private IEnumerable<long> Primes(int numPrimes)
{
    // Treat 2 separately.
    yield return 2;
    if (numPrimes == 1) yield break;

    int count = 1;
    for (long i = 3; ; i += 2)
    {
        if (IsPrime(i))
        {
            yield return i;
            if (++count == numPrimes) yield break;
        }
    }
}
```

The method first uses a `yield return` statement to return the first prime, 2. It then loops over odd numbers, looking for other primes.

Inside the loop, the method uses the `IsPrime` method to see if the current value is prime. If the value is prime, the method uses `yield return` to send it to the calling code. Then, if the method has returned the required number of primes, it uses a `yield break` statement to stop yielding values.

The main program uses the following code snippet to display the primes:

```
int numPrimes = int.Parse(numPrimesTextBox.Text);
int i = 1;
foreach (long prime in Primes(numPrimes))
    primesListBox.Items.Add(i++.ToString() + ": " + prime);
```

This code first gets the desired number of values entered by the user. It then uses a `foreach` loop to iterate through the primes returned by `Primes(numPrimes)` and adds them to the form's list box. It uses the count variable `i` to display each prime's position in the primes list, along with its value.

Download the `YieldingPrimes` example solution to see additional details.

80. Yielding Fibonacci numbers

The following method yields Fibonacci numbers:

```
// Yield Fibonacci numbers.
private IEnumerable<long> FibonacciNumbers()
{
    // Treat 0 and 1 separately.
    yield return 0;
    yield return 1;

    // Calculate other values.
    long fiboIMinus2 = 0;
    long fiboIMinus1 = 1;
    long fiboI = 0;
    for (;;)
    {
        try
        {
            fiboI = checked(fiboIMinus2 + fiboIMinus1);
        }
        catch
        {
```

```
            yield break;
        }

        fiboIMinus2 = fiboIMinus1;
        fiboIMinus1 = fiboI;
        yield return fiboI;
    }
}
```

First, the method yields the values 0 and 1. It then enters a loop where it uses previously calculated Fibonacci numbers to calculate the next number. The calculation uses the `checked` keyword to watch for integer overflow.

If no overflow occurs, the method uses `yield return` to return the new Fibonacci number. If the operation causes an overflow, the method uses `yield break` to stop generating values.

The program uses the following code snippet to display Fibonacci numbers:

```
int i = 1;
foreach (long fiboNumber in FibonacciNumbers())
    fiboListBox.Items.Add(i++.ToString() + ": " + fiboNumber);
```

This code simply loops through the values yielded by the `FibonacciNumbers` method and displays them in the program's list box.

Download the `YieldingFibonacciNumbers` example solution to see additional details.

81. Complex numbers

The `ComplexNumber` structure is fairly long, so I'll describe it in pieces.

You could make `ComplexNumber` either a class or a structure. Many programmers use classes exclusively. This isn't a terrible choice, in part because it frees you from having to deal with the differences between classes and structures.

I've decided to make `ComplexNumber` a structure for a couple of reasons. Microsoft's guidelines generally recommend using a structure if the item meets the following criteria:

- It is relatively small
- It logically represents a primitive type such as a number
- It is immutable, so its value does not change after it has been created
- It will not need to be boxed and unboxed often

 See `docs.microsoft.com/en-us/dotnet/standard/design-guidelines/choosing-between-class-and-struct` for a discussion of this issue.

A `ComplexNumber` clearly meets the first two criteria. The .NET Framework is good at allocating and deallocating small objects, so making the class immutable shouldn't hurt performance.

Finally, if you typically use a `ComplexNumber` for numeric calculations, then you shouldn't need to box and unbox it very often.

Having decided to make this a structure instead of a class, let's look at the structure's requirements. The structure uses the following declaration to indicate that it will implement the `IEquatable` interface:

```
public struct ComplexNumber : IEquatable<ComplexNumber>
```

I'll show you how the structure implements the interface later.

The structure uses the following code to store a number's real and imaginary parts.

```
// Auto-implemented properties.
private double Re { get; }
private double Im { get; }
```

These properties are read-only because they have no `set` accessors. This means that a program cannot change a `ComplexNumber` structure's value after the structure has been created. In fact, even the structure's private code cannot change the properties' values. This makes the structure immutable.

This is a structure, so if you create a `ComplexNumber` without using a constructor, its real and imaginary parts take the default values for the `double` type, which is zero.

The following code shows the structure's explicitly defined constructors:

```
// Constructors.
public ComplexNumber(double re, double im)
{
    Re = re;
    Im = im;
}
public ComplexNumber(double re)
{
    Re = re;
    Im = 0;
}
```

These constructors initialize the number's real and imaginary parts. If you use the second constructor, which omits the imaginary part, the code sets the imaginary part to 0.

All structures always have an implicit, parameterless constructor that takes no parameters and that leaves the properties at their default values. This means that you cannot create your own parameterless constructor for a structure.

Not having a parameterless constructor is okay in this example, but it could be an issue in other cases where you need that constructor to perform more complex actions. For example, suppose you want to make a `Circle` structure that represents a circle drawn on a `PictureBox`. You might want the constructors to give a new `Circle` an ID number. Because you cannot define a parameterless constructor for a structure, you can't do that.

Possibly worse, you cannot prevent the program from creating a new structure without using a constructor. For example, you might want to let the program draw a maximum of 10 circles. Because you can't create a paremeterless constructor, you can't prevent the program from creating as many `Circle` structures as it likes.

Finally, because you can't define a parameterless constructor, you cannot set a breakpoint in it.

If you need a parameterless constructor for any of those reasons, then you need to use a class instead of a structure.

Ideally, we could make another constructor that initializes a number from its polar coordinate representation. Unfortunately, that version would take two `double` values as parameters, so it would have the same signature as the first constructor in the preceding code, and C# would be unable to tell which version you were trying to use.

We cannot create a constructor that uses polar coordinates, but we can create the following factory method instead:

```
// Polar factory method.
public static ComplexNumber FromPolar(double magnitude, double angle)
{
    return new ComplexNumber(
        magnitude * Math.Cos(angle),
        magnitude * Math.Sin(angle));
}
```

A factory method creates a new instance of a structure or class. In general, a factory method can perform a lot of work getting the new object ready. For example, it could load data from a database or network, or perform complex validations on its parameters. This example simply uses the number's polar representation to calculate its real and imaginary parts and then uses them to create a new ComplexNumber.

The following code shows static read-only properties that return ComplexNumber objects representing the special values 0, 1, and i:

```
// Return 0, 1, or i.
private static ComplexNumber ComplexZero = new ComplexNumber();
private static ComplexNumber ComplexOne = new ComplexNumber(1);
private static ComplexNumber ComplexI = new ComplexNumber(0, 1);
public static ComplexNumber Zero
{
    get { return ComplexZero; }
}
public static ComplexNumber One
{
    get { return ComplexOne; }
}
public static ComplexNumber I
{
    get { return ComplexI; }
}
```

These read-only properties return static instances of ComplexNumber structures representing 0, 1, and i. Because the class is immutable, we don't need to worry about the program modifying these values after the properties return them. This means that it's safe to make these values static so that they are shared by any pieces of code that need to use them.

If the values were *not* immutable, then the program could modify these shared values. In that case, the static value, `ComplexZero`, for example, would no longer represent the number 0 + 0i and that could cause problems in other parts of the program. Therefore, if the items are not immutable, you should not return static values. Instead, you should return new objects for this kind of special value.

The following code shows the structure's `ToString` method:

```
// Display as in x + yi.
public override string ToString()
{
    return $"{Re} + {Im}i";
}
```

This method simply returns the number's real and imaginary parts in a string with the format x + yi.

When you override the `ToString` method, other controls can use that method to display a meaningful representation of the object. For example, a `ListBox` or `ComboBox` control uses `ToString` to display the items it contains. Similarly, the Immediate Window, Console window, code editor tooltips, and other Visual Studio features use `ToString` to display an object's value.

The following code shows the structure's `Parse` method:

```
// Parse from a string.
public static ComplexNumber Parse(string s)
{
    double re = 0, im = 0;
    if (s.Contains("+"))
    {
        // Real and imaginary parts.
        int pos = s.IndexOf("+");
        string rePart = s.Substring(0, pos - 1);
        re = double.Parse(rePart);

        string imPart =
            s.Substring(pos + 1).ToLower().Replace("i",
          "");
        im = double.Parse(imPart);
    }
    else if (s.ToLower().Contains("i"))
    {
        // Imaginary part only.
        string imPart = s.ToLower().Replace("i", "");
```

```
        im = double.Parse(imPart);
    }
    else
    {
        // Real part only.
        re = double.Parse(s);
    }

    return new ComplexNumber(re, im);
}
```

The `Parse` method looks for the + character to determine whether the string contains both real and imaginary parts. If the string contains the + character, the method separates the real and imaginary parts, parses them as `double` values, and saves them in the local variables `rePart` and `imPart`.

If the string does not contain +, then it contains either a real part or an imaginary part, but not both. If the string contains an `i`, then it contains an imaginary part. The code removes the `i`, parses the result, and saves it in the `imPart` variable.

If the string contains neither + nor `i`, then it contains only a real part. The code parses the string as a `double` and saves it in the `rePart` variable.

After it has the parsed the number's real and imaginary parts, the method uses them to create a new `ComplexNumber` and returns it.

This simple version of the `Parse` method can only understand the + sign when it is used to separate the real and imaginary parts. It cannot handle more complicated strings such as +1.2E+4 + 5.6E+7 i.

This method also handles negative imaginary parts rather awkwardly, as in 7 + -3i. You can try to improve this method if you like.

The following code shows how the structure implements the `IEquatable` interface and supports other equality tests:

```
// Equality and IEquatable<ComplexNumber>.
public bool Equals(ComplexNumber other)
{
    double dRe = Re - other.Re;
    double dIm = Im - other.Im;
    return (dRe * dRe + dIm * dIm == 0);
}
public override bool Equals(object obj)
```

```
    {
        if (!(obj is ComplexNumber)) return false;
        ComplexNumber other = (ComplexNumber)obj;
        return (Re == other.Re) && (Im == other.Im);
    }
    public bool Equals(ComplexNumber other, double precision)
    {
        double dRe = Re - other.Re;
        double dIm = Im - other.Im;
        return (dRe * dRe + dIm * dIm <= precision * precision);
    }
```

The first `Equals` method satisfies the `IEquality` interface. It compares two `ComplexNumber` structures to see if their real and imaginary parts are the same.

The second version overrides the default implementation of `Equals` to perform the same test with a generic `object` instead of a `ComplexNumber`.

As is true with all floating point data types, there may be times when two `ComplexNumber` values should be equal, but they differ slightly due to rounding errors. The final version of the `Equals` method returns `true` if two `ComplexNumber` values are within a certain distance of each other. For example, the `value1.Equals(value2, 0.01)` statement will return `true` if the values are within 0.01 of each other.

Note that this method calculates the distance between two values in the complex plane rather than by simply comparing the values' real and imaginary parts.

The following code show how the structure overloads the `==` and `!=` operators:

```
    // Comparison operators.
    public static bool operator ==(ComplexNumber c1, ComplexNumber c2)
    {
        return c1.Equals(c2);
    }
    public static bool operator !=(ComplexNumber c1, ComplexNumber c2)
    {
        return !(c1 == c2);
    }
```

The `==` operator simply invokes the `Equals` method. The `!=` operator invokes `==` and negates the result.

The == and != operators come as a pair. If you overload one, then you must overload the other.

If you override the Equals method (the second version), then Microsoft recommends that you also override the GetHashCode method. That method returns a hash code that objects such as dictionaries can use to quickly determine whether two objects are different. Because hash codes map complicated objects to comparatively simple codes, there will be cases where two different objects may have the same hash code. However, if two objects have different hash codes, then they are definitely not equal.

Being immutable is an advantage when it comes to hash codes because it means that an object's hash code can never change. In turn, this means that you can add a ComplexNumber to a dictionary and you don't need to worry about its values changing and preventing the dictionary from correctly finding it later.

The following code shows the ComplexNumber structure's GetHashCode method:

```
// GetHashCode.
public override int GetHashCode()
{
    return Re.GetHashCode() ^ (Re + Im).GetHashCode();
}
```

This method takes the number's real component and invokes its default GetHashCode method. It then adds the number's real and imaginary parts together and invokes the GetHashCode method for the sum. Finally, it uses the bitwise XOR operator to combine the two hash codes and produce its final result.

The reason GetHashCode doesn't simply calculate the hash codes for the real and imaginary parts and combine them is that the calculation would return the same hash code for the values a + b i and b + a i, and it seems somewhat plausible that an application might use two complex numbers having that relationship. The method shown here maps those values to different hash codes so that objects such as dictionaries can handle them more efficiently.

Of course, there are still many more possible ComplexNumber values than there are hash codes (which must fit in an int), so some collisions are unavoidable, but this change makes those collisions occur randomly. If you use the simpler version of GetHashCode and an application happens to use numbers of the form a + b i and b + a i, then collisions would be guaranteed.

The following read-only property returns a complex number's magnitude, which is also sometimes called its **modulus** or **norm**:

```
// Return the number's magnitude. (Also called its modulus or norm.)
public double Magnitude
{
    get { return Math.Sqrt(Re * Re + Im * Im); }
}
```

This property simply calculates the distance from the value to the origin on the complex plane.

The following read-only property returns the number's angle, which is also sometimes called its **argument** or **phase**:

```
// Return the number's angle. (Also called its argument or phase.)
public double Angle
{
    get { return Math.Atan2(Im, Re); }
}
```

This property uses the `Atan2` method to calculate the arctangent of the number's imaginary part divided by its real part.

> The `Angle` property's result is in radians. If you want the angle in degrees, multiply by 180/`Math.Pi`.

The following conversion operator converts a `double` into a `ComplexNumber`:

```
// Convert the double value re into the ComplexNumber re + 0i.
public static implicit operator ComplexNumber(double re)
{
    return new ComplexNumber(re);
}
```

The real number, R, is the same as the complex number R + 0i, so this operator simply creates and returns the appropriate `ComplexNumber`. Because this operation does not lose any data, this operator is declared `implicit`, so the program can use it without a cast operator. For example, the following statement creates a new `ComplexNumber` with the value 13 + 0i:

```
ComplexNumber f = 13;
```

The following operator converts a `ComplexNumber` into a `double`:

```
// Convert the ComplexNumber into a double by dropping
// the complex part.
public static explicit operator double(ComplexNumber c)
{
    return c.Re;
}
```

This operator drops the number's complex component. Because that causes a loss of data, the method is declared `explicit` to require the code to use a cast operator to perform the conversion. This prevents you from losing data accidentally. For example, the following statement converts the `ComplexNumber` f into the double g:

```
double g = (double)f;
```

Providing arithmetic operators for the `ComplexNumber` structure may seem like a daunting task. You would need to write methods to add, subtract, multiply, divide, and negate `ComplexNumber` values. Then, you would need to write methods showing how to perform those same operations for each of the numeric types `byte`, `sbyte`, `short`, `ushort`, `int`, `uint`, `long`, `ulong`, `float`, and `double`.

To further complicate matters, you would need to specify each method twice, once for the `ComplexNumber` on the left and one for the `ComplexNumber` on the right. For example, you would need methods showing how to calculate `int + ComplexNumber` and `ComplexNumber + int`. Mathematically those values are the same when you work with complex numbers, but C# doesn't know that. In general, operators could give different results when the operands are in different orders, or one of the orders might not be defined for a particular order.

Adding all of the combinations of operations, data types, and left/right orderings gives you more than 100 methods that you might need to write!

Fortunately, C# does something that greatly simplifies this problem. When it performs an arithmetic calculation, the program *promotes* values into the widest data type used by the expression. For example, if you add a `long` and a `double`, the `long` is promoted to a `double`, the two are added, and the result is a `double`.

Because we have already defined an implicit conversion operator that converts from a `double` to a `ComplexNumber`, C# will automatically make that conversion if necessary. This means that we only need to provide arithmetic methods to work with `ComplexNumber` values, and C# will automatically promote other values if necessary to perform the calculations. For example, suppose you add a `long` and a `ComplexNumber`. The program will promote the `long` into a `double`, then convert the `double` into a `ComplexNumber`, and finally perform the addition.

The following code shows the `ComplexNumber` structure's arithmetic operators:

```
// Arithmetic operators.
public static ComplexNumber operator +(ComplexNumber c1,
    ComplexNumber c2)
{
    return new ComplexNumber(c1.Re + c2.Re, c1.Im + c2.Im);
}
public static ComplexNumber operator -(ComplexNumber c1)
{
    return new ComplexNumber(-c1.Re, -c1.Im);
}
public static ComplexNumber operator -(ComplexNumber c1,
    ComplexNumber c2)
{
    return new ComplexNumber(c1.Re - c2.Re, c1.Im - c2.Im);
}
public static ComplexNumber operator *(ComplexNumber c1,
    ComplexNumber c2)
{
    return new ComplexNumber(
        c1.Re * c2.Re - c1.Im * c2.Im,
        c1.Re * c2.Im + c1.Im * c2.Re);
}
public static ComplexNumber operator /(ComplexNumber c1,
    ComplexNumber c2)
{
    double denominator = c2.Re * c2.Re + c2.Im * c2.Im;
    return new ComplexNumber(
        (c1.Re * c2.Re + c1.Im * c2.Im) / denominator,
        (c1.Im * c2.Re - c1.Re * c2.Im) / denominator);
}
```

These methods are straightforward, so I won't describe them in detail.

The ComplexNumbers example solution tests the ComplexNumber class. The code is long but straightforward, so I won't describe it in detail here. It tests a number of ComplexNumber features, including different constructors, the static Zero, One, and I properties, ToString, various arithmetic operations with ComplexNumber and integer values, GetHashCode, and more.

Download the ComplexNumbers example solution to see the results and to see additional details.

8

Simulations

This chapter describes some problems that involve simulations. In a simulation, a program uses rules to model the behavior of some sort of system. Often, the rules are simplified to make the simulation easier to manage. For example, to simulate the path of an object traveling through a solar system, you might apply forces based on the system's objects individually and at discrete time intervals instead of integrating those forces over time. Similarly, projectile simulations often ignore the effects of wind and air resistance.

Many simulations have a graphical component. Others examine processes that are easier to visualize graphically than by just looking at the data. If you don't have a lot of experience with graphics programming, these problems can give you some useful practice.

Most of the example solutions in this chapter are longer than those described in the previous chapters. Much of that code is relatively straightforward or user interface code, so it isn't presented here. Instead, the solutions focus on the key points and new techniques that are most central to the simulations. You can always download the example solutions from this book's website to see additional details.

You can use many different approaches to manage simulation steps. For example, you can use an infinite loop that continuously polls the system to see how much time has passed since the last time the loop executed and then move the objects appropriately. Alternatively, you can use the animation classes provided by WPF. The solutions shown in this chapter use a simpler approach. They are Windows Forms programs that use `Timer` components to perform steps at roughly equal intervals. The `Timer` component does not guarantee perfect timing, but the results are close enough for many simple simulations.

Problems

Use the following problems to test your skills at building simulations. Give each problem a try before you turn to the solutions and download the example programs.

82. Dawkins' weasel

Dawkins' weasel, also known as the **weasel program**, is a relatively simple text simulation that was intended to demonstrate how random variation and selection can lead to non-random results. The idea was inspired by the **infinite monkey theorem**, which states that a monkey typing randomly on a typewriter for an infinite amount of time will eventually reproduce all of the works of William Shakespeare. Thinking about that theorem, Richard Dawkins decided to write a simulation that would generate Hamlet's line, *"Methinks it is like a weasel."* (*Hamlet*, Act 3, Scene 2.)

The simulation starts with a completely random string of 28 letters and spaces. (The Hamlet quote is 28 characters long.) The program then creates a sequence of generations until the random string morphs into the target string.

During each generation, the program creates a certain number (the generation size) of copies of the best string found so far. Each copy is the same as the current best string, but there is a certain probability that any given character in the copy will be mutated into a random letter. After creating each of the generation's new values, the program saves the one that is closest to the target string as the new best string.

The process continues until the best string matches the target string exactly.

For this problem, write a Dawkins' weasel program. Allow the user to enter the generation size and mutation probability. After the program finishes running the simulation, display the best strings found during each generation and the total number of generations required to reach the target string.

83. Hailstone sequence

Suppose you start with some positive integer: N_0. After you have calculated N_i, you use the following operation to calculate N_{i+1}:

$$N_{i+1} = N_i/2 \text{ if } N_i \text{ is even}$$

$$N_{i+1} = 3N_i + 1 \text{ if } N_i \text{ is odd}$$

You stop if N_i ever reaches 1 (because, after that, the sequence repeats—1, 4, 2, 1,...).

The sequence of values that these rules generate has several names including the **hailstone sequence** or **hailstone numbers** (because the values tend to ascend and descend like hailstones in a storm cloud) or **wondrous numbers**.

For example, the following shows the sequence of values that you get if you apply the rules starting with the number 6:

- 6 is even, so the next value is 6 / 2 = 3
- 3 is odd, so the next value is 3 × 3 + 1 = 10
- 10 is even, so the next value is 10 / 2 = 5
- 5 is odd, so the next value is 3 × 5 + 1 = 16
- 16 is even, so the next value is 16 / 2 = 8
- 8 is even, so the next value is 8 / 2 = 4
- 4 is even, so the next value is 8 / 2 = 4
- 2 is even, so the next value is 8 / 2 = 1

The full sequence starting with the number 6 is {6, 3, 10, 5, 16, 8, 4, 2, 1} and has the length 9.

The **Collatz conjecture** is that, with any starting value, N_0, the hailstone sequence eventually reaches 1.

The **Collatz conjecture** was named after the German mathematician Lothar Collatz, who introduced it in 1937. The conjecture also has other names including the *3n + 1 conjecture* and several others named after people who worked on the problem.

One way to visualize a number's hailstone sequence is to graph its values.

For this problem, write a program similar to the one shown in the following screenshot.

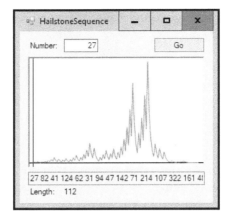

The form's upper area graphs the sequence's values, the text box below the graph shows the values, and the label at the bottom shows the sequence's length:

84. Hailstone sequence, Redux

The preceding problem described a way to visualize the values in a single hailstone sequence. It's also interesting to examine the lengths of a group of hailstone sequences.

Write a program similar to the one shown in the following screenshot that graphs the lengths of hailstone sequences. Speed up length calculations by using previously calculated lengths:

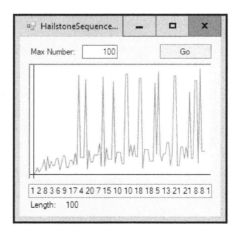

85. Langton's Ant

Langton's Ant is a simulation devised by Chris Langton in 1986. It uses remarkably simple rules to produce surprisingly complicated results.

The ant walks on a grid of black and white squares and obeys the following two simple rules:

- If the ant is on a white square, it turns 90° right, changes the color of its square, and moves forward one square
- If the ant is on a black square, it turns 90° left, changes the color of its square, and moves forward one square

For this problem, build a Langton's Ant program similar to the one shown in the following screenshot:

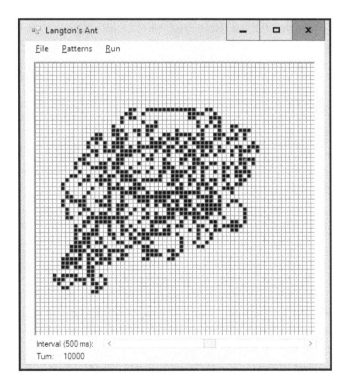

The rules that the ant follows are about as simple as you can imagine, but the ant's behavior is extremely complex. Initially, it follows a fairly restricted path and generates small, sometimes symmetric patterns.

After a few hundred steps, the patterns become much larger and more chaotic, but still remain bounded. Some time after 10,000 steps, the ant begins generating a repeating pattern that creates a *highway* leading away from the center of the ant's little world.

86. Life

In 1970, British mathematician John Horton Conway devised a simulation known as the **Game of Life** or simply **Life**. The rules are slightly more complicated than those used by Langton's Ant, although they are still quite modest.

The universe consists of an infinite grid of square cells. Each cell can be alive or dead (or occupied or unoccupied, if you prefer). Starting from some initial configuration, the cells obey the following rules:

- If a live cell has fewer than two live neighbors, it dies from underpopulation
- If a live cell has more than three live neighbors, it dies from overpopulation
- If a dead cell has exactly three neighbors, it becomes a live cell by reproduction

A cell's neighbors are the cells that are adjacent horizontally, vertically, or diagonally.

For this problem, write a **Life** program similar to the one shown in the following screenshot:

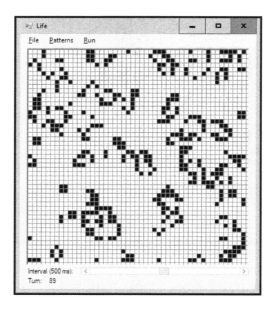

Let the user click cells to toggle their states and then start the program to see how it evolves. Also, let the user determine whether the program wraps cells at the grid's edges or treats locations outside of the grid as dead cells.

87. Sharks and Fish

Langton's Ant and Life use extremely simple rules. This simulation, which I call **Sharks and Fish**, uses much more complicated rules in an attempt to simulate real-world interactions between predators and prey. You can find similar simulations scattered around the internet that mimic predator/prey interactions between sheep and wolves, foxes and rabbits, lynxes and rabbits, moose and wolves, and even just generic predators and prey.

In the Sharks and Fish simulation, sharks and fish occupy the squares in a grid. The sharks use the following rules:

- Each shark has an energy level and each turn it loses some energy. If the shark's energy ever drops to zero, the shark starves and dies
- Each turn, every shark moves randomly left, right, up, or down into a neighboring square that is empty or that contains a fish
- If a shark moves onto a fish, it eats that fish and gains a certain amount of energy
- If the shark's energy level ever exceeds a set amount, it spawns a new shark in an empty neighboring square and splits its energy with the child

The fish use the following rules:

- Each turn, each fish moves randomly left, right, up, or down into a neighboring square that is empty
- If a fish survives a certain number of turns, it spawns a new fish in a neighboring empty square and resets its breeding counter

If a rule requires an empty square but none are available, then the rule is ignored. For example, if a fish should spawn but it has no empty neighboring square, then it resets its breeding counter without creating a new child fish.

For this problem, build a Sharks and Fish program similar to the one shown in the following screenshot:

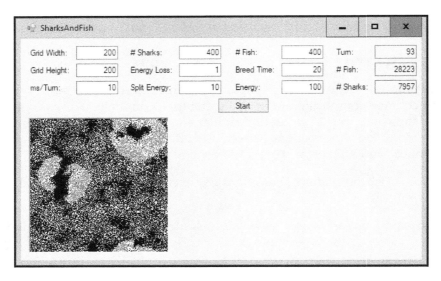

You can use a grid similar to the ones you used for the Langton's Ant and Life programs if you like. In the preceding screenshot, I chose to represent the sharks and fish as white and red and white pixels on a bitmap.

The user should enter the grid, fish, and shark parameters, and then click the **Start** button to begin the simulation.

This simulation is a bit more complicated than the previous ones, so you may want to use a slightly more complicated method for storing the world's information. In the example solution, I used an Ocean class to represent the world. I also defined Shark and Fish classes that inherit from a common Animal class. The program's Ocean object contains an array holding Animal objects and null values to represent empty locations.

88. Slingshot

The previous simulations used simple rules to produce complex behavior. Even the Sharks and Fish simulation, which uses a lot of parameters, doesn't really model the real world accurately.

To solve the current problem, you need to use a relatively realistic model for projectile motion. Create a slingshot program similar to the one shown in the following screenshot that lets the user fire projectiles:

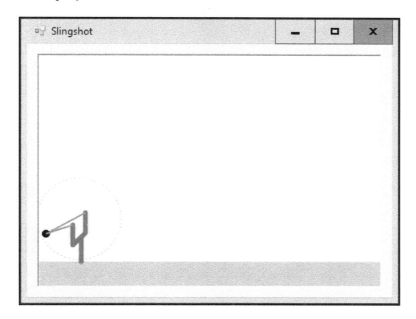

The user should be able to click and drag to pull the shot back at most a certain distance from the slingshot. In the screenshot, the faint dotted circle indicates the farthest that the user can pull the shot.

When the user releases the mouse button, the program should launch the projectile in the direction given by the rubber bands with an initial speed that depends on how far the shot has been pulled back. The program should then move the projectile appropriately until it leaves the form's sides or hits the ground.

If you don't know how to model projectile motion, you can read the first section of the solution later in this chapter for a brief overview. If you want more information, see http://en.wikipedia.org/wiki/ Projectile_motion or www2.hawaii.edu/~takebaya/lessons/lesson3.pdf, or search the web.

Note that physics web sites generally use equations for an object's position over time. In contrast, the example solution works incrementally, adding small amounts of acceleration and velocity at short time intervals.

89. Slingshot refinements

You can use the program that you wrote for the preceding example as a simple game, but it's missing a few key elements that would make it a lot more fun. Modify that program to add the following features:

- Draw a small building at a random position to act as a target.
- If the shot hits the target, replace the target with a picture of flames and display a new target.
- Draw shots where old shots hit the ground.
- Make the program play different sounds when a shot is released, when a shot hits the ground, and when a shot hits the target building. Use at least one WAV file and one MP3 file.

The following screenshot shows the example solution after the user has hit one target and missed several times:

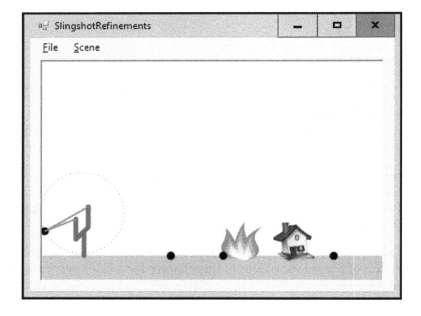

90. Space Force

Write a program similar to the one shown in the following screenshot:

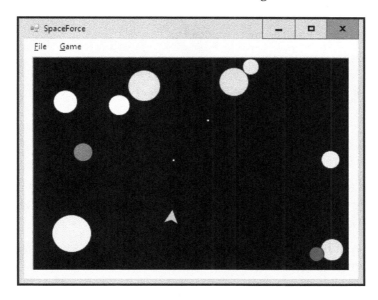

Pressing the up arrow key should accelerate the spaceship. Pressing the left and right arrow keys should turn the ship to the left or right. Pressing the spacebar should play a sound effect and make the ship fire a bullet. Require the guns to spend at least a quarter second between shots reloading.

When the user starts a new game, create bubbles with different sizes and colors moving in random directions. If a bubble leaves one side of the form, make it reappear on the opposite side.

If a bullet hits a bubble, pop the bubble and play a sound effect. If a bubble hits the ship, replace the ship with an explosion, again playing a sound effect. Finally, if the user pops all of the bubbles, play a celebratory sound effect.

Solutions

The following sections describe key pieces of the solutions to the preceding problems. You can download the example solutions to see additional details and to experiment with the programs at https://github.com/PacktPublishing/The-Modern-CSharp-Challenge/tree/master/Chapter08.

82. Dawkins' weasel

This program is actually quite simple. The following code shows how the example solution initializes itself:

```
private Random Rand = new Random();
private string Target, Letters;
private int TargetLength;

private vcid Form1_Load(object sender, EventArgs e)
{
    Target = "METHINKS IT IS LIKE A WEASEL";
    TargetLength = Target.Length;
    Letters = " ABCDEFGHIJKLMNOPQRSTUVWXYZ";
}
```

This code creates a `Random` object for use when generating strings. It defines variables to hold the target string, a string containing allowed characters (the letters A through Z, plus the space character), and the length of the target string.

The form's `Load` event handler sets the target string to `METHINKS IT IS LIKE A WEASEL`, saves the string's length, and initializes the `Letters` variable.

The following `RunWeasel` method performs the simulation:

```
// Perform the weasel transformation.
private vcid RunWeasel(int generationSize, double mutationProb)
{
    // Start with a random string.
    string parent = RandomString(Letters, TargetLength);

    // Repeat until we find the target.
    int error = FindError(parent, Target);
    while (error > 0)
    {
        // Display this parent.
        stepsListBox.Items.Add(error + ": " + parent);

        // Process a generation.
        int bestError = int.MaxValue;
        string bestOffspring = "";
        for (int i = 0; i < generationSize; i++)
        {
            // Make a mutated offspring.
            string testOffspring = "";
            foreach (char ch in parent)
            {
```

```
                if (Rand.NextDouble() <= mutationProb)
                    testOffspring += RandomLetter(Letters);
                else
                    testOffspring += ch;
            }

            // See if this is an improvement.
            int testError = FindError(testOffspring, Target)

            if (testError < bestError)
            {
                bestError = testError;
                bestOffspring = testOffspring;
            }
        }

        // Replace the parent with the best offspring.
        parent = bestOffspring;
        error = bestError;
    }
    numStepsLabel.Text = $"# Steps:
     {stepsListBox.Items.Count.ToString()}";

    stepsListBox.Items.Add(error + ": " + parent);
    stepsListBox.SelectedIndex = stepsListBox.Items.Count - 1;
}
```

This method calls the RandomString method described shortly to generate the initial string. It calls the FindError method, also described shortly, to see by how much that string differs from the target string.

The program then enters a loop that continues as long as the string in the parent variable does not match the target string. Inside the loop, the code adds the current parent string to a list box. It then creates a generation consisting of generationSize new child strings. The program makes each child string by copying the parent's characters, possibly mutating some randomly.

After it has created the new generation, the code saves the child closest to the target string in the parent variable and repeats the process until it finishes.

The following code shows how the program generates random strings and characters:

```
private string RandomString(string letters, int length)
{
    string result = "";
    for (int i = 0; i < length; i++)
        result += RandomLetter(letters);
    return result;
}

private char RandomLetter(string letters)
{
    int index = Rand.Next(0, letters.Length);
    return letters[index];
}
```

The `RandomString` method simply loops through the desired number of letters, calls the `RandomLetter` method to pick a random letter, and concatenates them.

The `RandomLetter` method simply picks a random letter from the `letters` string.

The following code shows the `FindError` method, which returns an indication of how far a test string is from the target string:

```
private int FindError(string string1, string string2)
{
    int error = 0;
    for (int i = 0; i < string1.Length; i++)
        error += Math.Abs((int)string1[i] - (int)string2[i]);
    return error;
}
```

This method just loops through the characters in two strings and subtracts the corresponding characters. It returns the sum of the characters' errors.

That's about all there is to this program. Download the `DawkinsWeasel` example solution to see additional details.

 Richard Dawkins originally intended this simulation to show how simple selection could produce evolutionary results relatively quickly. However, the program presupposes a goal, in this case, *"Methinks it is like a weasel."* Real-world evolution does not have a predetermined goal, so the program fails in that respect. However, it is still a useful example of a simple simulation. It also demonstrates a very useful *incremental improvement strategy* where a program makes small random changes to a potential solution to try to find a better one.

83. Hailstone sequence

The following method returns the values in a number's hailstone sequence:

```
// Find this number's hailstone sequence.
private List<int> FindHailstoneSequence(int number)
{
    List<int> results = new List<int>();
    while (number != 1)
    {
        results.Add(number);
        if (number % 2 == 0)
            number = number / 2;
        else
            number = 3 * number + 1;
    }
    results.Add(1);
    return results;
}
```

This method performs the actual hailstone simulation. It creates a list to hold the sequence's values and then enters a loop that continues as long as the number is not 1. Within the loop, the method adds the current number to the sequence and then uses the current value to calculate the next one.

When the loop ends, the method adds 1 to the list and returns the list.

The rest of the program displays the sequence. When you click the **Go** button, the following code draws the graph and shows the sequence's values:

```
private void goButton_Click(object sender, EventArgs e)
{
    resultTextBox.Clear();
    lengthLabel.Text = "";
    Refresh();

    // Find the hailstone sequence lengths.
    int number = int.Parse(numberTextBox.Text);
    List<int> sequence = FindHailstoneSequence(number);

    // Display the results.
    resultTextBox.Text = string.Join(" ", sequence.ToArray());
    lengthLabel.Text = sequence.Count().ToString();

    // Graph the results.
    int wid = sequencePictureBox.ClientSize.Width;
    int hgt = sequencePictureBox.ClientSize.Height;
```

```
Bitmap bm = new Bitmap(wid, hgt);
using (Graphics gr = Graphics.FromImage(bm))
{
    gr.SmoothingMode = SmoothingMode.AntiAlias;
    gr.Clear(Color.White);

    // We cannot graph it if there's only one point.
    if (number < 2) return;

    // Set up a transformation.
    RectangleF graphRect = new RectangleF(
        0, 0, sequence.Count(), sequence.Max());
    const int margin = 5;
    RectangleF bitmapRect = new RectangleF(
        margin, margin, wid - 1 - 2 * margin, hgt - 1 - 2 *
        margin);
    SetTransformation(gr, graphRect, bitmapRect, false, true);

    using (Pen pen = new Pen(Color.Black, 0))
    {
        // Draw axes.
        gr.DrawLine(pen, 0, -10000, 0, 10000);
        gr.DrawLine(pen, -10000, 0, 10000, 0);

        // Draw the sequence.
        pen.Color = Color.Red;
        List<PointF> points = new List<PointF>();
        for (int x = 0; x < sequence.Count; x++)
            points.Add(new PointF(x, sequence[x]));
        gr.DrawLines(pen, points.ToArray());
    }
}
sequencePictureBox.Image = bm;
}
```

This method clears the result text box and length label, and then parses the starting number that you entered. It calls the `FindHailstoneSequence` method to get the sequence, joins the values together in a string, and displays them. It also displays the sequence's length.

Next, the code builds the graph. It gets the size of the form's `PictureBox` control, makes a `Bitmap` object to fit, and creates an associated `Graphics` object. The code then sets the `Graphics` object's `SmoothingMode` property to draw a smooth curve and clears the image.

Now the method sets up a transformation to map the sequence's values onto the `Bitmap` object's surface. It creates a rectangle that holds the data's bounds. It then creates a second rectangle that gives the `Bitmap` object's bounds, minus a margin around the edges. The code then passes those rectangles to the `SetTransformation` method described shortly to make the `Graphics` object map the data area onto the `Bitmap`.

At this point, the method is ready to draw. It first creates a pen with a thickness of 0. It then uses the pen to draw the axes, $x = 0$ and $y = 0$.

A pen with a thickness of 0 always draw the thinnest possible line even if the `Graphics` object includes a transformation that would otherwise scale the pen.

Next, the code loops through the hailstone sequence and creates points to represent the sequence's values. It then calls the `Graphics` object's `DrawLines` method to draw lines connecting the points. The `Graphics` object's transformation automatically maps the graph onto the `Bitmap`.

The final interesting piece of the application is the following `SetTransformation` method:

```
// Map from world coordinates to screen coordinates.
private void SetTransformation(Graphics gr,
    RectangleF graphRect, RectangleF bitmapRect,
    bool invertX, bool invertY)
{
    PointF[] bitmapPoints =
    {
        new PointF(bitmapRect.Left, bitmapRect.Top),     // Upper left.
        new PointF(bitmapRect.Right, bitmapRect.Top),    // Upper right.
        new PointF(bitmapRect.Left, bitmapRect.Bottom), // Lower left.
    };

    if (invertX)
    {
        bitmapPoints[0].X = bitmapRect.Right;
        bitmapPoints[1].X = bitmapRect.Left;
        bitmapPoints[2].X = bitmapRect.Right;
    }
    if (invertY)
    {
```

```
                bitmapPoints[0].Y = bitmapRect.Bottom;
                bitmapPoints[1].Y = bitmapRect.Bottom;
                bitmapPoints[2].Y = bitmapRect.Top;
        }

        gr.Transform = new Matrix(graphRect, bitmapPoints);
    }
```

A `Graphics` object's `Transform` property is a `Matrix` object that describes the desired transformation. One of the `Matrix` class's constructors takes two parameters. The first is a rectangle giving an area in drawing coordinates where you want to draw. The second is an array containing three points that define the coordinates on the `Bitmap` where the rectangle's upper left, upper right, and lower left corners should be mapped.

The method initializes the `bitmapPoints` array to define those corners. If the method's `invertX` parameter is `true`, the method switches the roles of the rectangle's left and right sides. Then, if the `invertY` parameter is `true`, it performs a similar operation for the rectangle's top and bottom sides. The example program uses this feature because *Y* coordinates increase upward in mathematical space but downward on a `Bitmap`.

Having defined the `Bitmap` area points, the method creates a `Matrix` object and assigns it to the `Graphics` object's `Transform` property. Now the `Graphics` object is ready to draw and automatically map points in the drawing rectangle onto the correct part of the `Bitmap`.

Download the `HailstoneSequence` example solution to see the results and to see additional details.

84. Hailstone Sequence, Redux

This program is very similar to the preceding one. The main difference is that this program builds a list of sequence lengths and the preceding solution builds a list containing a single sequence.

You could build the list of lengths by simply using the `FindHailstoneSequence` method from the preceding solution to create each sequence in turn. The sequences aren't too long, at least for relatively small starting values, so that would work. However, there's a shortcut that you can use to make generating the lengths even faster.

The following method demonstrates that shortcut to find the lengths of hailstone sequences starting with numbers between 1 and `max`:

```
// Return the lengths of hailstone sequences for starting numbers 1
// through max.
private List<int> FindHailstoneLengths(int max)
{
    // Create an array to hold the lengths.
    int[] lengths = new int[max + 1];

    // Fill the lengths.
    for (int i = 1; i <= max; i++)
    {
        int length = 1;
        int number = i;
        while (number != 1)
        {
            // See if we know the length for the current number.
            if ((number <= max) && (lengths[number] > 0))
            {
                // We know lengths[number].
                length += lengths[number] - 1;
                break;
            }

            // Go to the next number.
            length++;
            if (number % 2 == 0)
                number = number / 2;
            else
                number = 3 * number + 1;
        }
        lengths[i] = length;
    }

    // Convert the array to a list and remove the entry 0.
    List<int> lengthList = new List<int>(lengths);
    lengthList.RemoveAt(0);

    return lengthList;
}
```

The method creates an array to hold the sequence lengths and then enters a loop to calculate those lengths. For each value within the loop, the code initializes a length counter. It then uses a `while` loop to generate values in the sequence until it reaches the value 1.

After generating the next number in a sequence, the method checks the `lengths` array to see if it already contains a length for the sequence starting at that number.

For example, consider the sequence starting at the value 8. The next value in the sequence is 4, but 4 is smaller than 8. If we're currently calculating the length of the 8 sequence, then we have already calculated the length of the 4 sequence. It took one step to get to this point, so the length of the 8 sequence is 1 greater than the length of the 4 sequence.

The `length` counter starts at 1 and the `while` loop adds steps to reach a previously calculated value, so we need to subtract 1 when we add the previously calculated value's length. (If you walk through the code for the value 8, you'll see how that works.) After adding the new value to the `length` counter, the code breaks out of its `while` loop.

After the `while` loop ends, the method saves the calculated sequence length in the `lengths` array and moves on to the next sequence.

After the method finishes finding all of the sequence lengths, it converts the `lengths` array into a list, removes the first entry (because no hailstone sequence is defined starting with the value 0), and returns the list.

The rest of the solution is very similar to the preceding one. Download the `HailstoneSequenceRedux` example solution to see additional details.

85. Langton's Ant

The example solution is fairly long but relatively straightforward, so I won't describe all of its code in detail. Instead, I'll describe the basic approach and a few selected pieces of code.

The program uses a `Timer` component to move the ant. When you select the **Run** menu's **Start** command or press *F5*, the following code starts or stops the simulation:

```
// Start or stop the simulation.
private void startToolStripMenuItem_Click(object sender, EventArgs e)
{
    if (startToolStripMenuItem.Text == "&Start")
    {
        startToolStripMenuItem.Text = "&Stop";
        moveTimer.Enabled = true;
    }
```

```
        else
        {
            startToolStripMenuItem.Text = "&Start";
            moveTimer.Enabled = false;
        }
    }
```

This code checks the menu item's current text and either starts or stops the program's Timer as appropriate. It also changes the menu item's text to **Start** or **Stop**, depending on whether the simulation is now running.

Each time the Timer ticks, the program uses the following code to update the ant's position:

```
// The ant's current location and direction.
private Point AntLocation = new Point(1, 1);
private enum Direction { Up, Right, Down, Left }
private Direction AntDirection = Direction.Left;

// Move the ant.
private void moveTimer_Tick(object sender, EventArgs e)
{
    // Get the ant's new direction.
    if (SquareIsBlack[AntLocation.X, AntLocation.Y])
        // Turn right.
        AntDirection = (Direction)(((int)AntDirection + 1) % 4);
    else
        // Turn left.
        AntDirection = (Direction)(((int)AntDirection - 1 + 4) % 4);

    // Toggle the current square's color.
    SquareIsBlack[AntLocation.X, AntLocation.Y] =
        !SquareIsBlack[AntLocation.X, AntLocation.Y];

    // Move the ant.
    switch (AntDirection)
    {
        case Direction.Left:
            AntLocation.X--;
            break;
        case Direction.Up:
            AntLocation.Y--;
            break;
        case Direction.Right:
            AntLocation.X++;
            break;
        case Direction.Down:
            AntLocation.Y++;
            break;
```

```
        }

        // Redraw.
        worldPictureBox.Refresh();
        TurnNumber++;
        if (TurnNumber == 20000) moveTimer.Enabled = false;
        turnLabel.Text = TurnNumber.ToString();
    }
}
```

The `AntLocation` variable holds the ant's current position. The `Direction` enumeration defines the possible directions that the ant could be facing, and `AntDirection` stores the ant's current direction.

The timer's `Tick` event handler uses the color of the square under the ant to determine the ant's new direction and then moves the ant appropriately.

After moving the ant, the program calls the `worldPictureBox` control's `Refresh` method to trigger that control's `Paint` event handler, which redraws the grid. The `Paint` event handler (and, in fact, the rest of the program) is fairly straightforward so it isn't shown here.

The last piece of information that I want to cover is the way the program handles the edges of the grid. In theory, the ant crawls across an infinitely large grid but, in practice, the grid cannot have infinite size. There are a few approaches that you can take to handle this problem.

One approach is to wrap the ant around when it reaches the grid's edges. If the grid has width W and height H then, at each step, the program takes the ant's new X position modulus W and its Y position modulus H. This makes the grid act as if it was on a torus (donut shape). If you go far enough in any direction, you wrap around to the other side.

A second approach is to make the program resize its grid whenever the ant reaches an edge. The program can resize the grid in the direction that the ant is moving to avoid creating large areas that are never visited. This strategy is limited only by the memory in your computer.

A third approach, and the one taken by the example solution, is to create a large grid and simply stop the simulation if the ant leaves the grid. In the example solution, if the ant steps off of the allocated grid, the program simply crashes. That allows the program to skip testing to see whether the ant has reached the grid's edges, so it makes the program slightly faster.

Download the `LangtonsAnt` example solution to see additional details.

86. Life

Like the Langton's Ant example solution, this one is fairly long but relatively straightforward, so I won't include a lot of code here. The most important piece of code is the following `Tick` event handler, which updates the world to create the next generation:

```
// The size of the world.
private int GridWid, GridHgt;

// The world.
private bool[,] World = null;

// True if we should wrap squares  across the world's edges.
private bool WrapEdges = true;

// Move objects.
private void moveTimer_Tick(object sender, EventArgs e)
{
    // See how many neighbors each squares has.
    int[,] numNeighbors = new int[GridWid, GridHgt];
    for (int y = 0; y < GridHgt; y++)
    {
        for (int x = 0; x < GridWid; x++)
        {
            // See if this square is occupied.
            if (World[x, y])
            {
                // Add this square to its neighbors' counts.
                for (int dx = -1; dx <= 1; dx++)
                    for (int dy = -1; dy <= 1; dy++)
                        if ((dx != 0) || (dy != 0))
                        {
                            if (WrapEdges)
                            {
                                // Wrap style.
                                int nx = (x + dx + GridWid) % GridWid;
                                int ny = (y + dy + GridHgt) % GridHgt;
                                numNeighbors[nx, ny]++;
                            }
                            else
                            {
                                // Discard style.
                                int nx = x + dx;
                                int ny = y + dy;
                                if ((nx >= 0) && (nx < GridWid) &&
                                    (ny >= 0) && (ny < GridHgt))
                                        numNeighbors[nx, ny]++;
```

```
                                    }
                                }
                            }
                        }
                    }

            // Repopulate the world.
            bool changed = false;
            for (int y = 0; y < GridHgt; y++)
            {
                for (int x = 0; x < GridWid; x++)
                {
                    // See if the square is currently populated.
                    bool value = World[x, y];
                    if (value)
                    {
                        // Currently populated. See if it survives.
                        if ((numNeighbors[x, y] < 2) ||
                            (numNeighbors[x, y] > 3))
                                value = false;
                    }
                    else
                    {
                        // Currently unpopulated. See if we should populate it.
                        if (numNeighbors[x, y] == 3)
                            value = true;
                    }
                    if (World[x, y] != value) changed = true;
                    World[x, y] = value;
                }
            }

            // If nothing changed, stop.
            if (!changed) startToolStripMenuItem_Click(null, null);

            // Redraw.
            worldPictureBox.Refresh();
            TurnNumber++;
            turnLabel.Text = TurnNumber.ToString();
        }
```

The form-level variables, GridWid and GridHgt, hold the size of the grid. The World array indicates which cells are live, with a true value meaning a live cell and a false value meaning a dead cell.

The `WrapEdges` value indicates whether the program should wrap the world around the grid's edges so cells along one edge are neighbors of cells on the opposite edge.

The `moveTimer_Tick` event handler creates an array to hold the number of neighbors that each grid cell has. It then loops over all of the cells. For each cell that is alive, the code loops through that cell's neighbors and increments their neighbor counts.

This is the step that wraps around the edges of the grid if desired. If the `WrapEdges` variable is `true`, then the code uses the modulus operator (`%`) to wrap the coordinates around the grid's edges vertically and horizontally.

Notice how the calculation adds the bounds before applying the `%` operator. That protects the program against negative indices. For example, suppose the width of the grid, `GridWid`, is 100, the code is considering cell [0, 0], and `dx` is -1. Then `(x + dx) % GridWid` would be `(0 - 1) % 100 = -1 % GridWid = -1`, which lies outside of the grid's valid indices. Adding `GridWid` to the calculation gives `(0 - 1 + 100) % 100 = 99 % 100 = 99`, which is a valid index.

The calculation of the neighbor's *Y* coordinate is similar.

After it has calculated each cell's neighbor count, the code rebuilds the world. It loops over each cell and uses the cell's current state and neighbor count to determine whether the cell should now be alive.

There are two reasons why the program counts neighbors and updates the cell population in two steps. First, it is slightly faster than updating the cells in one pass. Because the code only adds to the neighbor counts for cells that are alive, it performs roughly *8 × A* steps, where *A* is the number of live cells and 8 is the number of neighbors. In contrast, if the code examined every cell and counted its neighbors, it would need to examine 8 cells for every cell in the grid.

The second and more important reason for updating the world in two steps is to avoid using new cell values to update other cells. For example, suppose you update the cells one row at a time from top to bottom. After you have updated row 0, the new cell values in that row would affect the values in row 1, but we only want to consider the *previous* values in row 1 when calculating the new values in row 2. Storing neighbor counts in a separate array avoids that problem.

There's one more piece of code in this solution that I want to describe. The following `LoadPattern` method takes as an input an array of strings that uses zeros and ones to define a pattern of cells and uses those strings to initialize the program's cells:

```
// Load a pattern defined by strings of 0s and 1s.
private void LoadPattern(string[] pattern)
{
    World = new bool[GridWid, GridHgt];
    int x = (GridWid - pattern[0].Length) / 2;
    int y = (GridHgt - pattern.Length) / 2;
    for (int iy = 0; iy < pattern.Length; iy++)
        for (int ix = 0; ix < pattern[iy].Length; ix++)
            World[x + ix, y + iy] = (pattern[iy][ix] == '1');

    TurnNumber = 0;
    turnLabel.Text = "0";
    worldPictureBox.Refresh();
}
```

This method creates a new, blank `World` array. It then calculates starting *X* and *Y* positions where it should start building the pattern to center the pattern's cells in the world grid.

The code then loops through the strings in the pattern array. For each string, the code loops through the string's characters and sets the corresponding `World` entries to `true` where the pattern contains a 1.

The example solution uses the `LoadPattern` method to let the user load a number of predefined patterns. For example, the following code loads one of the most famous Life patterns, which is named *Glider*:

```
private void gliderToolStripMenuItem_Click(object sender, EventArgs e)
{
    string[] pattern =
    {
        "010",
        "001",
        "111",
    };
    LoadPattern(pattern);
}
```

Download the `Life` example solution to see additional details.

87. Sharks and Fish

This example solution is fairly long but relatively straightforward, so I won't include its code here. Instead, I'll describe the key features of each of the program's classes.

The Ocean class uses a two-dimensional array named Grid to hold the simulation's Animal objects. The class keeps separate lists of the current sharks and fish so it can loop through them easily. It also stores shark and fish parameters such as the amount of energy a shark loses each turn and the amount of energy a shark gains when it eats a fish.

This Ocean class also defines the following helper methods:

- MakeFish—Makes a specified number of randomly positioned fish.
- MakeSharks—Makes a specified number of randomly positioned sharks.
- FreeSpots—Returns a list of spots adjacent to a given position. If the ignoreFish parameter is true, the method includes positions containing fish. (So a shark can move onto a fish and eat it.)
- PickSpot—Picks a random position from a list of free spots.
- Move—Loops through the fish and sharks and calls their Move methods.

The Animal class defines an empty, virtual Move method. The Shark and Fish classes override that method to take appropriate action. For example, the following code shows the Fish class's Move method:

```
public override void Move()
{
    // Look for a free spot.
    List<Point> spots = Ocean.FreeSpots(X, Y, false);
    if (spots.Count > 0)
    {
        // Move.
        Ocean.Bitmap.SetPixel(X, Y, Color.Black);
        Ocean.Grid[X, Y] = null;

        Point moveTo = spots.Random();
        X = moveTo.X;
        Y = moveTo.Y;
        Ocean.Bitmap.SetPixel(X, Y, Fish.Color);
        Ocean.Grid[X, Y] = this;
    }

    // Breed.
    Breed();
}
```

This code calls the `Ocean` object's `FreeSpots` method to find a spot where the fish could move. If there are free spots, the fish erases its current position in the ocean's bitmap, moves to a randomly selected free spot, and draws itself on the bitmap in its new position.

The method then calls the following `Breed` method to see if the fish should breed:

```
// See if we should breed.
private void Breed()
{
    if (--TimeUntilBreeding > 0) return;

    // Breed.
    TimeUntilBreeding = Ocean.FishBreedingTime;

    // Position a child.
    List<Point> spots = Ocean.FreeSpots(X, Y, false);
    if (spots.Count == 0) return;

    Point childSpot = spots.Random();
    Ocean.Fishes.Add(new Fish(Ocean, Ocean.FishBreedingTime,
        childSpot.X, childSpot.Y));
}
```

This method decrements the fish's time until breeding. If that time is still greater than zero, the method returns.

If the fish's time until breeding has reached zero, the method resets the time until breeding to its starting value. It then gets a list of free spots adjacent to the fish. If there are no free spots, the method returns without breeding.

Finally, if there are empty spots adjacent to the fish, the method creates a new child fish in one of them.

The `Move` method of the `Shark` class is somewhat similar to the version of the `Fish` class, except it follows the rules for sharks.

Download the `SharksAndFish` example solution to see additional details.

88. Slingshot

The following section provides a brief introduction to modeling projectile motion. If this material is already familiar to you, you can skip to the section after that, which explains the problem's example solution.

Projectile motion

You can model projectile motion with two quantities—velocity and acceleration.

Velocity is a vector that indicates an object's current speed and direction. You can store that value directly as a speed (in pixels per second or some other unit) and a direction (degrees or another unit), but it's usually easier to store it as X and Y velocity components. If the components are Vx and Vy, then the object moves the distance Vx in the horizontal direction and Vy in the vertical direction per unit of time. You can adjust the components' values and the time unit to change the object's speed and to control the simulation's speed.

Acceleration is a force that acts on the object to change its velocity. Depending on the simulation, acceleration may be due to many forces such as the Earth's gravity, gravitational attraction due to other objects such as planets, current (for example, if the object is a boat or a plane flying through wind), or the object's engines (for example, if the object is a spacecraft).

You can model an acceleration with components Ax and Ay much as you can model velocity. To apply acceleration to an object, simply add Ax to Vx and Ay to Vy. To apply multiple accelerations to the same object, just add them all to the object's velocity one at a time. Just as you can adjust the velocity components to change an object's speed, you can also adjust an acceleration's components to change the amount by which that acceleration affects the object.

The final thing you need to know for this problem is that the acceleration due to the Earth's gravity on a projectile always points in the downward direction. In other words, if you consider Y coordinates to increase downward as they normally do in C#, then $Ax = 0$ and Ay should be positive.

More complicated models might involve drag forces such as wind resistance, water resistance, or friction, but the information in the previous paragraphs should be enough to get you started. If you like, you can give the problem a try before you read the next section.

Example solution

This example has several interesting pieces of code. The techniques used by the code are interesting, but the code itself is relatively long and straightforward, so I'll only show a little of it here. Instead, I'll describe the key pieces and you can download the example solution to see the details.

The program uses `MouseDown`, `MouseMove`, and `MouseUp` event handlers to allow the user to drag and release the shot. These work much as similar event handlers work in other programs with a few additional tests.

First, the `MouseDown` event handler calculates the distance from the mouse to the shot's center. If the mouse is not over the shot, then the event handler exits and does not start a drag.

Once a drag begins, the `MouseMove` event handler verifies that the user has not dragged the shot more than a given distance from the slingshot. If the user has dragged the shot too far, the event handler uses the following code fragment to adjust the shot's position:

```
// Adjust the shot position so it's inside the circle.
float dx = (e.Location.X - CrossCenter.X) * MaxR / (float)dist;
float dy = (e.Location.Y - CrossCenter.Y) * MaxR / (float)dist;
ShotPosition = new PointF(
    CrossCenter.X + dx,
    CrossCenter.Y + dy);
```

The event handler's `e.Location` parameter gives the mouse's position, `CrossCenter` gives the position of the center of the slingshot's crossbar, and `MaxR` is the maximum distance the user should be able to drag the shot. Finally, `dist` is the actual distance between the mouse and `CrossCenter`.

This code takes the difference between the mouse's and shot's *X* and *Y* coordinates. It multiplies the results by `MaxR / dist` to scale the coordinate differences. The final differences, `dx` and `dy`, have the same ratio as the original unscaled differences, so they give the same direction from the slingshot's center, but they can be at most `MaxR` distance from the center.

The code then uses the `dx` and `dy` values to adjust the shot's center.

The `MouseUp` event handler ends the drag operation just as any `MouseUp` event handler does, but it also launches the shot. The force exerted by normal springs (and the rubber bands used by a slingshot) depends linearly on the amount by which the spring is deformed. If you stretch a spring twice as far, it provides twice the force. For this program, that means the farther back the user pulls the shot, the faster it initially moves. The following code shows how the `MouseUp` event handler launches the shot:

```
// Stop dragging and launch the shot.
private void scenePictureBox_MouseUp(object sender, MouseEventArgs e)
{
    if (!Dragging) return;
    Dragging = false;
```

```
    // Get the shot's horizontal and vertical velocity components.
    ShotVx = VelocityScale * (CrossCenter.X - ShotPosition.X);
    ShotVy = VelocityScale * (CrossCenter.Y - ShotPosition.Y);

    // Start the timer.
    moveTimer.Enabled = true;
}
```

The ShotVx and ShotVy variables hold the shot's *X* and *Y* velocity components. The code sets them equal to the difference in the components between the shot's launch position and the slingshot's center. It then multiplies those values by a scale factor that was chosen to produce a nice result. In general, you may need to experiment to find the right scale factor for this kind of simulation.

After calculating the shot's velocity, the code enables the program's movement timer. The following code executes when the timer's Tick event occurs:

```
    // Acceleration due to gravity.
    private const float AccY = 3.2f * VelocityScale;

    // Move the shot.
    private void moveTimer_Tick(object sender, EventArgs e)
    {
        // Update the velocity components.
        ShotVy += AccY;

        // Calculate the shot's new position.
        ShotPosition.X += ShotVx;
        ShotPosition.Y += ShotVy;

        // See if the shot has left the scene.
        if ((ShotPosition.X < 0) ||
            (ShotPosition.X > scenePictureBox.ClientSize.Width) ||
            (ShotPosition.Y > GroundRect.Top))
        {
            // Stop.
            moveTimer.Enabled = false;

            // Reset the shot.
            ShotPosition = CrossCenter;
        }

        // Redraw.
        scenePictureBox.Refresh();
    }
```

The `AccY` constant represents acceleration due to gravity. In C#, *Y* coordinates increase downward, so `AccY` is set to a positive value to indicate acceleration downward. Like the `VelocityScale` value, `AccY` was set by trial and error to create a reasonable appearance.

The timer's `Tick` event handler adds `AccY` to the shot's current *Y* velocity component. The shot's *X* velocity component remains unchanged.

Next, the code adds the shot's velocity components to its current location to move the shot.

If the shot has reached the ground or left the sides of the form, the code disables the movement timer. Otherwise, if the shot should continue moving, the code refreshes the program's `PictureBox` to show the shot's new position.

The rest of the program is reasonably straightforward. Download the `Slingshot` example solution to see additional details.

89. Slingshot refinements

To draw the target building and the flames, I went online and found images that I liked. I then added the images to the project's resources.

To add a project resource, open the **Project** menu and select **Properties** from the bottom. In the project's resources window, click the **Add Resource** drop-down menu and select **Add Existing File**. Browse to select the resource file and click **Open**.

I also added WAV audio files for the program to play when the user releases a shot and when a shot hits the ground. The `System.Media.SoundPlayer` class can play WAV files stored as project resources, so I added those files to the project as resources. Working with those files is relatively easy.

You can find lots of interesting images free at `pixabay.com` and `commons.wikimedia.org`. You can find many free audio files at `freesound.org`.

When a shot hits the target building, the program plays an explosion sound stored in an MP3 file. The `WindowsMediaPlayer` class can play that kind of file, but it requires a bit of extra effort.

First, to use the media player, you need to add a reference to its library. To do that, open the **Project** menu and select **Add Reference**. Expand the **COM** branch and select the **Windows Media Player** entry.

Next, the media player only plays files, not project resources. To allow the player to find the file, I opened the **Project** menu and selected **Add Existing Item**. In the **Add Item** dialog, I selected the MP3 file and clicked **Add**. Next, in **Solution Explorer**, I selected the file, set its `Build Action` property to `Content`, and set its `Copy to Output Directory` property to `Copy if newer`. Now, when Visual Studio builds the executable program, it copies the MP3 file into the executable directory so the media player can find it at runtime.

With that preparation, the program is ready to use the sound files. The following form-level declarations define sound players for the three audio files:

```
// Sounds.
private SoundPlayer ShotSound, SplatSound;
private WindowsMediaPlayer BoomSound;
```

The form's `Load` event handler uses the following code snippet to initialize the players:

```
// Load the shot and explosion sound players.
ShotSound = new SoundPlayer(Properties.Resources.boing);
SplatSound = new SoundPlayer(Properties.Resources.splat);
BoomSound = new WindowsMediaPlayer();
BoomSound.settings.autoStart = false;
BoomSound.URL = "boom.mp3";

// Play the Boom sound at zero volume to pre-load it.
BoomSound.settings.volume = 0;
BoomSound.controls.play();
```

This code creates `SoundPlayer` objects associated with the `boing` and `splat` resources.

Next, the code creates a `WindowsMediaPlayer` and sets its `settings.autoStart` property to `false` so the player doesn't start playing the sound as soon as it is created. The code also sets the player's URL to the name of the MP3 file.

At this point, the media player is ready to play the sound file. Unfortunately, it has a significant delay before it plays the file for the first time, presumably because it hasn't yet loaded the file. To force the player to load the file, the code sets the player's volume to zero and then calls its `controls.play` method to make it play the file.

Later, the program uses the audio players to play their sounds. For example, the following statement plays the shot sound:

```
ShotSound.Play();
```

The media player is a bit different. Because we earlier set the player's volume to zero, we now need to reset it to a larger value so the user can hear the sound. One place we could do that is in the MouseUp event handler. That seems like a reasonable choice because the event happens before we might need to play the sound and it doesn't happen too often (so we don't waste time increasing the volume repeatedly).

Unfortunately, a really quick user might release a shot that hits the house before the initial silent sound has finished playing. In that case, the media player seems to play the new sound before it increases its volume. Later sounds work correctly, but the first shot might not.

The program uses the following code snippet in the MouseUp event handler to deal with this problem:

```
BoomSound.controls.stop();
BoomSound.settings.volume = 50;
```

The first statement makes the media player stop playing the soundless explosion if it is still in progress. The second statement increases the player's volume to 50, which is its default value.

Playing sounds requires a few steps but, once you figure them out, they're not too hard.

The other enhancements to the program require you to draw a target building, flames, and past missed shots. The program uses the following code to declare lists to keep track of past hits and misses:

```
// Past hits and misses.
private List<RectangleF> Misses = new List<RectangleF>();
private List<RectangleF> Hits = new List<RectangleF>();
```

When a shot hits the target or the ground, the program saves the shot's location in these lists. Later, the program's Paint event handler uses the following code snippet to loop through the lists and draw the hits and misses:

```
// Past hits.
foreach (RectangleF hitRect in Hits)
{
    e.Graphics.DrawImage(Properties.Resources.flames, hitRect);
}
```

```
// Past misses.
foreach (RectangleF missRect in Misses)
{
    e.Graphics.FillEllipse(Brushes.Black, missRect);
}
...
// House.
e.Graphics.DrawImage(Properties.Resources.house, HouseRect);
```

The first loop draws the `flames` image resource at the locations of earlier hits. The second loop draws filled circles where earlier misses occurred. Later, the event handler draws the `house` image resource to the current target location.

The rest of the program is long but reasonably straightforward. Download the `SlingshotRefinements` example solution to see additional details.

90. Space Force

I've already described some of the techniques that you need to use to solve this problem. For example, previous solutions have shown how to play sounds, use timers to control movement, add acceleration to velocity, and use velocity to update position.

I can't say that the rest of this example solution is exactly simple, but much of it is straightforward and it's too long to include all of it here, so I'll just describe the most interesting new techniques. You can download the program to see all of the details.

The following sections describe the program's `Sprite`, `Bubble`, and `Ship` classes, and techniques for handling keyboard events.

Sprite classes

In this context, a **sprite** is an object (in the object-oriented sense) that represents something in the scene that can move. This program uses sprites to represent the ship, bubbles, and bullets.

The example solution uses the following abstract `Sprite` class to define basic sprite behavior. The program's `Bubble` and `Ship` classes inherit from this class:

```
public abstract class Sprite
{
    // Position and velocity.
    public RectangleF Bounds;
    public PointF Velocity;

    // Brush. This should be a stock object.
    public Brush Brush = Brushes.Silver;

    // True if this sprite should be destroyed.
    public bool IsDestroyed = false;

    // Constructor.
    public Sprite(RectangleF position, PointF velocity, Brush brush)
    {
        Bounds = position;
        Velocity = velocity;
        Brush = brush;
    }

    // Move.
    public void Move(Rectangle spaceBounds, bool wrap = true)
    {
        // Update the position.
        Bounds.X += Velocity.X;
        Bounds.Y += Velocity.Y;

        // See if we should wrap around the sides of the bounds.
        if (wrap)
        {
            // If the sprite has left the space bounds, wrap around.
            if (Bounds.Right < spaceBounds.Left)          // Off left
                Bounds.X = spaceBounds.Right - 1;
            else if (Bounds.Left > spaceBounds.Right)     // Off right
                Bounds.X = spaceBounds.Left - Bounds.Width + 1;
            else if (Bounds.Top > spaceBounds.Bottom)     // Off bottom
                Bounds.Y = spaceBounds.Top - Bounds.Height + 1;
            else if (Bounds.Bottom < spaceBounds.Top)     // Off top
                Bounds.Y = spaceBounds.Bottom - 1;
        }
    }

    // Return true if the sprite is out of bounds.
    public bool IsOutOfBounds(Rectangle spaceBounds)
    {
```

```
        return (!Bounds.IntersectsWith(spaceBounds));
    }

    // Return true if the objects intersect.
    public bool IntersectsWith(Sprite other)
    {
        return (Bounds.IntersectsWith(other.Bounds));
    }

    // Draw the object.
    public abstract void Draw(Graphics gr);
}
```

The class begins with declarations for a `RectangleF`, which stores the object's position, and a `PointF`, which holds the object's *X* and *Y* velocity components. In this program, all of the items on the screen are filled shapes, so the class includes a `Brush` that the program can use the fill the object.

Next, the class defines an `IsDestroyed` property. The program uses this to mark objects as destroyed before their sprites are removed from the program's data structures.

The most complicated part of the `Sprite` class is its `Move` method. That method adds the sprite's velocity components to its position to get its new position. It then adjusts the location, if necessary, to make the object wrap around the sides of the screen.

The `IsOutOfBounds` method returns `true` if the sprite has left the playing area. The program uses this method to remove bullets that leave the playing area. (They do not wrap around so the playing area doesn't quickly become filled with bullets.)

The `IntersectWith` method determines whether the sprite's position rectangle intersects another given rectangle. The program uses this to determine whether a collision has occurred between two objects such as a bullet and a bubble or a bubble and the spaceship.

Because the program's objects are not actually rectangles, using bounding rectangles to check for collisions is somewhat inaccurate. For example, the spaceship might intersect the corner of a bubble's bounding rectangle without actually touching the bubble. In that case, the program would detect a collision when it shouldn't. Using bounding rectangles is quick and easy, however, and good enough for this program.

Finally, the class declares an abstract `Draw` method. Derived classes must override this method to draw their objects on the screen.

Bubble

The following `Bubble` class, which is derived from the `Sprite` class, represents one of the bubbles floating around in the playing area:

```
class Bubble : Sprite
{
    // Constructor.
    public Bubble(RectangleF position, PointF velocity, Brush brush)
        : base(position, velocity, brush)
    {
    }

    // Draw.
    public override void Draw(Graphics gr)
    {
        gr.FillEllipse(Brush, Bounds);
        gr.DrawEllipse(Pens.Black, Bounds);
    }

    // Used for making random bubbles.
    private static Random Rand = new Random();

    // Possible bubble brushes and pens.
    private static Brush[] BubbleBrushes =
    {
        Brushes.Red, Brushes.Green, Brushes.Blue,
        Brushes.Pink, Brushes.LightGreen, Brushes.LightBlue,
        Brushes.Yellow, Brushes.Orange, Brushes.Fuchsia,
        Brushes.Cyan,
    };

    // Factory method to make a random bubble
    // near the edges of the allowed rectangle.
    public static Bubble RandomBubble(Rectangle spaceBounds)
    {
        // Get random Bubble properties.
        int diameter = Rand.Next(20, 60);
        PointF center = spaceBounds.Center();
        PointF point;
        do
        {
            int px = Rand.Next(0, spaceBounds.Width - diameter);
            int py = Rand.Next(0, spaceBounds.Height - diameter);
            point = new PointF(px, py);
        } while (Distance(center, point) < 150);

        int speed = Rand.Next(3, 7);
```

```
        double angle = Rand.Next(0, 360) * Math.PI / 180.0;
        double vx = speed * Math.Cos(angle);
        double vy = speed * Math.Sin(angle);
        Brush brush = BubbleBrushes[Rand.Next(0,
          BubbleBrushes.Length)];

        RectangleF rect = new RectangleF(point.X, point.Y, diameter,
          diameter);
        return new Bubble(rect, new PointF((int)vx, (int)vy), brush);
    }

    // Return the distance between the two points.
    private static double Distance(PointF point1, PointF point2)
    {
        float dx = point1.X - point2.X;
        float dy = point1.Y - point2.Y;
        return Math.Sqrt(dx * dx + dy * dy);
    }
}
```

The class begins with a constructor and an overridden Draw method that simply draws the bubble as a filled circle. The rest of the class is used to generate random bubbles. The main program uses the RandomBubble method to create the obstacles that the user must shoot.

The program doesn't have a bullet class. Instead, it simply uses a small white bubble to represent a bullet.

Ship

The following code shows the beginning of the Ship class, which is also derived from the Sprite class:

```
class Ship : Sprite
{
    // The ship's direction in degrees. (Initially right.)
    public float Heading = 0;

    // Points to draw the ship at the origin pointing up.
    private PointF[] Points;

    // Constructor.
    private const float ShipRadius = 10;
    public Ship(Rectangle spaceBounds)
        : base(new RectangleF(
            spaceBounds.X + spaceBounds.Width / 2 - ShipRadius,
            spaceBounds.Y + spaceBounds.Height / 2 - ShipRadius,
```

```
                2 * ShipRadius, 2 * ShipRadius),
                    new PointF(), Brushes.Silver)
    {
        // Define the points used to draw the ship when Heading = 0.
        Points = new PointF[]
        {
            new PointF(-ShipRadius / 2, 0),
            new PointF(-ShipRadius, -ShipRadius),
            new PointF(ShipRadius, 0),
            new PointF(-ShipRadius, ShipRadius),
        };
    }
```

This class inherits its position from the `Sprite` class. It adds a `Heading` value to indicate the direction that the ship is facing.

The `Points` array, which is initialized by the class's constructor, contains a list of points that define the ship's simple shape centered at the origin when its `Heading` is 0 so it is pointing to the right.

The following code shows how a ship draws itself:

```
        // Draw.
        public override void Draw(Graphics gr)
        {
            if (IsDestroyed)
            {
                // Draw an explosion.
                gr.DrawImage(Properties.Resources.boom, Bounds);
            }
            else
            {
                // Draw a normal ship.
                // Transform to rotate and position the ship.
                GraphicsState state = gr.Save();
                gr.RotateTransform(Heading);
                gr.TranslateTransform(
                    Bounds.X + Bounds.Width / 2,
                    Bounds.Y + Bounds.Height / 2,
                    MatrixOrder.Append);
                gr.FillPolygon(Brush, Points);
                gr.Restore(state);
            }
        }
```

The `Draw` method first checks the ship's `IsDestroyed` value. If `IsDestroyed` is `true`, the code draws the `boom` resource at the ship's location to display an explosion graphic.

If `IsDestroyed` is `false`, the code saves the `Graphics` object's current state. It then uses a rotation transformation to rotate the ship for its current heading. It follows the rotation with a translation to move the ship to its correct location on the playing area. The method then draws the ship and restores the `Graphics` object's saved state so the rotation and translation are removed for future drawing commands.

The following code controls the ship's movement:

```
// Accelerate.
public void Accelerate()
{
    const float accceleration = 0.5f;
    double radians = Heading * Math.PI / 180;
    Velocity.X += (float)(accceleration * Math.Cos(radians));
    Velocity.Y += (float)(accceleration * Math.Sin(radians));
}

// Turn left.
private const float TurnDegrees = 6;
public void TurnLeft()
{
    Heading -= TurnDegrees;
}

// Turn right.
public void TurnRight()
{
    Heading += TurnDegrees;
}
```

The `Accelerate` method adds a small amount of acceleration to the ship's velocity, using some trigonometry to make the acceleration point in the direction that the ship is facing. This ship has no brakes and cannot move sideways. If you want to slow down, you need to turn the ship around and accelerate back in the direction opposite of the ship's velocity.

The `TurnLeft` and `TurnRight` methods change the ship's `Heading` by small amounts.

The last part of the Ship class deals with shooting bullets:

```
// Return the position of the ship's nose.
public PointF NosePosition()
{
    PointF center = Bounds.Center();
    double radians = Heading * Math.PI / 180;
    double x = center.X + ShipRadius * Math.Cos(radians);
    double y = center.Y + ShipRadius * Math.Sin(radians);
    return new PointF((int)x, (int)y);
}

// Make a bullet moving out of the ship's nose.
public Bubble MakeBullet()
{
    const int bulletSpeed = 10;
    const int bulletR = 2;
    double radians = Heading * Math.PI / 180;
    PointF velocity = new PointF(
        (int)(bulletSpeed * Math.Cos(radians)),
        (int)(bulletSpeed * Math.Sin(radians)));
    PointF nose = NosePosition();
    RectangleF bulletRect = new RectangleF(
        nose.X - bulletR, nose.Y - bulletR, 2 * bulletR, 2 *
        bulletR);
    return new Bubble(bulletRect, velocity, Brushes.White);
}
}
```

The NosePosition method calculates the position of the ship's nose. The MakeBullet method uses the nose position to create a new small Bubble object to represent a bullet placed at the ship's nose and moving away from the ship.

Keyboard events

One way to handle keyboard events is to set the form's KeyPreview property to true. Then the program can catch the form's KeyDown, KeyUp, and KeyPress events.

Unfortunately, those events have odd behaviors. If you press a key, the program receives a KeyDown event as you would expect. If you hold the key down, there is a small delay and then the program starts quickly receiving many KeyDown events. Generating many events by holding a key down isn't a problem. After all, you might want the ship to continue to accelerate as long as the up arrow is pressed. The trouble is that the events are not evenly spaced in time.

For example, suppose you press the up arrow key to accelerate the ship. The first KeyDown event occurs quickly, so the ship experiences a small acceleration. Next, there is a pause and then the ship receives many accelerations in rapid succession.

To avoid this problem, the example solution takes a different approach to handling keyboard events. Each time the move timer ticks, the Tick event handler calls the following ProcessKeys method to see if the user is currently pressing a key:

```
// Take action of the user has pressed an action key.
private void ProcessKeys()
{
    // Do nothing if the ship has been destroyed.
    if (TheShip.IsDestroyed) return;

    // Require at least 250ms between shots.
    const int msPerShot= 250;

    // Shoot.
    if (Keyboard.IsKeyDown(Key.Space))
    {
        // Make sure the required time has elapsed since the last shot.
        TimeSpan timePassed = DateTime.Now - LastShot;
        if (timePassed.TotalMilliseconds >= msPerShot)
        {
            Shoot();
        }
    }

    // Accelerate.
    if (Keyboard.IsKeyDown(Key.Up))
    {
        TheShip.Accelerate();
    }

    // Turn left.
    if (Keyboard.IsKeyDown(Key.Left))
    {
        TheShip.TurnLeft();
    }

    // Turn right.
    if (Keyboard.IsKeyDown(Key.Right))
    {
        TheShip.TurnRight();
    }
}
```

If the ship has been destroyed, the method returns without doing anything. That prevents the user from being able to control the explosion after the ship has been destroyed.

If the ship has not been destroyed, the method uses the `System.Windows.Input.Keyboard` class's `IsKeyDown` method to see if the spacebar is pressed. If the spacebar is pressed, the code checks that at least 250 milliseconds have passed since the last time the user fired a bullet. If the program doesn't make that check, the user can fire an endless stream of bullets making the game a lot less challenging. If at least 250 milliseconds have passed since the previous shot, the code calls the `Shoot` method to play a sound and calls the ship object's `MakeBullet` method. The `Shoot` method is straightforward so I won't show it here.

You must add references to the `PresentationCore` and `WindowsBase` libraries in order to use the `Keyboard` class and the `Key` enumeration in a Windows Form application. Also note that the `Keyboard` class's `IsKeyDown` method only works in .NET Framework versions 4.0 and later, so be sure your application targets one of the more recent versions.

After it finishes looking for the spacebar, the program similarly looks for the up, left, and right arrow keys. If any of those keys is pressed, the code calls an appropriate ship method to make the ship accelerate or turn.

Other details

The rest of the `SpaceForce` example solution deals with such tasks as adding and removing bubbles and bullets from lists, looping through sprites to make them move and draw themselves, and playing sounds. The code is long but not too complicated. Download the `SpaceForce` example solution to see additional details.

9

Cryptography

This chapter describes problems in cryptography. The first few problems ask you to use cryptographic systems that were once state-of-the-art but that are now insecure. They are purely for fun and are of historical significance. Later problems use modern, secure techniques, such as the .NET Framework's cryptographic library, to build secure programs.

When studying cryptography, it's useful to know a few basic terms. A **key** is a piece of secret information that you can use to encrypt and decrypt messages. Sometimes, a password is a key. Other times, a password is used to generate a key in a format suitable for use by a particular encryption algorithm. A message that is not encrypted is called **plaintext**. The encrypted version of plaintext is called **ciphertext**.

Traditionally, plaintext and ciphertext are written in five-letter groups of uppercase letters without punctuation or spaces, at least for older encryption systems such as the Caesar substitution and Vigenère ciphers. For example, the message, `This is the secret message`, would be written in plaintext as `THISI STHES ECRET MESSA GE`, and might be encrypted as `WKLVL VWKHV HFUHW PHVVD JH`. An **N-gram** is a sequence of *N* contiguous pieces of text or speech, so I call these groups *five-grams*. More modern systems encrypt and decrypt streams of bytes that can contain just about anything, including images, documents, and databases. In those systems, it doesn't make much sense to represent messages in five-grams.

Like most of the other topics covered in this book, cryptography is a huge subject, so this chapter covers only a tiny part of it. For more information, consult a book about cryptography, such as Bruce Schneier's excellent book, *Applied Cryptography*: *Protocols, Algorithms and Source Code in C* (John Wiley & Sons, 2015). You can also search the internet for general information and specific examples. For instance, Wikipedia has an overview at `https://en.wikipedia.org/wiki/Cryptography`, and Khan Academy has a course about cryptography at `https://www.khanacademy.org/computing/computer-science/cryptography`.

Most of the example solutions in this chapter use the .NET Framework's cryptography namespace, so you may want to add the following `using` directive to your code files:

```
using System.Security.Cryptography;
```

Problems

Use the following problems to test your skills at building cryptographic programs. Give each problem a try before you turn to the example solutions for help.

91. Caesar cipher

In a **Caesar cipher**, also called a *Caesar shift*, *Caesar substitution cipher*, or *shift cipher*, you shift the values of the letters in the message by some fixed amount. In the original Caesar cipher, Julius Caesar reportedly used a shift of three to send secret messages to his commanders, so each letter was replaced by the letter that comes three positions later in the alphabet. The letter A was encrypted as D, B was encrypted as E, and so forth. Letters at the end of the alphabet wrap around to the beginning so, for example, X becomes A, Y becomes B, and Z becomes C. In this example, the shift value, 3, was the cipher's key.

Write a program that uses a Caesar cipher to encrypt and decrypt messages. Let the user enter some text and a shift and then click a button to encrypt the message. Let the user then enter a new key and click another button to decrypt the message. Verify that decryption works only when the shift is correct.

To make this easier, write extension methods that encrypt and decrypt strings, strip punctuation and spaces from strings, and break strings into five-grams.

92. Vigenère cipher

The result of a Caesar cipher looks like gibberish, but it's actually quite easy to break a Caesar cipher. Simply try decrypting the message with each of the possible shifts 1 through 26 and look at the results. When the shift is incorrect, the result is still gibberish, but when the shift is correct, the result looks like words, albeit in five-grams without spaces or punctuation.

The Vigenère cipher improves on the Caesar cipher by using multiple interlaced Caesar ciphers. This cipher uses a word as its key. Each letter in the key represents a shift. For example, A represents a shift of 0, B represents a shift of 1, and so forth. The cipher matches letters in the plaintext with letters in the key, repeating the key if necessary. It then uses the key letters' shifts to modify the plaintext letters.

 The Vigenère cipher (Vigenère is roughly pronounced *vision-air*) is named after 17th century French cryptographer Blaise de Vigenère. He didn't invent the cipher, but it was misattributed to him and the name stuck.

Write a program similar to the one you wrote for the preceding problem but this time use a Vigenère cipher to encrypt and decrypt messages.

93. Cryptographic pseudorandom numbers

Several of the solutions in earlier chapters used the Random class to generate *random* numbers. In fact, those numbers are not really random at all. They use easily predictable algorithms to generate sequences of numbers that are random enough to simulate moving bubbles and random walks, but they are not cryptographically secure. Technically that means an attacker who learns some of the numbers in a sequence of *random* values may be able to predict the values that follow with some success. Even a small advantage at prediction may give an attacker a way to break an encryption system based on the random number generator.

To prevent that from happening, you can use a **Cryptographically Secure Pseudorandom Number Generator** (CSPRNG), which is also called a **Cryptographic Pseudorandom Number Generator** (CPRNG).

 Note that even these methods are not *truly* random, so they are still called **pseudorandom techniques**.

For this problem, create a method that uses the .NET cryptographic library to generate long integers between inclusive lower and exclusive upper bounds. (Similar to the way the Random class's Next method generates integers within a range.)

Make the test program generate an indicated number of random values and then display each value's number of occurrences, fraction of occurrences, and error (fraction minus expected fraction of occurrences), as shown in the following screenshot:

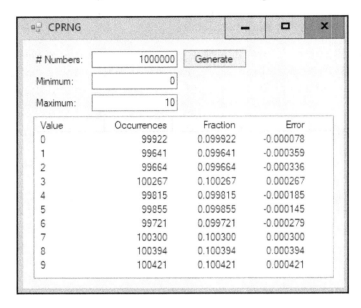

The error values will not be zero, but they should grow smaller when you perform more trials. They should also change relative positions if you click **Generate** repeatedly. For example, if the fraction or error for the value 8 is always greater than the results for the other values, then the values are not uniformly distributed.

94. Primality testing, redux

Some encryption methods, such as RSA (named after the inventors Ron Rivest, Adi Shamir, and Leonard Adleman), rely on large prime numbers. This problem and the next one ask you to find large primes.

Problem *11. Primality testing*, asked you to determine whether a number N was prime. The solution examined values between 2 and the square root of N to see if any of those values divided evenly into N. That approach works well for small numbers, but some cryptographic methods use very large primes.

Checking even a fraction of the values between 2 and the square root of a large number can take much too long to be practical. For example, suppose N has 100 decimal digits. Then its square root has around 50 digits. If you only need to check 10% of the numbers between 2 and the square root, then you still need to examine around 10^{49} values. If your computer can test 1 quadrillion numbers per second, then it would still take more than 10^{30} years to check every number. That's more than 66 billion billion times the current age of the universe.

Fortunately, there are ways that you can test a number to determine whether it is *probably* prime without checking all of those numbers. **Fermat's little theorem** says that, if P is prime and $1 \le N < P$, then $N^{P-1} = 1 \bmod P$. For example, suppose P is 5 and consider the following values:

N	N^{P-1}	N^{P-1} % P
1	$1^4 = 1$	1 % 5 = 1
2	$2^4 = 16$	16 % 5 = 1
3	$3^4 = 81$	81 % 5 = 1
4	$4^4 = 256$	256 % 5 = 1

In all of those cases, $N^{P-1} = 1 \bmod P$.

To see if P is prime, you can pick a number N between 2 and $P - 1$ and calculate $N^{P-1} \bmod P$. If the result is *not* 1, then P is definitely *not* prime or the calculation would violate Fermat's little theorem.

If the result *is* 1, then you don't know whether or not P is prime. P could be prime, or you may have been unlucky and picked a value for N that just happened to satisfy Fermat's little theorem.

 Pierre de Fermat (Fermat is pronounced *fer-mah*) was a 17th century French lawyer and mathematician who made important contributions to such fields as number theory, analytic geometry, and probability theory. One of his most famous theorems is **Fermat's last theorem**, which states that no three positive integers A, B, and C can satisfy the equation $A^N + B^N = C^N$ for any N greater than 2. Fermat proposed the theorem in 1637, but it was only successfully proven 358 years later in 1995 by British mathematician Sir Andrew Wiles.

It can be shown that, if P is *not* prime, then a randomly selected value N will have at least a 50% chance of proving that fact.

To see if *P* is prime, pick *M* random values for *N* and perform the test on them all. If *P* passes all of the tests, then there is at most a $1/2^M$ chance that *P* is not prime. For example, if *M* is 20, then there is at most a $1/2^{20} \approx 0.000001$ chance that *P* is not prime or a 99.9999% chance that *P* is prime.

For this problem, write a program that uses this technique to determine whether a number entered by the user is prime. Perform the number of steps indicated by the user and display the probability that the number is prime. Use the program to verify that 1,000,000,000,039 is probably prime.

Raising a large number to a big power will cause integer overflow. Use the `BigInteger` data type to allow the program to handle big values. You'll need to add a reference to `System.Numerics` to use that type, and you might want to add the `using System.Numerics` directive to your code.

95. Find primes

Use the methods that you used in the previous solution to make a program that looks for primes. Let the user enter a starting value and a desired probability. Make the program search upward from the starting value until it finds a number that is probably prime to the desired level of probability. Use the program to find the smallest prime larger than 1 trillion.

96. Hash files

In computer programming, **hashing** is the process of converting a larger piece of data, such as a string or file, into a shorter code that you can use to identify it. For example, the following value might be the hash for a large file:

```
F6-72-E5-7E-2E-09-6B-1A-9E-CE-9C-DE-F8-AE-13-98
```

Hashing has several uses. For example, you can use hash codes to identify files in a database, to determine whether two files are different, or to decide whether a file has been modified or corrupted since it was hashed.

For this problem, write a program that uses the MD5 hashing algorithm to find a file's hash code.

97. Steganography

Steganography is the process of hiding data inside a file, image, video, or other piece of data. For example, in **watermarking** you hide a copyright statement inside an image to later show that you own the rights to that file.

Write a program that defines `Bitmap` extension methods to perform steganography. The program should let the user load an image, hide a message in it, and save the result in a new image file. It should also be able to load an image and recover a message hidden inside it.

Hide the data in the low-order bits of the image's pixels. You don't need to encrypt the message for this problem; just hide it.

Use a lossless image format such as BMP or PNG. A lossy format such as GIF or JPG will destroy the message.

98. Encrypt and decrypt strings

Write a program similar to the one shown in the following screenshot to encrypt and decrypt strings:

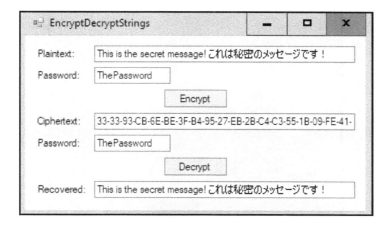

To do that, write an extension method that encrypts a string and returns a byte array. Write a second method that decrypts a byte array and returns the original string. To make it easier to display the values in a byte array, write extension methods that convert between byte arrays and hexadecimal strings.

To make this easier, write a method that encrypts or decrypts a byte array into another byte array. You may also want to create helper methods: `FindKeySize`, `MakeKeyAndIV`, and `MakeCryptoTransform`.

99. Encrypt and decrypt files

Write a program similar to the one shown in the following screenshot to let the user encrypt or decrypt one file into another file:

Enter the original filename, the name of a file to hold the encrypted results, and a password. When you click **Encrypt**, the program should encrypt the original file and save the result in the encrypted file.

Next, enter a decryption password and the name of a recovery file to hold the decrypted data. When you click **Decrypt**, the program should decrypt the encrypted file and save the result in the recovery file.

Make the program show the original file, the encrypted file (only display the first 1,000 bytes), and the decrypted file in separate tabs as shown in the preceding screenshot.

The program should be able to handle any kind of file. In the screenshot, I used an RTF file containing English, Japanese, and an image. Verify that the program cannot decrypt the encrypted file if the decryption password is wrong by even a tiny-amount.

100. CryptoPad

Write a program that lets the user open a file containing encrypted rich text data, edit it, and save it in the same or another encrypted file.

Do not use the methods from the preceding solution because that would require the program to save unencrypted versions of the file on the computer where an attacker might find them, either while the program is running or later, if the program crashes and does not clean up temporary files correctly.

Solutions

The following sections describe solutions to the preceding problems. You can download the example solutions to see additional details and to experiment with the programs at `https://github.com/PacktPublishing/The-Modern-CSharp-Challenge/tree/master/Chapter09`.

91. Caesar cipher

This problem is relatively straightforward. Simply loop through the message's letters and shift them by some amount.

The example solution uses the following string extension method to encrypt a string:

```
// Use a Caesar cipher to encrypt the plaintext.
public static string CaesarEncrypt(this string plaintext, int shift)
{
    plaintext = plaintext.StripText();

    // Encrypt.
    char[] chars = new char[plaintext.Length];
    for (int i = 0; i < plaintext.Length; i++)
    {
        int ch = plaintext[i] - 'A';
        ch = (ch + shift + 26) % 26;
        chars[i] = (char)('A' + ch);
    }
    return new string(chars).ToFiveGrams();
}
```

This method calls the `StripText` extension method described shortly to remove any non-letter characters from the string. It then loops through the message's letters, adding the shift to each and storing the results in a `char` array. When it has finished processing the letters, the method converts the `char` array into a string, calls the `ToFiveGrams` extension method (also described shortly), and returns the result.

The following code shows the `StripText` helper extension method:

```
// Convert to uppercase, and remove punctuation and spaces.
public static string StripText(this string text)
{
    text = text.ToUpper();
    text = new string(text.Where(
        ch => (ch >= 'A') && (ch <= 'Z')).ToArray());
    return text;
}
```

This method converts the message into uppercase. It uses a lambda expression to extract the characters between A and Z, and converts those characters into a new string. That removes any non-letter characters from the string. The method then returns the result.

 Unicode didn't exist back in Caesar's day, so this simple code was not intended to handle Unicode characters and this method doesn't even try. Later problems encrypt and decrypt non-letter characters and even more exotic items such as Unicode strings, formatting codes, and images.

The following code shows the `ToFiveGrams` helper method:

```
// Separate the string into five-character pieces.
public static string ToFiveGrams(this string text)
{
    StringBuilder result = new StringBuilder();
    for (int i = 0; i < text.Length; i += 5)
    {
        int length = Math.Min(5, text.Length - i);
        result.Append(" " + text.Substring(i, length));
    }
    result.Remove(0, 1);
    return result.ToString();
}
```

The code first creates a `StringBuilder` to hold the result. It breaks the text into groups of five characters and adds the groups preceded by a space character to the `StringBuilder`. After it has finished processing the text, the code removes the first space character, converts the rest of the `StringBuilder` contents into a string, and returns the result.

After you write the method to encrypt a string, decrypting a string is easy because decrypting a Caesar cipher message is the same as encrypting it with a negative shift. For example, if you encrypt a plaintext message with the shift 4, then you can decrypt it by encrypting the ciphertext with a shift of -4. The `CaesarDecrypt` method shown in the following code does that:

```
// Use a Caesar cipher to decrypt the ciphertext.
public static string CaesarDecrypt(this string ciphertext, int shift)
{
    return ciphertext.CaesarEncrypt(-shift);
}
```

This method simply calls the `CaesarEncrypt` method described earlier to encrypt the ciphertext with a negative shift value.

Download the `CaesarCipher` example solution to see additional details.

92. Vigenère cipher

The Vigenère cipher is only slightly more complicated than the Caesar cipher. The following method encrypts or decrypts a piece of plaintext and returns the resulting ciphertext:

```
// Use a Vigenere cipher to encrypt plaintext.
private static string VigenereEncryptDecrypt(this string plaintext,
    string key, bool decrypt)
{
    key = key.StripText();
    plaintext = plaintext.StripText();

    // Encrypt.
    char[] chars = new char[plaintext.Length];
    for (int i = 0; i < plaintext.Length; i++)
    {
        int shift = key[i % key.Length] - 'A';
        if (decrypt) shift = -shift;
        int ch = plaintext[i] - 'A';
        ch = (ch + shift + 26) % 26;
        chars[i] = (char)('A' + ch);
    }
    return new string(chars).ToFiveGrams();
}
```

This code calls the `StripText` method to remove non-letter characters as in the preceding solution. It then loops through the plaintext's letters.

For each letter, it uses the modulus operator (%) to get the matching character in the key word and subtracts the letter A from the key letter to get a shift value. If the method is decrypting, it negates the shift value. It then shifts the plaintext letter just as the preceding solution did. The method converts the ciphertext into five-grams and returns the result.

Download the `CaesarCipher` example solution to see additional details.

93. Cryptographic random numbers

This is much more complicated that you might imagine. (In fact, it's surprising that Microsoft didn't add methods to generate values within a range to its cryptographic random number generator so you wouldn't have to.) To understand why this is hard and to learn how to handle the difficulties, take the following discussion slowly. If you find that you're lost, you may want to start over.

The .NET Framework's `RNGCryptoServiceProvider` class generates cryptographic random values. It is fairly easy to use but it has a catch—it only generates bytes. If you want some other kinds of data, such as `double` or `int` that lies between two bounds, then you need to convert the bytes accordingly.

To make the discussion easier, I'll use the notation `[A, B)` to mean the range of numbers between A and B, including the A value (the `[` means include the end value) and not including the B value (the `)` means exclude the end value). I'll also work through a very simplified example that uses numbers that are much smaller than those typically used by real random number generators.

One simple method for generating numbers within a range is to generate a random number and then take that number mod the number of values that you want to generate. For example, suppose your random number generator creates numbers in the range [0, 9] and you want to pick a value in [0, 7]. Now suppose your random number generator gives you 5. The value *5 % 8 = 5*, so 5 is the number that you use. I'm using 8 as the modulus because we want one of eight values between 0 and 7 inclusive. Taking the result mod 8 ensures that the result lies between 0 and 7. So far so good.

Next, suppose the generator produces 9. In that case, *9 % 8 = 2*, so 2 is the number that you would use.

This method is easy to calculate, but it also has a big problem—the resulting values are not evenly distributed. In this example, there's only one way you can generate a 7, namely the generator produces 7. However, there two ways that you can generate the value 0—when the generator produces 0 or 8. That means you're twice as likely to end up with 0 as 7.

The following table shows all of the possible results created by the generator and the final numbers that they produce:

Generated	0	1	2	3	4	5	6	7	8	9
Result	0	1	2	3	4	5	6	7	0	1

You can see in the table that the results 0 and 1 appear twice while the other results appear only once.

Real random number generators produce much larger numbers, so the problem isn't as large. For example, if the random number generator produces values between 0 and 99 and we still map them into the range [0, 7], then there are 13 ways to produce some numbers. For example, you will get a result of 0 if the generator produces 0, 8, 16, 24, 32, 40, 48, 56, 64, 72, 80, 88, or 96. However, there are only 12 ways to get some other values. For example, you get the value 7 if the generator produces one of the values 7, 15, 23, 31, 39, 47, 55, 63, 71, 79, 87, or 95. That's a lot better than producing some values twice as often as others, but it's still a problem, particularly for a CRNG.

The goal of a CRNG is to ensure that an attacker cannot guess the next number in a sequence with even a slightly better than random chance of success.

One way to fix this problem is to discard any values that appear at the end of the range of generated values. To see how that works, let's go back to the example where you need to pick a value in [0, 7] and the generator produces values in [0, 9]. In that case, you simply discard any generated value larger than 7 and try again. You may need to try more than once to pick a number, but you probably won't need more than a few tries.

The following table shows the new results:

Generated	0	1	2	3	4	5	6	7	8	9
Result	0	1	2	3	4	5	6	7	Retry	Retry

The case where the generator produces values in [0, 99] is similar; you just discard any value above 95.

There's one more technique that you need to use to generate values within a range if the lower bound is not zero. In that case, subtract the upper limit from the lower limit to see how many values you need to consider. Pick a random number between zero and the number of values that you need, and add the result to the lower bound.

I know this is confusing, so let's look at an example. Suppose you want to pick a value in [10, 17]. That range includes eight values, so use the previous method to pick a value in the range [0, 7], which also holds eight values. Then add the result to the lower bound 10 to get the final number in the range [10, 17].

The following code shows how the example solution implements this technique to pick a random number in the range `[minValue, maxValue)`. Notice that the range does *not* include the upper limit, `maxValue`. That makes the method more consistent with the `Random` class's `Next` method and makes the math slightly easier:

```
// Generate a cryptographically secure long in [minValue, maxValue).
public static long NextLong(long minValue, long maxValue)
```

```
{
    // The biggest value we can create with 16 bytes.
    BigInteger biggest = BigInteger.Pow(2, 8 * 16) - 1;

    // Calculate the number of values in [maxValue, minValue).
    long numValues = maxValue - minValue;

    // The amount of unused space at the end of the biggest range.
    BigInteger numUnused = (biggest + 1) % numValues;

    // The largest usable value.
    BigInteger maxUsable = biggest - numUnused;

    // Generate random BigIntegers until we get one between
    // 0 and maxUsable.
    byte[] bytes = new byte[16];
    for (;;)
    {
        // Get a random BigInteger.
        BigInteger rand = RandomUBigInteger(16);

        // If the value is within the allowed range, use it.
        if (rand <= maxUsable)
            return (long)(minValue + (rand % numValues));
    }
}
```

In order to produce long integer values, the method must use a larger data type than `long` to perform its calculations. (You can't generate numbers in [0, 7] if the random number generator only produces values in [0, 5].) You might like to use the `double` data type, but it doesn't have enough resolution to represent all `long` values. For example, consider the following statement and result from Visual Studio's Immediate Window:

```
(long)(double)1234567890123456789
1234567890123456768
```

The value lost precision when it was stored in a `double`, so when it was turned back into a `long`, the last two digits were modified. Fortunately, the .NET Framework has a data type that can hold very large values and that has perfect integer precision—`BigInteger`.

To use the `BigInteger` data type, give your program a reference to the `System.Numerics` library. You may also want to add the following `using` directive to your code:

```
using System.Numerics;
```

The method sets the `biggest` variable to the largest value that it might generate. This is analogous to the value 9 in the example that generated numbers in [0, 9] and then converted them into the range [0, 7]. This example will use 16-byte values, so those values use 16 * 8 bits. The largest value that you can represent in 16 bytes is $2^{16*8} - 1$ when every bit is 1. (That's big enough to hold any `long` value because the `long` data type also uses 16 bytes.)

Next, the method calculates the number of values in the desired range. For example, if the range is [10, 17), then the number of values is 7.

The code then calculates the number of generated values in the range [0, biggest] that will be *unused*. Those are the values for which the method must try again. Earlier, when we wanted a value in [0, 7], if the random number generator produced 9, we tried again. In that example, `biggest` was 9 (the generator produced values in [0, 9]) and `numValues` was 8 (we wanted numbers in [0, 7]), so `numUnused` would be (9 + 1) % 8 = 2. That means we ignore the two largest values if we generate them. If you look back at the earlier table, you'll see that we retried if we generated the two largest values 8 or 9.

Next, the code uses `numUnused` to calculate the largest value that the method *will* use. For the previous example, `numUnused` is 2 and `biggest` is 9, so the largest usable value is 9 – 2 = 7, which matches the preceding table.

With all that set up, the method is finally ready to pick a number. It creates a `byte` array to hold 16 bytes and then enters an infinite loop.

Inside the loop, the code calls the `RandomUBigInteger` method described shortly to generate a `BigInteger` defined by 16 cryptographically secure random bytes. If the value is less than or equal to the largest usable value, the method adds it to `minValue` and returns the result. If the value is bigger than the largest usable value, the method continues its loop and tries again.

The following code shows the `RandomUBigInteger` method:

```
// A cryptographic pseudorandom number provider.
private static RNGCryptoServiceProvider
    Cprng = new RNGCryptoServiceProvider();

// Return a cryptographically secure random unsigned BigInteger
// with the indicated number of bytes.
private static BigInteger RandomUBigInteger(int numBytes)
{
    // Get the random bytes.
    byte[] bytes = new byte[numBytes];
    Cprng.GetBytes(bytes);
```

```
        // Convert the bytes into an unsigned value;
        BigInteger result = 0;
        BigInteger factor = 1;
        for (int i = 0; i < numBytes; i++)
        {
            result += factor * bytes[i];
            factor *= 256;
        }
        return result;
    }
```

The code creates a static CPRNG named `Cprng` at the class level so it is available inside all of the class's methods.

The `RandomUBigInteger` method creates an array big enough to hold the desired number of bytes and then calls the `Cprng` object's `GetBytes` method to fill the array with random bytes.

The method then uses the bytes to create a result by multiplying the values of the bytes by powers of 256. This is similar to the way that you calculate the value of a decimal number. For example, the decimal value 1729 is $9 * 10^0 + 2 * 10^1 + 7 * 10^2 + 1 * 10^3$. Similarly the bytes create the value $byte0 * 256^0 + byte1 * 256^1 + byte2 * 256^2 + ... + byteN * 256^N$.

After it finishes processing the bytes, the method returns the resulting `BigInteger`.

That ends the most interesting pieces of the example solution. The rest of the program's code performs such chores as displaying the counts, fractions, and errors. Download the CPRNG example solution to see additional details.

94. Primality testing, redux

The following method uses Fermat's little theorem to determine the maximum probability that a number is prime:

```
// Used to pick random N.
private static Random Rand = new Random();

// Return the probability that the number is prime.
public static double ProbabilityIsPrime(this BigInteger p, int
numTests)
{
    // Calculate the largest value we should generate randomly.
    int maxValue = int.MaxValue;
    if (p - 1 < maxValue) maxValue = (int)(p - 1);
    for (int test = 0; test < numTests; test++)
```

```
    {
        int n = Rand.Next(2, maxValue);
        if (BigInteger.ModPow(n, p - 1, p) != 1) return 0;
    }

    // Probably prime.
    return 1.0 - 1.0 / Math.Pow(2, numTests);
}
```

This code declares a Random object at the class level so methods in the class can use it.

The ProbabilityIsPrime method first sets maxValue to the largest value that it will use for *N* in Fermat's little theorem. Ideally that number would be p - 1, but in this method the p parameter is a BigInteger, so p - 1 might not fit in an integer. The Random class that the method uses to generate random numbers returns int values, so maxValue can be at most the largest int value.

Next, the method loops through the desired number of tests, generates a random n, and calculates n^{p-1} % p.

The BigInteger class's ModPow method calculates a number n raised to a power p - 1 in some modulus p. It uses special techniques to perform the calculation efficiently and is impressively fast even for large numbers.

If the result of any of those calculations is *not* 1, then we know that the number is *not* prime, so the method returns 0 to indicate that there is zero probability that the number is prime.

If all of the calculated values equal 1, then there is at most a $1/2^{numTests}$ probability that the number is actually composite (non-prime). The method subtracts that probability from 1 to get the probability that the number *is* prime and returns the result.

The following code shows how the program uses the ProbabilityIsPrime extension method to display a number's probability of being prime:

```
// Determine the probability that the number is prime.
private void testButton_Click(object sender, EventArgs e)
{
    BigInteger p = BigInteger.Parse(numberTextBox.Text);
    int numTests = int.Parse(numTestsTextBox.Text);
    probPrimeTextBox.Text = p.ProbabilityIsPrime(numTests).ToString();
}
```

This code gets the number that you want to test and the number of tests that you want to run. It then simply calls the `ProbabilityIsPrime` method and displays the result.

Download the `PrimalityTesting` example solution to see additional details.

95. Find primes

The preceding example solution makes this one relatively simple. To find a prime number larger than a given starting number, the program simply considers increasingly large numbers until it finds one that is probably prime. The following `FindNextPrime` method does just that:

```
// Find a prime at least as large a startNumber and with at least the
// given probability of being prime.
// Return the number, probability, and number of tests performed.
public static BigInteger FindNextPrime(this BigInteger startNumber,
    double desiredProb, out double primeProb, out int numTests)
{
    // Make sure the start number is odd.
    if ((startNumber != 2) && (startNumber % 2 == 0)) startNumber++;

    // Calculate the number of tests we need to run to achieve the
    // desired probability.
    numTests = (int)Math.Log(1.0 / (1.0 - desiredProb), 2) + 1;

    // Test values until we find a prime.
    for (BigInteger p = startNumber; ; p += 2)
    {
        primeProb = p.ProbabilityIsPrime(numTests);
        if (primeProb > 0.1) return p;
    }
}
```

The method first ensures that the number is either 2 or odd. If the number is 2, then it is prime. If the number is even and not 2, the code makes the number odd because no even numbers other than 2 are prime.

Next, the code calculates the number of tests that it must make to ensure the desired probability. The code then enters a loop that begins at `startNumber` and considers increasingly large numbers. It calls `ProbabilityIsPrime` for each number and returns that number if it is probably prime.

The `FindPrimes` example solution shows that the next prime larger than 1 trillion is 1,000,000,000,039. Download the example solution to see additional details.

96. Hash files

Hashing a file is relatively easy in C#. The following `CalculateMD5` method calculates an MD5 hash code for a file:

```
// Return a file's MD5 hash.
public static string CalculateMD5(string filename)
{
    // Make an MD5 hashing object.
    using (MD5 md5 = MD5.Create())
    {
        // Open the file and pass the stream into the MD5 object.
        using (FileStream stream = File.OpenRead(filename))
        {
            byte[] hash = md5.ComputeHash(stream);
            return BitConverter.ToString(hash);
        }
    }
}
```

This method first creates an `MD5` object.

 The `MD5` class is one of several .NET Framework classes that represent hashing algorithms. Other hashing classes work with different hashing algorithms such as MD160, SHA1, SHA256, SHA384, SHA512, HMAC, and HMACtripleDES. You can use any of the hashing algorithms as long as you use the same algorithm when you hash a file and later validate its hash code.

The code then opens a stream to the file that you want to hash. It calls the `MD5` object's `ComputeHash` method, passing it the file stream. The result is a byte array. The method finishes by using `BitConverter.ToString` to convert the array into a string with a format similar to `F6-72-E5-7E-2E-09-6B-1A-9E-CE-9C-DE-F8-AE-13-98` and returns that as its result.

Download the `HashFiles` example solution to see additional details.

97. Steganography

Hiding data in an image's least significant bits and then later recovering the data is simple in principle, but it's complicated by the way images store pixel values. A typical 32-bit color image uses 8 bits to store each of a pixel's red, green, blue, and alpha (transparency) color components. We won't use the alpha component because that might cause a noticeable change when parts of the image become slightly transparent. That means we can store three bits of data per pixel.

Unfortunately, data is usually stored in bytes, so a byte of data might start in one pixel and end partway through another pixel.

An alternative storage strategy would be to use three pixels (giving nine bits) to store each 8-bit byte and just ignore the extra unused bit in each group of three pixels. Even that is complicated, however, because a byte might start in one row of pixels and end in the next row.

As long as things are going to be somewhat complicated anyway, I'm going to use every pixel instead of the three-pixels-per-byte strategy.

This isn't really a matter of trying to squeeze every last bit of data out of the image. That may be a concern for some very large messages, but images can store a surprisingly large amount of data. For example, a small 300 × 300 pixel image can hold 300 × 300 × 3 / 8 bytes or roughly 33 KB of data. A larger 1,024 × 1,024 pixel image can hold more than a third of a megabyte of data.

It's actually pretty remarkable how much data you can store in an image without it being obvious. I've written other programs that store the four high-order bits of one image in the four low-order bits of another image and the result still looks good.

The general approach is to write a method that stores one bit of information in one of a pixel's red, green, or blue components. We then write another method that uses the first one to save a byte of data. Next, we write a method that uses the byte method to save an array of bytes. Finally, we write a method that uses the byte array method to store a string or other piece of data. To make it all work, each of the methods must keep track of the row, column, and color component of the pixel that we are using to hold data, so later calls to the methods know where to place future data.

The following code shows the example solution's bit-level method:

```
// The component where a bit should be stored.
private enum RGB { R, G, B }

// Hide a single bit in the image.
// The bit parameter should be true to set the bit, false to clear it.
private static void StegBit(Bitmap bm, bool bit,
    ref int x, ref int y, ref RGB component)
{
    Color color = bm.GetPixel(x, y);
    byte r = color.R;
    byte g = color.G;
    byte b = color.B;
    byte a = color.A;
    if (component == RGB.R)
    {
        if (bit) r |= 0b00000001;
        else r &= 0b11111110;
        color = Color.FromArgb(a, r, g, b);
        bm.SetPixel(x, y, color);
        component = RGB.G;
    }
    else if (component == RGB.G)
    {
        if (bit) g |= 0b00000001;
        else g &= 0b11111110;
        color = Color.FromArgb(a, r, g, b);
        bm.SetPixel(x, y, color);
        component = RGB.B;
    }
    else
    {
        if (bit) b |= 0b00000001;
        else b &= 0b11111110;
        color = Color.FromArgb(a, r, g, b);
        bm.SetPixel(x, y, color);
        component = RGB.R;
        if (++x >= bm.Width)
        {
            // Move to the next row.
            x = 0;
            y++;
        }
    }
}
```

The RGB enumeration indicates a red, green, or blue color component. The StegBit method takes as parameters the bitmap where we are storing data, whether the bit should be set or cleared, the pixel's *X* and *Y* location, and the color component to use. Notice that the x, y, and component parameters are passed by reference so the method can update them.

The code first gets the color components of the pixel at position (x, y). It then takes similar actions for each of the possible color components. If the bit should be set, the code uses the OR operator (|) to combine the component's current value with the binary mask 00000001. That sets the least significant bit to 1 and leaves the other bits unchanged.

If the bit should be cleared, the code uses the AND operator (&) to combine the component's current value with the binary mask 11111110. That sets the least significant bit to 0 and leaves the other bits unchanged.

After calculating the new color component, the code updates the pixel's color value. Next, if the code is storing information in the pixel's red or green color component, the code advances the component property to the next color component so the next bit of data will be stored in that component.

If the method is using the blue component, the code increments x to move to the next pixel in the row. If this was the last pixel in the row, the code resets x to 0 and increments y to move to the beginning of the next rows of pixels.

From here, things get easier. The following code shows the example solution's byte-level method:

```
// Hide a byte in the image.
private static void StegByte(Bitmap bm, byte aByte,
    ref int x, ref int y, ref RGB component)
{
    byte mask = 0b00000001;
    for (int i = 0; i < 8; i++)
    {
        bool setBit = (aByte & mask) != 0;
        StegBit(bm, setBit, ref x, ref y, ref component);
        mask <<= 1;
    }
}
```

This method loops through a byte's bits. It uses a mask to figure out whether each bit should be set and calls the earlier StegBit method to set or clear the next bit in the image.

The following code shows the example solution's byte array-level method:

```
// Hide an array of bytes in the image.
private static void StegBytes(Bitmap bm, byte[] bytes,
    ref int x, ref int y, ref RGB component)
{
    foreach (byte aByte in bytes)
        StegByte(bm, aByte, ref x, ref y, ref component);
}
```

This method simply loops through the bytes in the array and calls the earlier StegByte method to store each byte in the image.

Finally, the following method stores a string in an image:

```
// Return a copy of the bitmap with data embedded in it.
public static Bitmap StegMessage(this Bitmap bm, string message)
{
    // Make sure the image is big enough.
    byte[] messageBytes = Encoding.Unicode.GetBytes(message);
    int numMessageBytes = messageBytes.Length;
    byte[] lengthBytes = BitConverter.GetBytes(numMessageBytes);
    int numLengthBytes = lengthBytes.Length;
    int numMessageBits = 8 * (numMessageBytes + numLengthBytes);
    int numAvailableBits = 3 * bm.Width * bm.Height;
    if (numMessageBits > numAvailableBits)
        throw new IndexOutOfRangeException(
            "The message is too big to fit in the image.\n" +
            $"The message is {numMessageBits} bits long but " +
            $"the image can hold only {numAvailableBits} bits.");

    // Hide the message length.
    Bitmap bmCopy = new Bitmap(bm);
    int x = 0, y = 0;
    RGB component = RGB.R;
    StegBytes(bmCopy, lengthBytes, ref x, ref y, ref component);

    // Hide the message bytes.
    StegBytes(bmCopy, messageBytes, ref x, ref y, ref component);

    // Return the bitmap.
    return bmCopy;
}
```

When we later want to decode the data, we need to know how long the message is so we know how many bits to pull out of the image. This method solves that problem by first storing the length of the message in the data.

The method begins by converting the message string into an array of bytes. The code uses Unicode encoding, so it can store Unicode messages. After converting the string into an array, the code gets the array's length.

Next, the code uses the `BitConverter.GetBytes` method to convert the message's length into an array of bytes. It also gets that arrays' length. The code then calculates the number of bits needed to store the message together with its length, and the number of bits that are available in the image. If there isn't enough storage space, the method throws an exception.

The rest of the method is fairly straightforward. It makes a copy of the bitmap and then uses the `StegBytes` method to store the length of the message in the image. It then uses `StegBytes` again to store the message's bytes and returns the new bitmap.

The example solution's decoding methods undo the steps performed by the encoding methods in reverse order. They're reasonably straightforward if you understand how the encoding methods work, so I won't show them here. You may want to try to write them yourself before you download the example solution.

The example solution includes code to load and save image files. It also includes some code to prevent you from closing the program without saving a newly encoded image. (Because I kept doing that accidentally during testing.)

 This example stores a Unicode message, but the `StegBytes` method just stores an arbitrary array of bytes so it can store just about anything. For example, you could encrypt a message and then store the encrypted version in an image. Then someone else cannot read your message, even if they suspect it is there. Just remember that all data is destroyed if you save the image in a lossy format such as JPG of GIF.

Download the `Steganography` example solution to see additional details.

98. Encrypt and decrypt strings

Before you can use the .NET Framework's cryptography tools to encrypt and decrypt strings (or files, arrays of bytes, or just about anything else), you need to perform some setup. The following method creates an `ICryptoTransform` object that you can use to encrypt or decrypt data:

```
// Prepare a cryptographic transformation for this password
// and SymmetricAlgorithm.
private static ICryptoTransform MakeCryptoTransform(
    string password, bool doEncryption, SymmetricAlgorithm
cryptoProvider)
{
    // Find a valid key size for this provider.
    int numKeyBits = FindKeySize(cryptoProvider);
    Console.WriteLine($"Key size: {numKeyBits} bits");

    // Get the block size for this provider.
    int blockSizeBits = cryptoProvider.BlockSize;

    // Generate the key and IV.
    byte[] key = null;
    byte[] iv = null;
    byte[] salt = { 0x03, 0x07, 0x11, 0x22, 0xAB, 0xCD, 0x1F,
        0xF1, 0xF1, 0x00, 0xA4, 0x6B, 0xC4, 0x99 };
    MakeKeyAndIV(password, salt, numKeyBits, blockSizeBits,
        out key, out iv);

    // Make the AES encryptor or decryptor.
    ICryptoTransform cryptoTransform;
    if (doEncryption)
        cryptoTransform = cryptoProvider.CreateEncryptor(key, iv);
    else
        cryptoTransform = cryptoProvider.CreateDecryptor(key, iv);
    return cryptoTransform;
}
```

This method takes as parameters a password, a flag indicating whether you want to encrypt or decrypt, and a `SymmetricAlgorithm` provider object. You'll see how the last one works later when I show you how to use this method.

The code first needs to find an appropriate **key size** for the cryptographic provider that it will use. The key sizes that you can use depend on your version of Windows, and that depends on the country where you bought Windows. For example, the US government may allow Windows to use a 256-bit key in the United States but a shorter, less secure key size in some other countries. The `FindKeySize` method described shortly returns a key size that the algorithm can use.

Next, the program must create a **key** and **initialization vector** (**IV**) to initialize the algorithm. The key is sort of like the password after it has been processed. The IV is an array of bytes that determines the encryption algorithm's initial internal state. The algorithm uses both of those to initialize itself.

The `MakeKeyAndIV` method described shortly creates a key and IV. Most of its parameters are straightforward. The most confusing is the salt.

A **salt** is an array of *random* values that you pick to make it harder for an attacker to build a dictionary of possible passwords. If different programs use different salts, then the attacker cannot use a single dictionary to try to attack them all. You should pick a different salt for your programs. In particular, do not use the one shown here. (Of course, if one program needs to decrypt messages produced by another program, then they need to use the same salt.)

Next, the code calls the cryptographic service provider's `CreateEncryptor` or `CreateDecryptor` method to create the object that will actually encrypt or decrypt messages. Finally, the method returns the resulting transform object.

The following code shows the `FindKeySize` helper method:

```
// Find a valid key size for this algorithm.
private static int FindKeySize(SymmetricAlgorithm algorithm)
{
    for (int i = 1024; i > 1; i--)
    {
        if (algorithm.ValidKeySize(i)) return i;
    }
    throw new InvalidOperationException(
        $"Cannot find a valid key size for
            {algorithm.GetType().Name}.");
}
```

This method loops through possible key sizes starting at 1,024 bits and moving through smaller sizes. It uses the cryptographic provider's `ValidKeySize` method to check each potential key size and returns that size if the method returns `true`.

If the method cannot find a valid key size, it throws an exception.

The following code shows the `MakeKeyandIV` method:

```
// Use a password to make a key and IV.
private static void MakeKeyAndIV(string password, byte[] salt,
    int keySizeBits, int blockSizeBits, out byte[] key, out byte[] iv)
{
    Rfc2898DeriveBytes deriveBytes =
        new Rfc2898DeriveBytes(password, salt, 1000);
    key = deriveBytes.GetBytes(keySizeBits / 8);
    iv = deriveBytes.GetBytes(blockSizeBits / 8);
}
```

This method creates an `Rfc2898DeriveBytes` object. That object is sort of like a CPRNG that initializes itself from a password and salt that you pass into its constructor. The final parameter to the constructor is the number of times that the constructor should run its algorithm (which for this object is the HMACSHA1 algorithm) before generating the key and IV.

Microsoft recommends that you set the iteration count to at least 1,000, at least partly to make the operation take longer. (See the *Remarks* section at `https://docs.microsoft.com/dotnet/api/system.security.cryptography.rfc2898derivebytes.iterationcount`.) If an attacker wants to break your code by trying random passwords, this makes each attempt take longer. Most programs only need to create an `Rfc2898DeriveBytes` object once, so it doesn't hurt you too much to use a large iteration count.

After creating the `Rfc2898DeriveBytes` object, the method calls its `GetBytes` method twice to get the necessary number of bytes for the key and IV.

At this point, you're ready to use the `MakeCryptoTransform` method to encrypt or decrypt strings. The following extension method encrypts or decrypts an array of bytes:

```
// Encrypt or decrypt a byte[].
private static byte[] EncryptDecryptBytes(string password,
    byte[] inputBytes, bool doEncryption)
{
    try
    {
        // Make the encryptor or decryptor.
        ICryptoTransform cryptoTransform = MakeCryptoTransform(
            password, doEncryption, new AesCryptoServiceProvider());

        // Make the output stream.
        using (MemoryStream outputStream = new MemoryStream())
        {
            // Attach a CryptoStream.
            using (CryptoStream cryptoStream = new CryptoStream(
```

```
                    outputStream, cryptoTransform, CryptoStreamMode.Write))
            {
                // Write the bytes into the CryptoStream.
                cryptoStream.Write(inputBytes, 0, inputBytes.Length);
                cryptoStream.FlushFinalBlock();
                return outputStream.ToArray();
            }
        }
    }
    catch (CryptographicException ex)
    {
        // The password is incorrect.
        throw new CryptographicException("Invalid password.", ex);
    }
    catch
    {
        // Re-throw.
        throw;
    }
}
```

This method calls the `MakeCryptoTransform` method to create an `ICryptoTransform` object. That object only works with streams, so the program creates a `MemoryStream` to hold the encrypted output. It then makes a `CryptoStream` associated with the output stream and the `ICryptoTransform` object.

The code then writes the message bytes into the `CryptoStream`. That stream automatically uses the `ICryptoTransform` object to encrypt the message and writes the result into the output stream.

The method then returns the resulting output stream converted into an array of bytes.

Note that the whole method is enclosed in a `try-catch` block. When a cryptographic object fails, it is usually because the program tried to decrypt a message with the wrong password. Unfortunately in that case, the exception usually doesn't tell you that the password was wrong. Instead, it gives you some other cryptic message (no pun intended) that isn't very helpful. This method catches those kinds of exceptions and raises a new one that makes more sense.

Now you can use the `EncryptDecryptBytes` method to encrypt or decrypt strings. The following method encrypts a string:

```
// Encrypt a string into a byte[].
public static byte[] Encrypt(this string plaintext, string password)
{
    byte[] plainbytes = Encoding.Unicode.GetBytes(plaintext);
    return EncryptDecryptBytes(password, plainbytes, true);
}
```

This code converts a Unicode string into a byte array, calls `EncryptDecryptBytes` to encrypt the array, and returns the result.

The following method decrypts a string:

```
// Decrypt a string from a byte[].
public static string Decrypt(this byte[] cipherbytes, string password)
{
    byte[] plainbytes = EncryptDecryptBytes(password, cipherbytes,
     false);
    return Encoding.Unicode.GetString(plainbytes);
}
```

This method calls `EncryptDecryptBytes` to decrypt the encrypted array, converts the resulting bytes into a Unicode string, and returns the result.

Those methods encrypt a string into a byte array and decrypt a byte array into a string. The example solution also displays the encrypted bytes as a string with a format similar to 33-33-93-CB-6E-BE-3F-B4-95-27-EB-2B-C4-... The following method converts a byte array into that kind of string:

```
// Convert a byte[] into hexadecimal values.
public static string BytesToHex(this byte[] bytes)
{
    return BitConverter.ToString(bytes, 0);
}
```

This method simply calls `BitConverter.ToString` to convert the array into a string representation. The last parameter 0 tells the method to start at byte 0 in the array.

Unfortunately, the `BitConverter` class does not have a simple method to convert back from a string representation to a byte array. The following method makes that conversion:

```
// Convert two-digit hexadecimal values into a byte[].
public static byte[] HexToBytes(this string hexString)
{
    // Separate the bytes.
```

```
        char separator = hexString[2];
        string[] hexPairs = hexString.Split(separator);

        // Allocate the array.
        int numBytes = hexPairs.Length;
        byte[] bytes = new byte[numBytes];

        // Parse the pairs.
        for (int i = 0; i < numBytes; i++)
            bytes[i] = Convert.ToByte(hexPairs[i], 16);
        return bytes;
    }
```

This method assumes that the string's third character is a separator such as – or a space. It uses the separator to split the string into pieces, each of which holds two hexadecimal digits that represent a single byte. The code allocates a byte array large enough to hold the bytes and then loops through the values converting the pieces into bytes.

The rest of the example solution uses the methods described earlier to encrypt and decrypt strings. Download the `EncryptDecryptStrings` example solution to see additional details.

99. Encrypt and decrypt files

You could adapt the techniques for encrypting strings from the preceding solution to encrypt files. You would simply use `File.ReadAllBytes` to read a file into a byte array, call the `EncryptDecryptBytes` method to encrypt or decrypt the bytes, and then use `File.WriteAllBytes` to save the results into the output file.

That method would work reasonably well for small files, but holding the file's bytes in memory could be a problem for very large files. Fortunately, there's a better approach.

The encryption methods read and write data through streams. If you use the same setup methods used by the preceding solution, then you can use file streams to easily encrypt and decrypt files. The following code shows the `CryptFile` method that encrypts or decrypts files:

```
        // Encrypt or decrypt a file into another file.
        private static void CryptFile(string password, string inputFilename,
            string outputFilename, bool doEncryption)
        {
            try
            {
                // Make the encryptor or decryptor.
```

```
            ICryptoTransform cryptoTransform = MakeCryptoTransform(
                password, doEncryption, new AesCryptoServiceProvider());

            // Make streams for the input and output files.
            using (FileStream inputStream = new FileStream(inputFilename,
                FileMode.Open, FileAccess.Read))
            {
                using (FileStream outputStream = new FileStream(
                    outputFilename, FileMode.Create, FileAccess.Write))
                {
                    // Attach a CryptoStream.
                    using (CryptoStream cryptoStream = new CryptoStream(
                        outputStream, cryptoTransform,
                        CryptoStreamMode.Write))
                    {
                        // Read and write in blocks.
                        const int readingBlockSize = 16 * 1024;
                        byte[] buffer = new byte[readingBlockSize];
                        while (true)
                        {
                            int numBytesRead = inputStream.Read(
                                buffer, 0, readingBlockSize);
                            if (numBytesRead == 0) break;

                            // Write the bytes into the CryptoStream.
                            cryptoStream.Write(buffer, 0, numBytesRead);
                        }
                        cryptoStream.FlushFinalBlock();
                    }
                }
            }
        }
        catch (CryptographicException ex)
        {
            // The password is incorrect.
            throw new CryptographicException("Invalid password.", ex);
        }
        catch
        {
            // Re-throw.
            throw;
        }
    }
```

The method encloses all of its code in a try...catch block in case it is trying to decrypt a
file with the wrong password. Inside the block, the code uses the MakeCryptoTransform
method used by the preceding solution to prepare a cryptographic transform.

Next, the code creates an input file stream to read the input file and an output file stream to write the output file. It then makes a `CryptoStream` object that attaches the cryptographic transform to the output stream.

The method then enters a loop that processes the input file in blocks. Each time through the loop, the code reads a block. If the read returns no bytes, then the program has finished reading the input file so it breaks out of its loop. If the read returns some bytes, the method writes those bytes into the `CryptoStream`, which automatically encrypts or decrypts the bytes and writes the results into the output stream. After the loop ends, the code calls the `CryptoStream` object's `FlushFinalBlock` method to flush any pending data into the output stream.

The following two methods use the `CryptFile` method to encrypt and decrypt files:

```
// Encrypt a file into another file.
public static void EncryptFile(string password,
    string plainFilename, string cipherFilename)
{
    CryptFile(password, plainFilename, cipherFilename, true);
}

// Decrypt a file into another file.
public static void DecryptFile(string password,
    string cipherFilename, string plainFilename)
{
    CryptFile(password, cipherFilename, plainFilename, false);
}
```

These methods simply call `CryptFile`, passing it the appropriate parameters.

The rest of the example solution's code allows you to open a file, encrypt it into a new file, and decrypt an encrypted file. It also displays the original, encrypted, and recovered files. Download the `EncryptDecryptFiles` example solution to see additional details.

100. CryptoPad

This program could use the techniques used by the preceding solution to save data in an encrypted format. When you wanted to load a file, the program would decrypt it into a temporary file, load that file, and then delete the temporary file. When you wanted to save data, the program would write the data into an unencrypted temporary file, encrypt it, and then delete the temporary file.

That method would work, but using unencrypted temporary files is risky. An attacker might be able to grab the temporary file before the program can delete it. Even worse, if the program happens to crash at the wrong moment, the temporary file might not be deleted.

Another, safer approach is to encrypt data directly between the program and the encrypted file so the decrypted file is never stored on the computer's hard drive.

The CryptoPad example solution uses a RichTextBox to allow you to edit Rich Text. The program is not a full text editor, however, so it does not provide tools that let you indent text, make bulleted and numbered lists, change fonts, and perform other text editing tasks. You can add those tools if you like. The program does, however, allow you to copy and paste formatted code and even images into its RichTextBox control, so you can still test it with complex data.

The RichTextBox control's Rtf property returns the control's contents as a string containing formatting codes. To save its data, the program encrypts that RTF string directly into a file. To load an encrypted file, the program decrypts the file directly into an RTF string and sets the RichTextBox control's Rtf property to the result.

The following method encrypts string data into a file:

```
// Encrypt a string and save the results in a file.
public static void EncryptIntoFile(this string plaintext,
    string password, string cipherFilename)
{
    try
    {
        // Make the encryptor.
        ICryptoTransform cryptoTransform = MakeCryptoTransform(
            password, true, new AesCryptoServiceProvider());

        // Make streams for the input text and output file.
        byte[] plainbytes = Encoding.Unicode.GetBytes(plaintext);
        using (MemoryStream inputStream = new MemoryStream(plainbytes))
        {
            using (FileStream outputStream = new FileStream(
                cipherFilename, FileMode.Create, FileAccess.Write))
            {
                // Attach a CryptoStream.
                using (CryptoStream cryptoStream = new CryptoStream(
                    outputStream, cryptoTransform,
                    CryptoStreamMode.Write))
                {
                    // Read and write in blocks.
                    const int readingBlockSize = 16 * 1024;
                    byte[] buffer = new byte[readingBlockSize];
```

```
                        while (true)
                        {
                            // Read a block of bytes.
                            int numBytesRead = inputStream.Read(
                                buffer, 0, readingBlockSize);
                            if (numBytesRead == 0) break;

                            // Write the bytes into the CryptoStream.
                            cryptoStream.Write(buffer, 0, numBytesRead);
                        }
                        cryptoStream.FlushFinalBlock();
                    }
                }
            }
        }
        catch (CryptographicException ex)
        {
            // The password is incorrect.
            throw new CryptographicException("Invalid password.", ex);
        }
        catch
        {
            // Re-throw.
            throw;
        }
    }
```

After reading the last few solutions, this code should seem familiar. It uses the MakeCryptoTransform method to make an encryptor, creates an input stream attached to the string to encrypt, makes an output stream attached to the file, and makes a CryptoStream that connects the encryptor to the output stream. The method reads the input and writes into the output in blocks. When it has finished processing the input string, the method flushes the CryptoStream and is done.

The following code shows how the program decrypts an encrypted file into an RTF string:

```
// Decrypt a file and return the result in a string.
public static string DecryptFromFile(string password,
    string cipherFilename)
{
    try
    {
        // Make the decryptor.
        ICryptoTransform cryptoTransform = MakeCryptoTransform(
            password, false, new AesCryptoServiceProvider());

        // Make streams for the input file and output MemoryStream.
```

```
        using (FileStream inputStream = new FileStream(cipherFilename,
            FileMode.Open, FileAccess.Read))
    {
        using (MemoryStream outputStream = new MemoryStream())
        {
            // Attach a CryptoStream.
            using (CryptoStream cryptoStream =
                new CryptoStream(outputStream, cryptoTransform,
                    CryptoStreamMode.Write))
            {
                // Read and write in blocks.
                const int readingBlockSize = 16 * 1024;
                byte[] buffer = new byte[readingBlockSize];
                while (true)
                {
                    // Read a block of bytes.
                    int numBytesRead = inputStream.Read(
                        buffer, 0, readingBlockSize);
                    if (numBytesRead == 0) break;

                    // Write the bytes into the CryptoStream.
                    cryptoStream.Write(buffer, 0, numBytesRead);
                }
                cryptoStream.FlushFinalBlock();

                // Return the string.
                byte[] plainbytes = outputStream.ToArray();
                string plaintext =
                    Encoding.Unicode.GetString(plainbytes);
                return plaintext;
            }
        }
    }
}
catch (CryptographicException ex)
{
    // The password is incorrect.
    throw new CryptographicException("Invalid password.", ex);
}
catch
{
    // Re-throw.
    throw;
}
}
```

This code is very similar to the preceding method. The only real difference is that this version converts the output `MemoryStream` into a string and returns it.

The rest of the example solution performs document management tasks such as keeping track of whether the data has been modified so it can warn you if you try to close the program without saving changes. Download the `CryptoPad` example solution to see additional details.

Other Books You May Enjoy

If you enjoyed this book, you may be interested in these other books by Packt:

C# 7 and .NET Core 2.0 Blueprints
Dirk Strauss, Jas Rademeyer

ISBN: 978-1-78839-619-6

- How to incorporate Entity Framework Core to build ASP .NET Core MVC applications
- Get hands-on experience with SignalR, and NuGet packages
- Working with MongoDB in your ASP.NET Core MVC application
- Get hands-on experience with .NET Core MVC, Middleware, Controllers, Views, Layouts, Routing, and OAuth
- Implementing Azure Functions and learn what Serverless computing means
- See how .NET Core enables cross-platform applications that run on Windows, macOS and Linux
- Running a .NET Core MVC application with Docker Compose

Hands-On Microservices with C#
Matt R. Cole

ISBN: 978-1-78953-368-2

- Explore different open source tools within the context of designing microservices
- Learn to provide insulation to exception-prone function calls
- Build common messages used between microservices for communication
- Learn to create a microservice using our base class and interface
- Design a quantitative financial machine microservice
- Learn to design a microservice that is capable of using Blockchain technology

Leave a review - let other readers know what you think

Please share your thoughts on this book with others by leaving a review on the site that you bought it from. If you purchased the book from Amazon, please leave us an honest review on this book's Amazon page. This is vital so that other potential readers can see and use your unbiased opinion to make purchasing decisions, we can understand what our customers think about our products, and our authors can see your feedback on the title that they have worked with Packt to create. It will only take a few minutes of your time, but is valuable to other potential customers, our authors, and Packt. Thank you!

Index

www.ingramcontent.com/pod-product-compliance
Lightning Source LLC
Chambersburg PA
CBHW080616060326
40690CB00021B/4710